Privacy

For Seija and Graham Tattersal

Privacy

A Short History

David Vincent

polity

First published in 2016 by Polity Press

Polity Press
65 Bridge Street
Cambridge CB2 1UR, UK

Polity Press
350 Main Street
Malden, MA 02148, USA

ISBN-13: 978-0-7456-7112-3
ISBN-13: 978-0-7456-7113-0(pb)

A catalogue record for this book is available from the British Library.

Library of Congress Cataloging-in-Publication Data

Names: Vincent, David, 1949- author.
Title: Privacy : a short history / David Vincent.
Description: Cambridge ; Malden, MA : Polity, 2016. | Includes bibliographical references and index.
Identifiers: LCCN 2015025091| ISBN 9780745671123 (hardback) | ISBN 9780745671130 (paperback)
Subjects: LCSH: Privacy, Right of. | BISAC: HISTORY / General.
Classification: LCC JC596 .V56 2016 | DDC 323.44/8–dc23 LC record available at http://lccn.loc.gov/2015025091

Typeset in 10.5 on 12 pt Sabon
by Toppan Best-set Premedia Limited
Printed and bound in the United Kingdom by Clays Ltd, St Ives PLC

For further information on Polity, visit our website:
politybooks.com

Contents

Preface

The history of privacy is a curious mixture of noise and silence. There is a large and inconclusive literature on the concept of privacy, and a boiling debate about contemporary threats to the protection of personal information. However, much of the commentary treats the decades before 9/11 as privacy's medieval period, and the centuries before the internet are lost in the mists of time. The requirement for an historical perspective is usually satisfied by brief, second-hand references to Jeremy Bentham or George Orwell. The first official review of privacy in the United Kingdom, the Younger Report of 1972, lamented the absence of any historical writings on the subject at all. As it happened the first monograph, David Flaherty's now classic account of colonial New England, was about to be published, and since then there has been a scattering of excellent studies of privacy reaching as far back as the medieval period and into the classical world. However, apart from the heroic, multi-volume, multi-author survey piloted by Philippe Ariès and Georges Duby in the late 1980s and early 1990s, the field has presented an archipelago of books and articles, rarely linked together. Critical areas of culture and practice, including housing, religious observance, literacy and reading, are for the most part only tangentially related to the main narrative of change, and there is a range of topics, including the ways in which people in the past sought solitude and conducted private relationships outside their homes, which have yet to receive any systematic historical treatment.

The following brief history seeks to give an account of the long-run development of privacy, not just to provide those involved in current debates with a clearer temporal perspective, but also to narrate the concepts and practices on their own terms in successive centuries. Given the fragmented nature of the existing scholarship, it is partly a literature survey and partly a review of adjacent bodies of research, particularly in the fields of mass communication, housing, religion, domestic relations, and surveillance. There is throughout an engagement with primary evidence; condensed though the account must be, there is a need to keep close to the texture of emotions and practices of those struggling to balance complex aspirations. The book is organized on a straightforward chronological basis, beginning in the late Middle Ages and ending with the fallout from the Snowden revelations. Each of the five chapters has dates, but given the nature of the subject matter, these are only approximations. Many of the themes cross the boundaries between one period and another. Even in the final chapter on the digital revolution, the impact of computers could be seen as beginning both earlier and later than the nominated date of 1970. The book concludes with a note on further reading, which summarizes the current field of publications on privacy, relevant work in related fields, and those topics requiring further research.

An enterprise of this kind is not so much standing on the shoulders of giants as stumbling about in the long grass hoping not to be trodden on. The pursuit of a long-run account has forced me out of my comfort zone in nineteenth-century history, and I am particularly grateful to Anne Laurence and Amanda Goodrich for helping to reduce the errors and solecisms in the earlier chapters of the book, to John Naughton for his informed and balanced understanding of the course and consequences of the digital revolution, and to audiences in various parts of Britain and Europe who have commented on versions of the argument. Elliott Karstadt and Andrea Drugan at Polity have shown faith in what turned out to be a lengthy short project. Charlotte Vincent has examined every word and phrase in the text, patiently asking at every point that necessary question, 'what does this mean?' To her, as always, my profound thanks. The dedication is for a life-long friendship; a true value of privacy.

Shrawardine, June 2015

1

Privacy before Privacy 1300–1650

ᏽᏯ

On Friday 13 July 1341, it was recorded at the London Assize of Nuisance that 'Isabel relict of John Luter complains that John Trappe, "skynnere", who has a tenement adjoining her garden in the par[ish] of St. John de Walbrok, has four windows of which the glass is broken, through which he and his servants can see into her garden.' The site was visited, and judgment given that the defendant should repair his windows within 40 days. Isabel, however, was not finished. She next successfully complained that 'John de Thorp, "skynnere", has seven windows overlooking her adjoining tenement in the par[ish] of St. Stephen de Walbrok, less than 16ft. from the ground, through which he and his servants can see into the pl[aintiff]'s tenement.' Then 'John de Leche, fishmonger' was summoned by the litigious widow. She charged that this neighbour 'has a leaden watch-tower (garritam) upon the wall of his tenement adjoining hers in the same par[ish] upon which he and his household (familiares) stand daily, watching the private affairs of the pl[aintiff] and her servants.' Finally she turned her attention to a fourth householder who overlooked her property: 'The same Isabel complains that Joan relict of Simon Corp has twelve apertures (foramina) overlooking her adjoining tenement in the same par[ish] through which she and her servants can see the private business of the pl[aintiff] and her servants.' Following visits, all the cases resulted in 40 days' notice to rectify the problems, 'subject to the customary penalty'.[1]

These disputes in the crowded streets of late-medieval London challenge the frequent assumption that privacy did not emerge as an aspiration until the seventeenth century and was not a reality for the

mass of the population for at least a further two centuries. At issue
in the court hearings was the claim to protection from the surveillance
of domestic life. There was a working distinction embedded in the
Latin term *privatus* between matters which belonged to the collective
arena and were subject to public authority, and those which pertained
to an enclosed community governed by the head of the household.[2]
This boundary is invisible to some historians because they are looking
for the wrong situation.[3] During the modern era an individualistic
conception of privacy has gained traction, given its most resonant
definition as 'the right to be let alone' in the influential 1890 article
of Warren and Brandeis.[4] The emphasis is on the isolated, self-sufficient citizen, protecting their personal archive from invasion or theft
by every kind of outside agency.[5] Unsurprisingly this figure is hard to
locate amid the crowded households and thin walls of urban or rural
communities anywhere in fourteenth-century Europe. Except possibly in the specialized environment of the growing monastic orders,
almost everyone shared their lives with others, whether spouses,
children, servants, fellow workers or passing visitors. 'The mistaken
assertion that the notion of physical privacy was absent in medieval
society', writes Diane Shaw, 'perhaps derives from the modern
assumption that privacy is individual and absolute, rather than communal and relative.'[6]

The narrative of privacy is not a journey from absence to invention, from less to more, or even, as we will see in later chapters, from
collective to personal. There are no beginnings in this history, only
threatened endings. As William Reddy has argued, it is possible to
locate values and behaviours that exist over long periods, interacting
with but not fully conditional on changing physical and normative
contexts.[7] The task is to identify those features of privacy which are
recognizable over the centuries and those which were specific to the
aspirations and constraints of particular eras. Privacy was so deeply
associated with the conduct of intimate social relations that its complete absence is difficult to imagine in any era of recorded history. In
the words of Diana Webb's account of the medieval period, 'there
was surely never a time when individuals, families or groups did not
sometimes claim the right to withdraw from public scrutiny into a
space of their own.'[8]

There were three distinct motives for such a retreat that over time
were consistent neither in themselves nor in relation to each other.
There was the nurturing of intimate relations whose conduct required
a realm of protected discourse. There was the search for an inner
sanctum where individuals could manage their mental archive and
conduct their bodily functions. And there was the defence of thought

and behaviour from invasion by external structures of authority. Each of these was visible in the late-medieval period, but in forms that were to change radically over the succeeding centuries. What could be expected of intimacy in the multi-functional, shape-shifting households of fourteenth-century London had only a distant relation to the emotions invested in the tight domestic units of the late-modern era. Privacy as an arena of retreat and reflection had a long journey to make from the world of secret prayer that will be examined later in this chapter. And the private realm as opposed to the state which became a defining feature of liberal democracy can only distantly be glimpsed in the conflicts between households and authorities in this period. Over the years the terminology of privacy is inexact, and as the final chapter will argue it has become no less so in our own times, when the social and political functions have tended too easily to be subsumed into the right to control personal information.

Amidst the complex evolution of privacy there were several features of the cases at the London Assize of Nuisance that have remained constant throughout the period. The first was that in the definition and defence of privacy, there was a critical distinction between the inside and the outside of the dwelling place, however confined, insubstantial and overcrowded it might be. The expectation of what could be known of thoughts and behaviours changed radically once the threshold was crossed. The door might be flimsy, the fastening nominal, the party walls porous to sound, smell and damp, but the act of entering the domestic space from the street generated a specific set of requirements. For this reason, the nascent legal defence of privacy was bound up in a broader set of rights associated with the occupancy of property. The action of trespass began to take shape in the early-fourteenth-century courts, giving householders recourse against the physical invasion of their space. The concept of nuisance embraced every kind of behaviour by inhabitants of neighbouring buildings that diminished the value of the complainant's occupancy of his or her premises. An individual could not construct or occupy their property in a way that materially damaged the use of another.[9] In the packed medieval urban communities this meant above all ensuring as far as possible that the materials out of which a house or tenement was constructed did not present a fire hazard to all those around it. It meant that rainwater should not leak into an adjoining building, nor sewage and its associated odours. And it also meant that the occupants' enjoyment of an enclosed universe of communication should not be compromised by sight or by sound. In terms of windows, even if only shuttered at a time when glass was a luxury, it implied both that the occupants should be able to see out of their property, and also that neighbours should not be able to see in. Attempts were made to ensure that party walls were of sufficient quality, and where there were holes caused by decay or poor materials, adjacent occupiers were expected not to listen at them or to make such noise about their business that it interfered with the lives that were being led next door. Litigants were unconcerned about the difference between these assaults on their use of their property. It is possible to calculate that about one in six of the cases at the Assize of Nuisance involved the invasions of privacy through doors and windows,[10] but these cases were often combined with other grievances. Thus for instance it was recorded that on 29 February 1348, 'Simon de Worthstede complains that Robert Bisshop and Roger Madour have six windows and two apertures in their tenement adjoining his in the par[ish] of St. Alban de Wodestrete through which they can see his private business; and his tenants throw sewage and other refuse through the apertures on to his land.'[11]

A second feature was that the conflicts were for the most part between two social groups. The head of household brought a case on behalf of all those for whom he or she was responsible, including dependent relatives and servants, against the behaviour of another householder and his or her domestic community. The Assize recorded on 26 February 1350 that 'Adam de Buri, citizen and skinner, and Alice his wife complain that for lack of a fillet-gutter (filetti) 6½ ells 2 ins. long, the rainwater from the tenement of Maud relict of John le Leche, "pessoner", adjoining theirs in the par[ish] of St. John de Walbrok, falls upon their land; and that she has two windows through which she and her servants can see the private business of the pl[aintiff] and their servants.'[12] There was no nominal distinction in the late-medieval and early-modern period between the household as the totality of individuals under one roof and the family as a body of co-residing kin.[13] Together they constituted both an authority structure and a bounded communication network. All of the household's members, regardless of age, gender or employment status, expected to interact with each other without being overseen or overheard. Husband and wife, parent and child, master and servant, shared intimacies which would be distorted or betrayed if they escaped the physical boundaries of the domestic space. The more complex and fragile boundaries of knowledge and discourse within the household were a matter for its head and the relationships between its members. The law applied only beyond the threshold of the building that they occupied.

The cases that came before the Assize of Nuisance represented a failure of informal negotiation. They were dealt with by a system of public conciliation involving nominated individuals physically visiting the site of the dispute. The process reflected a third feature of privacy which in many different variants and contexts was consistent across time. In fourteenth-century London, privacy was a scarce and contested commodity. It was not a possession or a secure right, but rather an aspiration whose achievement had to be traded against other objectives and whose pursuit required constant vigilance, endless adjustment, frequent defeat and occasional outright conflict. Judgements as to what was desirable and possible were conditioned by changing normative and physical structures.[14] In the cramped, multi-functional domestic spaces of the medieval homes, as in the middle-class apartments of modern-day Chicago studied by Christena Nippert-Eng, privacy, however conceived and described, was a practice involving effort, choice and compromise.[15] As the historian and privacy commissioner David Flaherty writes, 'privacy has always been under challenge throughout recorded Western history.'[16]

The error in many long-term treatments of the concept is in eliding difficulty with absence, and the average with the universal. Maintaining a balance between seclusion and intimacy was a profound challenge in all but elite homes and even then presented problems, given the state of sanitation and the inescapable presence of servants. Directing conversation at one set of ears and not another in a room almost always containing other people was never easy. But attempts were made. Individuals and groups differentiated by inclination, by prosperity, by the mix of personalities, pursued aspects of privacy with varying degrees of energy and tolerance. There is no knowing why Isabel, relict of John Luter, gave up informal protests and decided to settle scores with all her neighbours in one go in July 1341. Heads of households had a choice of tactics in their unending struggle to police the privacy of domestic communities. The law was a device of last resort, although even at this early stage of legal history, it is notable that the courts were open to women of the servant-employing class as well as men.

The final feature was that the conflicts involved, in some way, the transmission of information. The cases were about what could be seen and heard, and how the boundaries of discourse were policed. This study embraces a history of face-to-face communication and how it interacted with more formal means of expressing and recording thought and emotion, ranging from the emergence of personal correspondence and the invention of printing in the fifteenth century to the arrival of social media in the early twenty-first. From the moment that pen was put to paper to connect those separated by time and distance, it is possible to add the category of this virtual privacy to that of physical interactions between familiar individuals. Each development both extended and compromised the management of privacy; the anxieties surrounding the receipt and reception of letters were endlessly re-worked by successive technologies. The resolution of these dilemmas depended not just on the machinery of communication but on the codes and contexts of exchanging information in each particular register, beginning with the wordless glances between those sharing a past and an expected future together.

The association of privacy with property has placed the evolution of housing design at the centre of accounts of its early history. In a realm constituted of oblique behaviours and unspoken attitudes, there is evidential comfort to be derived from the sheer physical presence of at least a scattering of buildings stretching back to the late-medieval period. A combination of archaeological and documentary research has established that the housing of at least the more prosperous members of the peasantry had acquired a degree of permanence and solidity.[17] Living quarters were becoming separated from livestock, and the domestic and productive activities of the household were being conducted in buildings with internal divisions between several rooms. If there was a distinction of function between the spaces it was purely relative. In a three-bay dwelling no room was exclusively for the conduct of any identifiable activity, including sleeping. Seasonal labour demands and variations in light and warmth were the most powerful forces shaping how the inhabitants managed their domestic interactions over the course of the daily round. Windows were small and unglazed, hearths were open and smoky. The lower gentry and upwards enjoyed the use of a single-storey hall with a few adjacent smaller rooms, but as with their social inferiors, eating, socializing, conducting business and sleeping took place wherever there was a need and an unoccupied space.[18] There were few pieces of furniture, and beds were put to variable occupancy as the household expanded and shrank with births and deaths, and the coming and going of employees and visitors. The nearest to a wholly private space was a coffer, or small trunk, in which personal clothing or other valued possessions could be kept.[19]

The narrative of change over the next two centuries centres on a process of increasing differentiation in the provision and use of rooms. More recent scholarship has qualified W. G. Hoskins' thesis of a 'great rebuilding' between 1570–1640.[20] The process is now seen to have taken place over a longer period, with many regional and temporal variations. Nonetheless, the general direction of travel is unaltered. There was increasing differentiation by wealth, as those benefitting most from the expansion of the economy were able to display their disposable income in the size and furnishings of their homes, and there was growing specialization in the internal design of living spaces. More prosperous peasants and yeomen gained a first floor to their dwellings, and increased the number of separate rooms to six or more.[21] The medieval hall, open to the rafters, acquired a ceiling and a chimney, with the upper floor reached by a staircase. A great chamber, apart from the hall, enabled the multiple functions of the household to be conducted at a remove from outsiders.[22] Around the central core were clustered smaller rooms in which a diversity of activities could take place.[23] Storage spaces for food were created, and the heat and smells of its preparation were as far as possible separated from the rest of the house. A new nomenclature emerged, with the appearance of terms such as parlour, bedchamber, closet, study and library.[24] As larger sums of money were spent on homes and their contents, so the range of specialized trades associated with house building was extended to encompass the notion of architecture. One of the earliest texts, Henry Wotton's *The Elements of Architecture* of 1624, described the positioning of the new roster of rooms in the ideal country house:

> All *Studies* and *Libraries*, be towards the East: For the Morning is a friend to the Muses. All Offices that require heat, as *Kitchins, Stillatories, Stoues*, rooms for *Baking, Brewing, Washing*, or the like, would be *Meridionall*. All that need a coole and fresh temper, as *Cellers, Pantries, Butteries, Granaries*, to the *North*. To the same side likewise, all that are appointed for gentle Motion, as *Galleries*, especially in warme Climes, or that otherwise require a steadie and unvariable light.[25]

As Lena Cowen Orlin has observed, such prescriptions 'represent a degree – if not more – of wishful thinking'.[26] Only the largest of landowners could contemplate Wotton's list of specialized spaces, whichever direction they faced, and for those able to rebuild their property or add a new floor and extra rooms to their existing residence, it is far from clear that either the intention or the outcome of change was a unilinear enlargement of privacy. In the founding account of early-modern housing, the driver of so much investment in bricks and stone was straightforward. 'We must look for the cause of the Great Rebuilding', wrote W. G. Hoskins, 'in the filtering down to the mass of the population, after some two centuries, of a sense of privacy that had formerly been enjoyed only by the upper classes.'[27] In this view, the pattern of renovation or new construction reflected an increasing desire for seclusion and a growing opportunity of achieving it. The journey towards the modern private home began with ambition fuelled by wealth, and accelerated as more of the population moved away from subsistence living. More recently there has been a reaction against what Tim Meldrum has described as 'architectural determinism', the notion that the value and practice of privacy can be read back from the physical spaces in which lives were conducted.[28] The temptation to do so is strong. As we have seen, there was, and remained, a basic association between the privacy and the occupancy of a domestic residence. As Nicole Castan writes, 'an open or closed door was both a symbol and a reality, whether in a rich man's house or a poor farmstead.'[29] Permission was required to pass the threshold during the day. Visits were not expected if the head of the household was absent, or at all at night when the door was shut. By the fifteenth century, burglary, the act of breaking and entering a house, had become an indictable felony in English law.[30] The crime presupposed the existence of locks and of doors and frames robust enough to hold them, an assumption confirmed by contemporary court roll evidence.[31] There was an expectation that they would be secured against outsiders, particularly when it was too dark to observe their countenance.

Whilst the surviving record does suggest a long-term process of multiplication and specialization of domestic spaces, there remains a gap between language and practice. The nominal distinction, for instance, between parlour and bedchamber was taking form in the early-modern period, but in practice only the houses of the elite could aspire to sufficient rooms and specialized beds to separate fully the activities of the day and the night. For the great majority of those enjoying their enlarged accommodation, adults, children, servants and visitors could still be found bedding down all over the house and eating and socializing in the same space when morning returned. The new vocabulary of domestic usage failed to capture the breadth of functions to be found in most households, where earning and consuming were still spatially coextensive. For the bulk of the population the activities of entertaining, conversing, relaxing, playing, sleeping, procreating, cooking, eating, washing bodies and clothes, urinating and defecating, earning, making, serving, managing and accounting could rarely be walled off from each other. Indeed a fundamental element of privacy, passing bodily waste, became in this period more integrated into living space, as the separate latrine was replaced by the commode in a sleeping area.[32]

The more permanent the building, the more likely that its occupants were not living in the architectural present, but rather adapting their

requirements and behaviours to the expectations of the earlier generation that constructed it. And even in the case of a carefully considered
new residence, there was no guarantee of how it would be used. For
most of the population, occupation was in the form of a tenancy permitting easy movement between properties as household fortunes
waxed and waned. At the top end of society there was little sense of
confinement to one property. There were frequent comings and goings
for pleasure or business. Lady Anne Clifford's early-seventeenth-cen-
tury diary records a life of regular journeys to the homes of relatives,
or to London.[33] Whole households moved regularly from estate to
estate.[34] A striking example of locational uncertainty is the rebuilding
of Wollaton Hall in the late sixteenth century, which has been meticu-
lously documented by Alice Friedman. The owner, Sir Francis
Willoughby, employed the architect Robert Smythson to fulfil ideas
derived from the latest European pattern books:

> Unlike the old manor house, the new Hall easily accommodated a
> number of smaller spaces in the basement and corner towers. These
> small rooms served as privies, private studies or places for storing both
> personal effects and official documents. Reflecting a new emphasis
> both on personal privacy and on the written word, whether in printed
> form or in manuscript, closets and chambers were tucked away in the
> four corners of the house on the principal floors and formed the inner
> recesses of the suites.[35]

At the end of the account, however, it is revealed that because of
long-term marital difficulties involving a bitter conflict between Lady
Willoughby and the servants employed by her husband, this model
of early-modern private living was rarely occupied. Sir Francis preferred to inhabit another of his houses, and after half a century of
intermittent use by his descendants, the Hall was closed down
altogether.

Prosperity was not just the enabler of a desire for privacy, but in
itself the driver of change. As personal wealth increased, more objects
were purchased and more spaces were required to accommodate
them.[36] The earliest and most pervasive form of differentiation was
in the storage and preparation of an increasing abundance of food-
stuffs. Elsewhere there were more cupboards, more tables and chairs,
and, in particular, more of the most expensive items in a household:
beds and bedding. There was pressure to increase the number of
rooms to contain the furniture, and a gradual tendency to describe
them in terms of one category of possession rather than another. This
ambiguity between wealth and withdrawal was particularly apparent

in the increasing presence of the closet as a place of private meditation and reading. As the Wollaton Hall plans indicated, this room
was usually constructed as an enclosed space leading off the principal
bedchamber. In the corridor-less early-modern house where each
room opened into another, its door could be closed or even locked
without impeding the circulation of the rest of the household.[37] There
are grounds for seeing the closet as a harbinger of modernity, 'the
first expression', as Raffaella Sarti writes, 'of a new need for privacy
and personal comfort which was to develop in the coming centuries'.[38] It was evidence of a growing equality between men and women
in the search for individual seclusion. A godly wife had a claim on a
place of withdrawal for personal reflection, as well as her husband.
But there is also a case for not overloading with meaning what was
generally a cramped space in a large house. The very existence of the
closet was a function of wealth, an impossible ambition for any
household below the level of the lesser gentry or successful merchant.
Where it was afforded, its furnishing and use could not be abstracted
from larger structures of power and function within the household.
As Ronald Huebert has observed, the available evidence suggests that
the husband had the right to enter his wife's closet at will but to
protect his own enclave against all-comers.[39] For the male, the retreat
was an extension of his education and a facility for expanding his
economic and intellectual role in society. Whereas the wife might
furnish her room with a desk and a few precious books and items to
assist in household management, her husband's space, which could
also be described as his study, was more likely to include the papers,
maps and scientific instruments necessary to manage an estate or a
business, or pursue a career of research and publication.[40] His enclosed
and lockable room was as much a safe repository of portable possessions as it was a retreat from the workaday world. It was the forerunner of a cabinet of curiosities, a display of both the mind and the
wealth of its owner. It was also a place of business, where two men
might converse on confidential matters.[41]

A final argument against the architectural determinism of privacy
lies in the territory on the other side of the threshold. Front doors let
people out as well as in. If the physical space of the home defined the
unit of the private community and supplied such legal defence against
intrusion and surveillance as existed, it was not the sole arena for
maintaining intimate relationships or of engaging in solitary contemplation. For the inhabitant of the crowded, multi-functional household, the simplest means of conducting a conversation out of the sight
and hearing of others was just to step outside. In the packed urban
centres, life was as much led on the street as in the house or tenement.

In the countryside, where the majority of the population lived until the mid-nineteenth century, most men spent their labouring days out of doors, and their wives and children worked, talked and played in the open spaces around their dwellings.[42] The weather and the seasons shaped opportunity, but given the need, the means of escaping oversight were always present. Here courtships were conducted, friendships maintained, confidences made and upheld. Like the retreat into the closet, withdrawal from the company of the household might be noted, but there were plenty of informal opportunities for sheltered discourse in the diurnal round of labour and in the weekly rituals of the market or the church service. Longer journeys were almost always made in company, providing further possibilities for talk hidden from the surveillance of family and servants.[43] The geography of privacy was bounded by the distance that could be walked or ridden in a day, not by the extent of the built or rebuilt landscape.

From the late-medieval period onwards, the casual use of the outdoors was supplemented by the provision of enclosed spaces. As early as the fourteenth century, substantial investment was being made in formal gardens around royal palaces, monasteries and the residences of the greater nobility.[44] Peasants and urban householders cultivated small plots of land adjacent to their homes.[45] Professional seedsmen and nurseries emerged in response to the growing demand for trees, flowers and vegetables. To exclude predatory animals, and also to indicate that the managed soil was an extension of the privacy domain of the property to which it was attached, gardens were protected by hedges and ditches or, where they could be afforded, walls, and legal action was taken against trespass.[46] Like interior rooms, the external spaces had overlapping functions. The principal use was growing or, in the case of the larger estates, pursuing food. Where there were ponds or river banks, that most meditative outdoor activity, catching fish for pleasure rather than sustenance, was already an established pastime by the fifteenth century.[47] The diary of the Lancashire gentleman Nicholas Assheton, for instance, is almost entirely taken up with his life out of doors, planting his orchard, fishing and hunting with friends, riding to their houses for convivial evenings.[48] They were places of relaxation that were relatively hidden from both strangers and those inside the domestic residence.[49] Lady Anne Clifford found that the best place to build her friendship with her cousins was out of doors: 'My Coz. Frances Bourchier & my Coz. Francis Russell & I did use to walk much in the Garden & were great one with another.'[50] As with internal locations, it was possible to switch between different registers of seclusion, encompassing recreation, business and spiritual meditation.[51] 'In the afternoon', Lady Anne recorded, 'I went abroad in the garden & said my Prayers in the Standing [a copse] in the garden.' The next day she took the opportunity to engage in a confidential business discussion with her husband out of the sight and hearing of the servants: 'I walked abroad with my Lord in the Park & the Garden, where he spake to me much of this Business with my Uncle.'[52] Amongst the landed elite, strolling in the fresh air within the confines of the garden became a recreation in its own right, conferring both physical health and the prospect of ambulatory conversation or contemplation. Francis Bacon's essay of 1625 extolled the layout of a garden with 'Varieties of Alleys, Private, to give a full Shade', which would permit walking 'wheresoever the Sun be' and 'when the Wind blows Sharpe.'[53] To ensure that the opportunities for this kind of exercise were available all the year round, the newly built larger country houses began to be supplied with long galleries, enclosed walkways in an upper storey.[54]

It is tempting to substitute walking for the built environment as the principal focus of the history of the privacy not just in the early part of this survey but through to the twentieth century when the motor car became the most available location for secluded reflection and discourse. In practice, from the medieval period onwards, those seeking to protect their thoughts and intimacies viewed their physical environment as a continuum of more or less transient opportunities. Where there were sufficient resources to provide specialized spaces, the walled exterior served the same function as the enclosed room. The late-sixteenth-century Nuremberg merchant wrote home to his fiancée, 'for If dear God cannot immediately reconcile us, I still trust he will spare us this time and help guide us joyfully back together again in our little chamber or flower garden.'[55] For the more prosperous, there were always choices about where time was spent. Lady Margaret Hoby's diary entry for 24 August 1599 recorded how she moved between a series of locations during the course of a summer evening as she engaged in intimate converse with her friends, her husband and God:

> I presently went to dinner, after which I passed the time in talk with some freinds, and then went to priuat praier: that don I took the aire in the Coach with Mr Hoby, and so cam in and walked in the garden, medetatinge of the pointes of the sarmon and prainge tell hard before I went to supper: and after supper went to publeck praier and thence to bed.[56]

Those below the coach-owning class had fewer opportunities for such complete withdrawal and instead relied on purloined moments during

the course of the day's business and pleasure. The single most important consequence of the rising standard of housing was not the com-
paratively rare provision of a lockable study, or a bedchamber used
only for the repose of a married couple, but rather the multiplication
of casual opportunities for private intercourse. More and smaller
rooms meant that there was a greater chance that one might be temporarily empty in the interstices of the household's activities. The
construction of a first-floor storey, accessed not by a ladder and trap-
door but by an enclosed staircase, created a vertical passageway in
which encounters could take place outside the rooms in the house.
Within the walls, converse remained ever vulnerable to interruption.
To escape it, there were always the gardens and fields, the lanes and
streets, where purposeful business could be translated into opportun-
istic or planned encounters.

At the beginning of the early-modern period, the most frequent use
of the word private is to be found in the personal writings of godly
men and women. The second entry in the diary made by the Puritan
Margaret Hoby summarizes a busy morning from the moment she
was dressed:

> After I was redie I betooke my selfe to priuat praier, wherein it pleased
> the Lord to deall mercifully: after, I went about the house and instructed
> Tomson wife in som principles of religion, and then eate my breakfast,
> and then walked abroad tell all most :11: of the Clock: and after I had
> read :2: chapters of the bible, I went to diner.[57]

There is a case for arguing that prayer in the post-Reformation era
represented the true beginning of privacy as a withdrawal from the
society of others for the purpose of managing a personal archive of
emotion and knowledge. Like her fellow Puritans, Margaret Hoby
insisted on a sharp distinction between general belief and inward
meditation, and on communing with God in spatial isolation in contrast to more collective practices in the household or the community.
Private prayer was a framed activity both physically and mentally. It
took place in a distinct location separated as far as possible from the
surrounding company, and required a process of intense spiritual
self-examination. As a later guide explained, such devotion occurred
'when a person gets alone by himself, and makes his requests known
to God. When being sequestred from all company whatsoever, and
withdrawn from his nearest and dearest Relations, his most intimate
Friends, and by himself in a most close and private retirement.'[58] The
closet was the ideal environment, but in its absence the corner of a

room would suffice, or a bed, or, as we have seen with Lady Clifford and Lady Hoby, walking in a garden. The stress in the diaries of godly men and women is on the sheer effort that was involved. Time and space had to be found, when both were at a premium, to avoid a superficial accounting of the soul's doings with the Almighty.

Prayer itself was neither the prerogative of Protestantism nor an invention of the Reformation. Christianity had long contained a tension between personal piety and ecclesiastical observation. Personal prayer for a range of spiritual and instrumental purposes was commonplace amongst medieval believers. Monastic tradition in its different forms emphasized retirement and seclusion. Catholicism emerged from the Council of Trent with an enhanced respect for personal piety and spiritual meditation. Morning and evening family prayers were commended and encouraged. As the locus of sin shifted from the act to the intention, reflection on the mental inventory of the believer became more important. But the post-Tridentine Church renewed its insistence on the sacraments and the clergy as intermediaries between the believer and God whereas the Protestant believer at prayer was engaged in an unmediated discourse with the Almighty. The distinction was not between individualistic and collective faiths. In practice, Catholic priests had difficulty getting their flock to confession even once a year, and the fifteenth-century Protestant churches strongly emphasized the role of communal activities and the responsibilities of parish officials. The concept of private prayer gained meaning in its relation to other necessary forms of social worship in the household and at the regular church service.[59] Women's domestic role did not excuse them from public observances.[60] Margaret Hoby was fully a member of a religious community, and the content of the Sunday services, in particular the sermon, provided spiritual and intellectual sustenance for the course of personal reflection during the rest of the week. She also exercised her responsibilities within the household, ensuring that its dependent members, including the servants, knew and practised their Christian beliefs. But when she withdrew to her inward self she was face to face with God. There was no other person or practice that could intercede for her.

It would be misleading, however, to conflate private prayer with the kind of privacy represented by the secular 'right to be let alone'. 'Solitariness', warned Samuel Slater, 'is looked upon as having Melancholly for its usual Companion; and a Life of loneliness and retirement is reckon'd a very disconsolate life.'[61] An enclosed preoccupation with personal thoughts and actions was not the function of successful prayer but rather a measure of its absence. Withdrawal was necessary in order to repair and deepen the connection with the all-embracing presence of the Almighty. The sense of guilt that informed the spiritual discourse was founded on an apprehension that God had been too easily forgotten in the daily round of business and pleasure. 'I blesse god this weeke my minde hath not run out after some foolish vanities as formerly,' wrote Ralph Josselin, 'yett I find Sathan like the lapwing crying before mee with one temptacion or vanitie, to drawe my minde from my god of my salvacion.'[62] That kind of individualism belonged to the realm of the Fallen Angel. In such devotions, urged Daniel Featley, 'we ought most of all to *deny our selves.*'[63] If those at private prayer were physically by themselves, in their minds they could not have been less alone. They talked and argued with a real, active presence from whom no aspect of the believer's life was hidden or beyond intervention. Isaac Archer's diary was but a pale imitation of the record kept by his maker: 'all my thoughts, words, and actions, with every sin and debt of mine, are recorded in heaven, and the whole series of my life perfectly knowne to God.'[64] This was surveillance in its fullest sense, ranging from the most detailed insight to the most comprehensive reaction. 'Every night God setteth his watch about us, and every day he commands his Angels to pitch their tents for our safeguard', wrote John Beadle. 'And alas, what is all our care and prudence, without his watchful eye and providence over us!'[65]

In Parson Woodford's diary, as in others, a distinction was drawn between private and secret prayer. At times the terms merely specified relative stages of withdrawal. On 26 December 1637, Woodford recorded that 'I prayed in secret, & in private with my wife & in publiq.'[66] Private in this context was a social term, referring to the variable relationship between individuals and those about them in the conduct of spiritual observance. Prayer did not have a fixed social or spatial location, and even in the closet was not necessarily silent.[67] But secret also described the quality of the discourse with God. 'There are some duties we seldome or never perform', lamented John Beadle. 'Where is the man that makes conscience of private fasting and prayers, that shuts himself up in his closet, and wrastles with God in secret, that his Father that seeth in secret may reward him openly?'[68] It embodied a conception of the Deity whose person and knowledge were never fully transparent. And it constituted an increasing emphasis on the role of silent auditing as a means of engaging in the most profound form of spiritual communion. As Peter Burke writes, it was a 'technique for opening the inner ear'.[69] Through secrecy and silence, the superficial could be dissolved. An intense form of self-interrogation opened a channel between the innermost being of the penitent believer and the veiled personage of their Redeemer. Practices which had taken form in the medieval monasteries were now translated to the everyday life of godly folk.

The strict temporal rituals of the Carthusians or the Cistercians could not be fully replicated in the busy life of the secular believer, but the silent intercourse with God remained a time-infused event, at least for those freed from a life of manual labour. The most popular manuscript text in the late Middle Ages was *The Book of Hours*, based on the monastic round of worship.[70] The secret self-examination comprised a review of the recent past, and in turn the recipient of the prayers was assumed to maintain his own record of his dealings with supplicants. As John Beadle observed, 'God himself seems to keep a Journall by him of all the care he hath of us, the cost he bestows upon us, and the good things he gives to us.'[71] The notion of the celestial diarist was a projection of the growing importance that was attached to the compilation of a regular written record of daily affairs. From the closing decades of the sixteenth century it became an increasingly common practice amongst the upper reaches of society. The form embraced a range of secular and spiritual preoccupations and its practice was not confined to Northern Europe. Manuscript notebooks were becoming necessary adjuncts of commercial and professional life.[72] The merchants of Renaissance Florence extended their practice of financial accounting to record the progress of their business affairs and by extension the rise of their family's prosperity. In the execution of contracts, the manoeuvrings for political position and the management of dynastic succession, it was valuable to have access to a written record of dates and events.[73] The adoption of the diary for spiritual purposes, particularly amongst Protestants, who lacked the regular oral review of the confession, served several purposes. It reinforced the memory of failings and supplications; it selected from the mass of daily thoughts and actions those which had meaning for spiritual transactions; and at its most celebratory it set down the material signs of God's intercession. The diary was both an aide to prayer and a religious meditation in its own right. Parson Woodford began keeping a diary in 1637 with a reflection on his marriage that was addressed both to God and to himself and his wife:

> But Lord I pray thee make us very Carefull & wise for time to come as thou hast in m[er]cye given us speciall love one to another so I humbly pray thee give us discretion, & power over every passion, that no jarre may at any time come at all to interrupt that true affection betweene us and Lord I pray thee give my deare wife harty affection to my poore mother, & wisdome in her Cariage & expressions.[74]

Diaries were also a reflection of the growing importance of reading and writing in the definition and management of the self. Philippe Ariés set out the agenda for his *History of Private Life* project by arguing that 'it is no accident that in England, the birthplace of privacy, diaries were widely kept from the late 1500s.'[75] The most obvious qualification of this view is that literacy itself was a restricted skill in the early sixteenth century. Between 1530 and 1730, signature literacy in England ranged from being more or less universal for the gentry, clergy and professions, around two thirds for yeomen, less than half for tradesmen and craftsmen, and a fifth or lower for husbandmen and labourers. Women as a whole were slightly less literate than the lowest category of men.[76] As would be the case until the nineteenth century, across the more developed European countries literacy consistently declined with social and economic status, and by gender.[77] Signature literacy was a surer indication of reading than writing ability. Only amongst the sons of gentry and professional families who were crowding into schools and universities in the later sixteenth century was there any certainty of a fluent command of written communication.

The distinction between literacy as an individual and a collective practice was inherently fluid. The Reformation was driven by print and the insistence on the believer's engagement with the Bible and other religious texts. But Protestant clergy soon recognized that the bulk of the population would at best encounter God's word not as readers but as groups of listeners, seated in church or receiving instruction from the head of their household. The practice of slow, prayerful reading took form in the medieval monasteries and gradually spread amongst the laity.[78] Yet even in the cloistered world, as Jessica Brantley writes, 'these most "private" of fifteenth-century encounters between people and books depended nonetheless upon social and communal practices.'[79] As need and occasion arose, the same texts were read or were listened to, were performed in the interior mind and in debate and conversation. The emergence of written vernacular languages from the later Middle Ages increased the direct access of the educated elite to the written word, but in a manuscript culture, texts were so precious that possession was as much collective as personal. Although the printing revolution hastened the transition towards silent reading and facilitated the abstraction of readers from surrounding company, the constant tendency of demand to outstrip the supply of literature and literacy entrenched the practice of borrowing materials and skills and sharing their contents amongst networks of readers, both male and female.[80]

The tension between the personal and the social was particularly apparent in the early history of what can be termed virtual privacy, the use of the communications technology of the era to extend the realm of affective relations. By the fifteenth century, correspondence was spreading out from specialized, often religious practitioners to encompass the secular concerns of men and women.[81] Many of the surviving letters were about matters of business, whether financial or political, but amongst them are messages whose central purpose was the maintenance of intimacy in the face of physical separation. An indication of changing practice was the replacement of the medieval study of epistolary composition, the *ars dictaminis*, with a growing genre of humanist guides to letter-writing. The first published English manual was William Fulwood's 1571 *The Enemie of Idlenesse. Teaching the manner and stile how to endite, compose, and wryte all sortes of Epistles and Letters: as wel by answer.* This set out the central purpose of correspondence in a dedicatory epistle:

> by letter well we may
> communicate our hart
> Unto our frende, though distance farre
> Have us remov'd apart.
> By letter we may absence make
> Even presence for to be,
> And talke with him as face to face
> Together we did see.[82]

The written message was the substitute for the distant body. 'Pay me a visit with a little letter', wrote the young Nuremberg merchant Balthasar Paumgartner to his fiancée Magdalena as he travelled abroad.[83] It made separation bearable. Another Nuremberg merchant working away from home, Lucas Friedrich Behaim, wrote to his future bride:

> seeing that [this] has been ordained by God, and that I am now at my life's work, I can freely choose patience. The only thing that could possibly strengthen and increase my endurance is a short, friendly letter from you. That would console my deepest sadness and, so to speak, make alive again in me what is now dead. Dear love, I look entirely to you to grant me this, my heart's desire, but to do so at your own good opportunity.[84]

Whether it was the businessman conducting his affairs in other countries, or the landowner moving between residences, or the cohorts of children in Western Europe who were sent away as servants or apprentices, there was no lack of 'distance farre' separating lovers from lovers, husbands from wives, parents from offspring.[85] The capacity to engage in epistolary intercourse was not confined to men. Sending and receiving letters was one of the few means available for able and intelligent women to escape the physical constraints of the home.[86] It was not necessary that they should be able to read and write themselves.[87] Margaret Paston, the most prolific letter writer of fifteenth-century England, may not herself have been literate at all. She made extensive use of scribes to take down dictation and perhaps read aloud the replies. The editor of her correspondence has found that 104 letters bearing her name were written by as many as twenty-nine different hands.[88] With her husband frequently away in London, over a hundred miles from her Norfolk home, letters were embedded in her daily routines. As her biographer notes, 'She wrote at any time and at all hours: on Sundays; on saints' days; on All Souls' Day, Christmas Eve, Easter Monday, Ascension Day, and Holy Rood Day; to her husband on the same day "that ye departyd hens" and again "at xj of the clok in the nyth the same day I departyd fro yow"; "by candel light at evyn", "at ix of the belle at nyght" and "at nyght, in hast." '[89]

Epistolary communication at once relieved and created stress. It gave assurance that a distant partner was still alive and well, that a child was progressing in his studies, that the affections of an absent lover had not cooled. In the early-modern world, death was never far from the calculations of correspondents. They wrote to ensure that the worst had not befallen those who had last been seen in good health, and speculated endlessly about the causes of a slow reply. The process of sending and receiving letters added a layer of anxiety to intimate discourse. In England, the royal post that was set up by Henry VIII was not meant for private correspondence. Not until the reforms of 1635 was civilian mail formally incorporated into the national service.[90] In the meantime reliance was placed on the many friends, relations and employees who were on the road for other purposes.[91] Such favours made possible virtual privacy but they offered little security. It was never certain whether a delayed reply was a fault of the recipient or of the mode of delivery. Margaret Paston wrote anxiously to her husband:

> May it please you to know that I received a letter from you sent by Laurence Read last Friday, from which I understand that you had no tidings from me at the time your letter was written, which I am surprised about, because I sent you a letter by Chittock's son, who

is an apprentice in London, which was given to him the first Thursday after Lammas Day. And he promised to set off the same day and that you would have it as quickly as possible after he arrived in London.[92]

The element of calculated risk grew as the volume of correspondence expanded in the fifteenth and sixteenth centuries and the expectations of private communication widened. Whilst collective composition or reception remained commonplace, there was at the heart of the process an exchange between individuals. The letters bore a signature, whoever actually put pen to paper, and were addressed to a specified person who expected to receive them unopened and unread, no matter with whom their information was then shared.[93] Devices such as seals were used to conceal the contents. The fragile missives were written in code or with invisible ink such as vinegar, urine and citric juices to protect business or family secrets. Persecuted political or religious groups adopted techniques of concealment as governments began to use the spread of correspondence as an opportunity for espionage.[94] Recipients of sensitive confidences were urged to destroy incriminating messages in case they might later fall into the wrong hands. Conversation could always be overheard, but letters had a physical substance which made them a hostage to time and unknown eyes. As eavesdropping was countered by thicker walls and glazed windows, so another dimension of surveillance was created. Alongside other aspects of privacy, the gain from its extension required effort, ingenuity and a constant balancing of estimated gains against likely dangers.

Correspondence was both a consequence and an extension of privacy. Its conduct reflected the increasing mobility of the population, ranging from wealthy merchants and gentry with business away from home to the apprentices and tradesmen often carrying the letters as they went about their affairs. It was aided by the changes in the domestic environment. Letters were written in studies and closets by those who could afford them, and stored in locked rooms and desks away from prying eyes. They were composed and read in the fugitive spaces in the enlarged houses, or in the surrounding gardens and fields.[95] 'I am sending you with this letter', wrote Balthasar's Magdalena, 'the flower from our garden, which I do not forget to do because I write to you from there.'[96] The substance of the epistolary exchange demonstrated an enhanced aspiration for enclosed communication. William Fulwood's introductory epistle stressed the association of affection and concealment:

When loving letter trots betwene,
And mynde to mynde declares,
It blabbeth not abroade the hid
And secret of our mynde.
To any one, save unto him
To whome we have assigned.[97]

The individualism that was promoted by this form of virtual privacy was essentially social. If the correspondents had to abstract themselves from the company of the home in order to read or write, they did so in order to sustain distributed networks of friends, relatives and colleagues. Less literate communicators had to involve their immediate connections in order to take part in the practice at all. Epistolary intercourse diminished the dependence of intimacy on physical space. In return it enlarged the realm of the secret, with all its attraction and vulnerability.

In 1612, John Dod and Robert Clever published a lengthy guide to domestic living. *A godly Forme of Household Government: for the ordering of private families, according to the direction of God's word* commenced with what had become a conventional metaphor for the well-managed family unit: 'An Householde is as it were a little com-mon-wealth, by the good Government whereof, Gods glorie may be advanced, the commonwealth which standeth of severall families benefited, and all that live in that familie receive much comfort and commoditie.'[98] There was a division of labour between 'the *Chiefe Governour*, which is the *Husband*', and 'secondly a *Fellow-helper*, which is the *Wife*'.[99] The governor's role was ordained by God and in turn he possessed important spiritual responsibilities. He had to ensure that his household went to church on Sunday, and during the week he was required to 'performe to all in his familie...private instruction, and dealing with them in matters of religion'.[100] The authors were not content, however, to sketch the formal roles and duties. They proceeded to describe the relations between husband and wife in terms which were less hierarchical than their initial model and more aware of the significance of boundaries of communication within a household and between its members and the surrounding neighbourhood.

For Dod and Clever, a marriage was founded on an intimate exchange of physical and personal knowledge. 'And therefore it were convenient,' they wrote,

and also much better, that both parties should disclose the one to the other, the imperfections, infirmities, and wants, in either of their bodies;

as also the mediocrity and meannesse of their goods and substance, as
in truth it is: yea, though it should be with the perill and losse one of
the other, rather than the one to obtaine and get the other, with fraude,
guile, and discord.[101]

A marriage was a union of two histories, and these should be fully
shared in the expectation that each partner would accept the demerits
as well as the virtues of the other. Trust and secrecy were mutually
supportive. If the couple were to be open within their relationship
they had to police what was communicated to outsiders: 'It doth
greatly increase Love, when the one faithfully serveth the other: when
in things concerning marriage, the one hideth no secrets nor privities
fro the other, & the one doth not utter or publish the frailties, or
infirmities of the other.'[102]

The authors were realistic enough to accept that however successful the marriage, there would be moments of conflict: 'It can hardly
be avoyded, but there will be some squaring, and diversitie betweene
the man and his wife.'[103] The management of such events was partly
an issue of speed, of not letting grievances fester. But it was also, and
crucially, a matter of controlling what was known of disputes, within
and beyond the household; the couple 'must labour to compose such
matters privately and quickly'.[104] In the first instance, discord should
as far as possible be kept from those with whom the couple were
sharing their limited domestic space. When a husband and wife
argued, advised Dod and Clever, 'Let it bee done privately betweene
themselves, and not before children or servants.'[105] The children
lacked the maturity to understand the matter, the servants the self-
discipline not to foment more grief. The curiosity of those employed
to keep the household and its economy functioning was a permanent
threat to its survival.[106] The smaller the domestic unit, the more its
members were thrust into each other's company, the larger, the
greater the risk that the servant community would form its own
centre of information and intervention. At Wollaton Hall, rebuilt
with such care and expense to provide a model for modern family
living, the rancorous conflict between Sir Francis and Lady
Willoughby was exploited by the officers and upper servants, who,
Alison Friedman writes, 'manipulated their private relationships and
undermined their public image' in a way that denied all prospect of
reconciliation.[107] Church courts were full of servants giving evidence
of misconduct by their superiors based on what they had seen and
heard through doors and walls. Informally they gossiped with each
other, and outside the house or on visits, with the servants of other
families. Once the married couple lost control of their own secrets,

their capacity to maintain a relationship of mutual confidence was fatally weakened.

Beyond the household lay the street or the village. Here again there were boundaries of communication which required constant attention, particularly at times of difficulty within the marriage. 'And if any unkindnesse or displeasure should happen to be at any time betwixt the husband and wife,' cautioned Dod and Clever, 'yet neither of them ought to impart, or to make it knowne unto any one of their neighbours: for if they be such as wish them evill, they will rejoice at it, and if they be such as wish them well, then they minister matter whereof to talke.'[108] As within the walls of the home, it was a matter of negotiating between the desirable and the possible. The material and social interdependency of households demanded a level of shared knowledge about their circumstances.[109] Gossip was a necessary process of embodying collective values and disciplining unacceptable behaviour, including the excessive mis-treatment of dependent members of a household.[110] If there was to be an effective response to a family that had fallen into crisis, there had to be a flow of information about what was required, what was deserved, and what could be supplied.[111] The network of credit and debt that sustained the local economy was fuelled by reputa-tion. Decisions were based on what was collectively known about the moral and material history of the household and its members. This in turn generated dialogue between neighbours about misun-derstandings and false allegations. Where possible a resolution was found informally, although an increasing number of disputes were becoming the subject of litigation.[112] At issue was not the com-munication of information itself, but the means by which it had been obtained and the extent to which it had been wilfully mis-construed. A fifth of all cases in the late-sixteenth-century courts involved scolding or eavesdropping.[113]

Absolute secrecy about personal affairs was neither feasible nor acceptable. In the critical arena of the post-mortem transmission of property, testamentary dispositions were expected to follow custom-ary practice; not until the later seventeenth century did it become possible to exclude people from wills for private reasons. Individuals about whom nothing was known were an immediate source of sus-picion. Household members who refrained from conversation about their own affairs generated mistrust and sacrificed essential mutual support. The task, which had to be addressed daily, was finding a working balance between needs and expectations. A value was placed on the privacy of intimacy. 'What greater pleasure', wrote the young fifteenth-century Venetian scholar Francesco Barbaro, 'than to decide together all things, even while spared the concerns of the household? Than to have a modest wife, a companion in good days and bad, a spouse and a friend? To whom you can confide your most private thoughts regarding your affairs?'[114] For all the press of people within the domestic interior, the modest couple could conceive of some kind of enclosed arena of communication within it. Even amongst those engaged in transgressive sexual relations, there were anticipated possibilities. The numerous cases of adultery exposed by servants or neighbours can be read in two ways. On the one hand they demonstrated the frailty of house construction and the constant threat of interruption. 'In Elizabethan England,' writes John L. Locke, 'domestic walls lulled occupants into thinking they were alone when, in fact, neighbours and strollers were only a structural defect away.'[115] On the other hand they were evidence of the repeated calculation by hopeful lovers that they could find moments of seclusion amidst the comings and goings of the household. There were rules, some recognized by the courts, about how the household's body of knowledge was transmitted. It was improper to obtain secrets secretly. Eavesdropping, literally or metaphorically, was the subject of censure. Implicit in this judgement was the assumption that those in possession of intimate information had the right to influence its communication whilst recognizing what their neighbours had a right to know.

The fraught balance between public and private archives within the community was threatened at two levels. The decline of the great hall and the increasing tendency of elite families to dine and relax apart from both their poorer neighbours and the household servants disrupted the sense of a local society constituted by a shared discussion of its affairs.[116] For the wealthy, withdrawal became easier to achieve, for the less prosperous it became more difficult to justify. The rise of Puritanism forced a reconsideration of the legitimacy of domestic privacy.[117] By the 1630s Protestantism had finally gained ascendancy over the Church of Rome in Britain, and its radical wing was determined to transform the culture of unlettered labourers. Zealous reformers were increasingly intolerant of enclosed realms of belief and behaviour. They demanded public accountability for what was done and thought inside the household, and for how its members behaved as they went about their business or pleasure. Where amicable neighbourly relations had been a shared aspiration, irrespective of wealth or social standing, now ministers and godly laymen drawn from the ranks of the minor gentry, yeomen and artisans took satisfaction from the conflicts their .

interventions engendered. The customary calendar of recreation came under attack together with year-round threats to sober living such as alehouses. Attempts were made to cleanse the Sabbath of profane activities, including working and dancing, and to ensure that once it returned home from the church service, the congregation led God-fearing lives during the rest of the week. The church courts were deployed to enforce moral discipline. Successful prosecutions required the assemblage of evidence derived from the inspection of the labouring poor by their respectable neighbours. Non-reciprocal forms of surveillance were undertaken which cut across the complex systems of mutual disclosure and conditional privacy. In turn the fierce and often successful resistance to cultural policing generated new structures of evasion and concealment.

What contained the threat of surveillance, then and in later centuries by other means and agencies, was the largely unacknowledged nature of intimate communication. In a subsequently famous passage in his *Essays*, Michel de Montaigne drew attention to the wealth of non-verbal devices employed in everyday conversation:

> After all, lovers quarrel, make it up again, beg favours, give thanks, arrange secret meetings and say everything, with their eyes...
>
> And what about our hands? With them we request, promise, summon, dismiss, menace, pray, supplicate, refuse, question, show astonishment, count, confess, repent, fear, show shame, doubt, teach, command, incite, encourage, make oaths, bear witness, make accusations, condemn, give absolution, insult, despise, defy, provoke, flatter, applaud, bless, humiliate, mock, reconcile, advise, exalt, welcome, rejoice, lament; show sadness, grieve, despair; astonish, cry out, keep silent and what not else, with a variety and multiplicity rivalling the tongue.
>
> What of the head? We summon, dismiss, admit, reject, deny, welcome, honour, venerate, disdain, request, refuse, rejoice, lament, fondle, tease, submit, brave, exhort, menace, affirm and inquire.
>
> And what of our eyebrows or our shoulders? None of their movements fails to talk a meaningful language which does not have to be learned, a language common to us all.[118]

In a world where all but a tiny fraction of information was exchanged face-to-face this late-sixteenth-century insight had far-reaching implications. It applied to any level of discourse but particularly to those familiar with the language of each other's body. As Montaigne recognized, lovers knew each other by how much they could say with their eyes alone. Words themselves, whether spoken or written, were only one element of communication, and the more familiar the interlocutors the less important words were. Those who held 'no secrets nor privities from the other', whose mutual knowledge was based on time and trust, had at their disposal a range of means for exchanging information that diluted the effect of overheard or retold conversation. The greater danger posed by the eavesdropper and the gossip was the misconstruction rather than the betrayal of intimacy.

2

Privacy and Communication 1650–1800

During the early-modern period, face-to-face discourse was challenged by two forces of change. Urbanization and mass communication were interdependent events. Print oiled the machinery of living in the expanding towns and cities, and literacy and literature flourished in the urban environments. In each case, the key question was the impact on informal means of communication. Where once individuals managed their personal archive principally through conversation – whether verbal or, in Montaigne's terms, visual – with those in their immediate physical proximity, now they encountered teeming populations that presented new questions about who could know what about whom. Anonymity, the bedrock of 'the right to be let alone', was seen as a possibility. In its bleakest form, privacy became a synonym for isolation as meaningful engagement with the lives of others was overwhelmed by the press of numbers. At the same time the two manifestations of the contemporary communication revolution, print and correspondence, seemed capable of facilitating greater withdrawal from everyday sociability. 'Between 1500 and 1800', writes Roger Chartier, 'man's altered relation to the written word helped to create a new private sphere into which the individual could retreat, seeking refuge from the community.'[1] It was a process of growing interiority and independence:

> The ability to read was an essential prerequisite for certain new practices around which people built their private lives. Personal communication with a read or written text liberated the individual from the old

mediators, freed him or her from the control of the group, and made it possible to cultivate an inner life.[2]

By this means a new sense of the framed self could be nurtured apart from the orally constructed society. The following two sections will take a measure of each of these potential developments in turn.

During the seventeenth century, London almost tripled in size. By 1700, it was the largest city in Europe, with over 500,000 inhabitants. It contained as many as one in ten of the British population, and perhaps one in six lived in it at some point in their lives.[3] Its continuing growth, with around 8,000 migrants arriving annually, presented a double problem of knowledge. How was it possible to comprehend the scale and complexity of this endless enlargement? London was still a walkable city, but no pedestrian, no coachman could know every street. How were the inhabitants to recognize their neighbours and manage the shifting boundaries of private and public identity? As Richard Sennett writes, 'the material conditions of life made people question marks to each other.'[4] In 1698 Ned Ward, a high Tory pamphleteer and satirist, commenced a publication entitled *The London Spy* which supplied a means of answering these questions without the need for physical exposure to the teeming streets.[5] 'Herein,' he wrote, 'Town gentlemen may see the view of the Town (without their experience), and learn the better to avoid those snares and practised subtleties which trepan many to their ruin.'[6] The title of the serial, which was published as a book the following year, constituted London as a secret that required decoding on behalf of the reader. Ward adopted the classical form of the rural visitor accompanied by a local guide, which was repeated by a host of imitators through to Pierce Egan's *Life in London* more than a century later.[7] To learn, it was necessary to walk, or ramble, a term that did not translate from an urban to a rural setting until late in the nineteenth century.[8]

In smaller urban communities, and in the countryside where most of the population still lived, there was much occasion to be out of doors but little consciousness of the act of moving from one place to another. The metropolitan pedestrian was a special case, calling forth a host of handbooks and pocket maps. In 1716, John Gay, the future author of *The Beggar's Opera*, wrote a poetical guide to the 'long perplexing lanes untrod before' entitled *Trivia: or, the Art of Walking the Streets of London*.[9] As with the *London Spy*, the enterprise emphasized the physical distinction between the domestic interior and the roofless exterior. Even more so than Ward, Gay drew attention to the sheer discomfort of being out of doors. As John Bancks wrote in 'A Description of London', 'Streets, unpleasant in all weather'.[10] At every turn those – like Gay himself – who could not afford their own coach were assaulted by smells and noise, buffeted by other pedestrians, and soaked 'when dirty Waters from Balconies drop'.[11] While the guides to rambling were appearing, the grip of the 'Little Ice Age' was beginning to relax.[12] It was not quite so cold and damp in the London streets. At the same time there was a growth in expectations of domestic comfort, sharpening the spatial dimension of privacy.

The construction standards of the capital's houses had been improved under the 1667 Act for Rebuilding the City of London following the Great Fire, which specified that exterior walls should be built of brick or stone, and interior walls of sufficient thickness to act as a firebreak.[13] Evasion of the regulations, particularly in outlying districts, was countered by further Building Acts in 1764, 1772 and 1784. Life outside the houses was kept at bay by panelling, by the greater use of glass in windows and by the more frequent hanging of curtains.[14] The journey from the front door to the domestic life of the household was lengthened. Houses in the capital were of three or four storeys and one or two rooms deep, with the living quarters constructed above the workshop, and the sleeping chamber above the parlour.[15] Prosperous artisans might command up to five rooms, and the upper reaches of the middling orders as many as eight. In larger urban and country houses, corridors became more common, permitting greater specialization of activities within each room.[16] Where possible, activities that generated odours, particularly cooking, were increasingly separated, with distinct spaces for brewing, for preparing food and for consuming it. There was less employment of temporary truckle beds for children, servants and visitors, and greater investment in beds and bedding, at least for the married couple.[17]

The pace of change was uneven, and for the poorer classes often imperceptible.[18] Crowded, multi-functional interior spaces continued to be a reality for the bulk of the population whether in towns or the countryside.[19] As Peter Guillery writes of London, 'most houses had in-built flexibility, and there was a great deal of the *ad hoc* about room use; in smaller houses, few rooms did not contain a bed.'[20] In the smallest, life in all its aspects was still conducted in a single room. Developments that were later to transform the hygiene of the home, such as the 'S-bend' patented by Alexander Cumming in 1775, and Joseph Bramah's float valve of 1778, were in this period the preserve of the rich and the experimental.[21] Most households still used close stools and commodes adjacent to the beds in which everyone slept.

But gradually a new model of domestic life was taking shape, at a greater distance both from the workplace and from the public arena beyond the front door. Prosperous householders increased their expenditure on furniture during the eighteenth century.[22] Larger windows brought more light into rooms, facilitating seated activities demanding close attention, such as sewing or reading.

As the interior of the home became marginally quieter, so the streets outside became significantly noisier.[23] There were more artisans disturbing the peace with their labours, more tradesmen crying their wares, more pedestrians in pattens clinking on pavements, and above all there was more horse-drawn traffic rumbling across paved surfaces.[24] The noise was most resented when it was destructive of expected quiet. Quotidian church bells were rendered soundless by their predictability; the early-morning cacophony described by John Gay occurred when all the world was up and about its business. The eruption of drunken singing when the weary household was abed was much less welcome. The more it became possible to control assaults on the senses inside the home, and the greater the opportunity for quiet domestic pastimes such as reading or correspondence, the more noticeable were the sounds and smells of the world outside.

The guidebooks were a product of a new interiority. They vividly described the physicality of street life but at the same time insulated the reader from it. The printed page offered silenced noise, deodorized smell, unthreatening violence, uncontagious disease. By their own account these guides supplied a prophylactic against the multiple forms of moral and physical downfall to be found out of doors. 'Reader,' proclaimed John Dunton's serial guide to London's prostitutes, 'if the Time and Moneys spent in these *Six Nights Rambles* may reclaim or hinder the Debauchery of one single Person, I shall think it all worth my Labour.'[25] Their success in the expanding literary marketplace rested on a claim to an authenticity that was powerful precisely because of its abstraction from direct experience. Gay described the plight of the rural visitor:

> Here oft the Peasant, with enquiring Face,
> Bewildered, trudges on from Place to Place;
> He dwells on ev'ry Sign with stupid Gaze,
> Enters the narrow Alley's doubtful Maze,
> Trys ev'ry winding Court and Street in vain,
> And doubles o'er his weary Steps again.[26]

Left to his own devices, the incoming pedestrian would become in every sense a lost soul. The urban insider who acted as the guide in texts from Ward to Egan was a fictional construct, an avatar of the author rather than a real being. The sheer variety of street life made the abstract figure the more feasible companion. There was no single, authoritative perspective. All but the very rich had to walk, day in and day out, about their work and their pleasures. The eighteenth century was the high tide of pedestrian freedom before the modern era. Pavements began to separate walkers from wheeled traffic and streets were better lit at night.[27] The prosperous and respectable mixed with those who lacked either quality. Un-veiled women were permitted to go abroad, whether to make money or to spend it. Visitors and residents made a virtue of their perambulations, celebrating the effect of exercise on health, and enjoying the possibilities of viewing and being viewed. Streets and open spaces began to be constructed not just as thoroughfares but as places to dawdle and stop. Specialized venues were established for enjoying the company of friends and lovers and like-minded strangers. The most famous of these, Vauxhall Gardens in Lambeth, began as New Spring Gardens sometime before the Restoration, and was developed as a fashionable venue from 1728 onwards.[28] 'The people of London are as fond of walking as our friends at Pekin of riding', observed Oliver Goldsmith; 'one of the principal entertainments of the citizens here in summer is to repair about nightfall to a garden not far from town, where they walk about, shew their best clothes and best faces, and listen to a concert provided for the occasion.'[29]

The function of the literary guide was both to celebrate the chaos and to distil the rules required to manage it. The immediate challenge was visual contact with passers-by. John Gay announced the purpose of his enterprise:

> How to walk clean by Day, and safe by Night,
> How jostling Crouds, with Prudence to decline,
> When to assert the Wall and when resign,
> I sing.[30]

Street etiquette was founded on the oblique glance.[31] Wholly to ignore other pedestrians was to risk embarrassing collision, but to stare at them was an invasion of personal privacy. It was necessary, as Gay advised, to anticipate an approaching encounter by taking or ceding the inside route along the pavement. Women by growing convention should be allowed to take the path furthest from the puddled, manure-covered road. Disregarding the buildings lining a route threatened disorientation. Not to notice urban facades made failure to reach a destination more likely. But to look directly at a face or in through a window was to cause offence. The courteous rambler demonstrated consideration, refined to instinct, in achieving an appropriate balance between seeing and not seeing. This cast of mind calls into question the conventional attribution of anonymity to the early-modern and modern urban community. It implies a transition from a knowable to an unknowable community that is perhaps more absolute than any that was made by those who arrived in the city from what is held to be the face-to-face world of the village or the small town.

Escaping the surveillance of neighbours and the authorities was a perennial attraction of the urban world and, as we saw in the previous chapter, was increasingly so for those who were subject to the censorious gaze of their superiors. As London became more conscious of itself, so its spokesmen projected a rural way of life that was the mirror image of the assumed virtues of their emerging civilization. Writing in the *Spectator*, the founding text of the eighteenth-century public sphere, Joseph Addison celebrated the contrast:

> It is indeed high time for me to leave the Country, since I find the whole Neighbourhood begin to grow very inquisitive after my Name and Character: My Love of Solitude, Taciturnity, and particular way of Life, having raised a great Curiosity in all these Parts...I shall therefore retire into the Town, if I may make use of that Phrase, and get into the Crowd again as fast as I can, in order to be alone.[32]

But the point of the crowd, as the urban guidebooks insisted, was that it denied complete isolation, whether physical or psychological. It presented instead tiers of knowledge. To proceed along the street or to enter a public building in total ignorance of the company was neither feasible nor safe. Instead the newcomer was advised to recognize types of individual as an interim stage to greater familiarity. The *London Spy*, for instance, described a character in a public house: 'he that sat over against him, in the plate-buttoned suit and white beaver hat, is a kind of amphibious rascal, a compound of two sorts of villainy. He is one half town-trap and the other half sweetener.'[33] The advice revealed both the expertise and the limitations of the guide; he possessed a bottomless archive of performing characters but could never identify an actor. Such information did not preclude a closer acquaintance which might in due course involve an exchange of names and identities; it merely gave the stranger help in determining whether or not to pass by. The notion that it was impossible to be alone in the country, in mind or body, demonstrated how little Addison understood rural society. There were fugitive opportunities within domestic accommodation and, as they had been in previous centuries, gardens and fields were places of retreat. Furthermore there existed varying levels of familiarity within the streets of the city, even one as large as London. Incoming migrants might for a while experience the shock of the strange, but once they had found a home and a job, a map would form, distinguishing known from unknown thoroughfares, and conversable faces of neighbours from less recognizable pedestrians further afield.

The second difficulty with the trope of anonymity is that it treats the street as a synecdoche for the city. It may have been the most visible manifestation of urban modernity, but it was only one element of the way of life. Most urban dwellers spent some part of the day moving out of doors in heterogeneous streams of people, but they left and returned to homes and workplaces. Despite the constant flood of migrants from the countryside, almost all the residents had a roof over their heads. As in other centuries, incomers tended to make for the homes and neighbourhoods of existing acquaintances or family connections.[34] Single men or women found lodgings in households willing to sub-let their cramped space, or jobs as apprentices or servants which came with a bed. They walked along the new pavements but rarely slept on them. The tolerance of crowded rooms made it less likely for those seeking accommodation to be turned away. Once inside the property, however small and insubstantial the doors, people had a right to resist entry by others. Whether they were renting or sub-letting from tenants, occupation rather than ownership defined private space. Even if he was calling for the rent, the landlord had to ask permission to cross the threshold.[35] As London grew, so did the legal rights of its residents. The ruling that 'the house of everyone is his castle' was set forth in 1604 and by 1700 it was as, Amanda Vickery writes, 'already a hoary cliché of English Common Law'.[36] Burglary and housebreaking were capital offences, and locks were widely used to secure both the front door against strangers and internal doors against lodgers.[37] There was an established arms race between householders and criminals, with inventors offering mechanisms that would defeat those 'furnished by a number and variety of keys, or other instruments, adapted to the purpose of picking, or opening Locks'.[38] In the 1760s, the general principle of the occupancy of property embodying the ability to exclude others was enshrined in Blackstone's *Commentaries* and dramatized by John Wilkes' attack on the use of general warrants to mount a search for incriminating documents.[39] 'My house [has been] ransacked and plundered,' he protested, 'my most private and secret concerns divulged...Such inhuman principles of star-chamber tyranny will, I trust, by this court...be finally extirpated.'[40] Heavy fines were imposed on the king's revenue agents in 1770 for committing trespass in pursuit of unpaid excise. 'This is an unlawful entry into a man's house (which is his castle),' stated the lord chief justice, 'an invasion upon his wife and family at peace and quietness therein.'[41] The long-standing regulations controlling the surveillance of one neighbour by another were strengthened by a ruling in 1709 that windows could not be altered 'if before...they could not look out of them into the yard...for privacy is valuable'.[42]

None of these rights were invented in the period. They were re-stated and extended as the power of the crown was challenged by an increasingly assertive urban society and as the continuing press of people and buildings demanded clearer regulation. In principle, these rights applied equally to town and country, but in practice it is doubtful whether the local squire was much influenced by Cope or Blackstone as he called upon the cottagers on his estate. What was changing, more rapidly in towns and cities than in smaller, dispersed settlements, was how knowledge of individuals and their intimate lives was being communicated and managed. London, like every other urban centre, was full of neighbourhoods that were reshaped as populations grew.[43] Eighteenth-century Paris, the second city of Europe, was not, David Garrioch has argued, a society full of strangers, but rather one of intricate, knowable communities.[44] Everyone had a place in a network of familiar co-residents. At issue was not anonymity displacing named and known identity, but the means by which personality and personal relationships were exposed and controlled. Just as encounters in the street increasingly avoided close face-to-face contact, so the deployment of sight and conversation to embody and enforce standards began to decline. Character became less dependent on its projection by visual signs of dress and demeanour in the hasty, half-noticed passage of people on the pavements. It was more infrequently fixed by language spoken or shouted out of doors. Pausing to exchange words became a diminished element of the exterior experience. Robert Shoemaker has traced the decline of defamation as a contestable offence in the later seventeenth century and throughout the eighteenth.[45] Reputation still mattered across a range of registers, from creditworthiness and employability to more diffuse forms of self and household worth, but it was perceived to be less vulnerable to what was said about it.[46] Speech delivered from the doorstep to all in earshot, or muttered in conversations which were overheard by chance or deliberate eavesdropping, began to lose its perceived power to damage. As it did so, the female gossip as a pivotal figure of authority became less threatening. She was more frequently viewed as someone damaging her own reputation by her incontinent inquisition. In part, the concern was displaced to physical violence as a disruptive force in social and communal relationships; in part the growing ease of getting into print following the 1695 Licensing Act shifted the anxiety from slander to libel.

The dilution of face-to-face communication outside the home was accompanied by a decline in the principal institutional means of dealing with deviant behaviour. Since the Reformation, the church consistory courts, as we have seen, had been a critical opponent of enclosed domestic privacy.[47] They were abolished during the Commonwealth and never regained their former authority after the Restoration.[48] In their heyday they gave agency to neighbours, relying on their oral evidence, and defending their reputations against malignant conversation. The courts dealt with both the personal damage caused by slanderous words and the harm caused by scolding or argumentative discourse to the general texture of neighbourly relations.[49] Together with the bearers of gossip, they disputed the right of households to constitute themselves as privileged spheres of intimate knowledge and behaviour. During the eighteenth century, the reach of the courts contracted to matters directly relating to ecclesiastical regulation. No new institutional or legal entity was called into being to replace them; instead, greater reliance was placed on the domestic unit as the principal agency of social discipline. The household had long been viewed as central to the maintenance of communal and political order, but in the stressed period that culminated in the Civil War, it could not be trusted to perform its responsibilities without external supervision and sanction. Its private nature was itself a threat to the collective wellbeing, fomenting or concealing spiritual, sexual or physical misconduct. Increased confidence was now placed in the household's capacity to constitute a self-sufficient agency of moral health, which in turn depended on the nature of its communication practices in the world beyond its walls.

In 1701 Richard Gough set out to construct a prosopography of the Shropshire village of Myddle. His enterprise rested on the relative stability of the community. Most of the inhabitants attended the Anglican service each Sunday. Odd individuals were missing from the congregation, such as John Ralphs, who 'has imbibed some phanaticall oppinions, and comes not to Church',[50] but it proved possible to encompass the local society by the simple expedient of proceeding pew by pew and writing compact histories of each of the families that occupied them. Although there were comings and goings, including the occasional migration to London, it was a knowable society, in contrast to the urban settlements where so many of the inhabitants had been born elsewhere. Gough's biographical strategy combined personal detail with behavioural types which in their way were just as generalized as those used by Ned Ward in his guide to the streets of the distant capital. Gough was particularly concerned to delineate good conduct within and between families. A description of a local farmer captured all that was to be admired in early-eighteenth-century society:

> This Mr William Watkins is now (1701) owner of this farme, and very happy in that it hath pleased God to give him such skill, care, and industry in good husbandry as his grand-father and father had, for hee is not inferiour to eyther of them therein. Hee is alsoe happy in a prudent, provident and discreet wife who is every way suitable for such an husband. They live very loveingly togeather, very loveing to their neighbours, and very well beloved by theire neighbours, and they are both happy in that itt hath pleased God in toaken of his love to them, and theire mutuall love to one another to blesse them with many comely and witty children.[51]

Here and throughout the account there is a double stress on affection. Those who loved each other also generated warmth and goodwill amongst those they lived alongside. Gough wrote of another villager, 'his wife was a good, discreet woman, they were both peaceable and well-beeloved.'[52] There was a sense of a collective appreciation of what Lawrence Stone termed 'affective individualism', although, as elsewhere in early-modern society, there is no indication that the sentiment was confined to the middling and upper strata of the population.[53] At the same time it was taken for granted that a successful marriage enhanced rather than reduced relations with surrounding households. There remained a range of emotional and practical interdependencies between one domestic unit and another. William Watkins' business as a farmer required not just his husbanding skills but his effective negotiation of the local structure of borrowing and lending goods, services and money during the course of the agricultural year. This in turn rested on his reputation as a stable family man, whose time and money were spent not in the public house but on his dependents and on his continuation of the dynastic farm. Despite the apparent blessing of the Almighty on his family, there was no guarantee that his domestic unit would not in the future suffer illness or death for which the emotional or material assistance of neighbours was the only resource available. In this sense the closeness of the couple's relationship made it more open to the social network in which it was embedded. It attracted rather than repelled charity. At the same time, where there was disharmony or worse within the family, its members had every interest in keeping it quiet. As Linda Pollock has noted, the wealthier and more powerful the family in this period, the more effort was invested in keeping secret any matrimonial discord.[54]

Richard Gough had a keen appreciation of the mechanism by which relations were nourished within and beyond the family. It was a matter of self-discipline in the communication of private information. The key term in his assessment of a successful marriage was 'discreet'. It applied to how the couple interacted with each other, with a particular emphasis on the wife's capacity to control herself. And it referred to how the household managed its dealings with the neighbourhood. On the debit side of the ledger Gough constructed for Myddle were those who combined aggression with verbal indiscipline. He described Daniell Wicherley as 'a spare leane person, whose countenance shewed that he was a passionate cholerick man, and his actions proved him soe; for hee was allways at strife with his neighbours, and much in debt'.[55] What was particularly deplored, as it had long been in English society, was the propensity to translate verbal confrontation into legal dispute. Gough's review of the church pews arrived at Bartholomew Peirce: 'Hee was a taylor by trade, and was a crosse, troublesome, litigiouse person amongst his neighbours. His wife was as bad in that behalf as hee was.'[56] Litigation was a well-used option for dealing with intra-communal strife. Micro studies of early-modern society have demonstrated the accessibility of the law to those of merely modest means, and the damage to the texture of neighbourly relations that this caused.[57] In neighbouring Staffordshire a resident was described as 'a comen pyker of quarrels a comen haunter of Alehouses a dronkard and a comon mayntener and partaker of dyvers and manye accions and sutes that have growed...within the parish of Norton and Lyttle Wyrley to the great disagreement trouble and expense of moste of the neighbours there'.[58] Where possible, various forms of neighbourly conflict resolution were attempted in order to prevent the cost and long-term harm of court cases. Better still was the instinct to curb the passions altogether, and keep within the family such grievances as were harboured.

Managing the boundaries of knowledge within and between families was a matter of constant effort. Much time was spent talking about talking. On 11 November 1715, the young London lawyer Dudley Ryder made a note of an informal soirée he had attended with his mother and sister: 'The conversation turned entirely upon the manners, behaviour, way of living, clothes, dress, &c., of their neighbours and though at the same time they were blaming others for prying into the secrets of families and talking about others.'[59] Ryder's main preoccupation, apart from his nascent career, was getting a wife with whom to establish his own sphere of bounded intercourse. He was so tongue-tied that he resorted to hiring prostitutes not for sex, but for practice in addressing women.[60] Amidst his embarrassment, he kept a clear sight of his goal:

> I wish I could reason myself into an easy state of mind under the thoughts of never being married, but I find a strong inclination towards it, not from any principle of lust or desire to enjoy a woman in bed, but from a natural tendency, a prepossession in favour of the married state. It is charming and moving, it ravishes me to think of a pretty creature concerned in me, being my most intimate friend, constant companion and always ready to soothe me, take care of me and caress me.[61]

Finding the friend with whom affection could deepen into unspoken intimacy was an enterprise that exposed a painful tension between transparency and secrecy. On the one hand courtship was a legitimate concern of both families and the community more broadly; it might well involve the transmission of property, and everyone in the neighbourhood had an interest in the establishment of a new member of the local constellation of domestic units. Undue secrecy in the affair was mistrusted as it heightened the possibility that inexperienced lovers might make an irrevocable decision unsupervised by their more responsible elders. At the same time marriages were not formally arranged by parents in the absence of children. The couple had an accepted right for the relationship to be an expression of their will and affection, however much their choice might require compromise with a range of material considerations. They therefore needed an opportunity to develop some kind of knowledge of each other. In the intensity of his first courtship, Roger Lowe of Ashton-in-Makerfield sought a double withdrawal from the company of his family and friends:

> Att my comeing home I cald att Roger Naylor's and partly ingagd to come beare them company that night; I comeing downe to shop and stayd awhile, and then went againe and privatly ingagd to Mary to sit up awhile to let us discourse, which she promisd, and the maine question was because we lived seaverally that we wuld not act soe publickely as others, that we might live privately and love firmely, that we might be faithfull to each other in our love till the end: all which was

firmely agreed upon. This was the first night that ever I stayd up a wooing ere in my life.[62]

As so often in the crowded domestic spaces it proved possible to find time alone, on this occasion with the assistance of a conspiring friend. And between them the couple agreed to set up a wall around them, the better to get close to each other. Although the relationship soon foundered, the couple's ambition to 'live privately and love firmely' expressed a more general aspiration of conjugal life, however difficult its achievement might be.

Once the household was established, the most pervasive threat to marital privacy came from those hired to assist in its maintenance. It has been calculated that in early-modern Europe about 40 per cent of all children spent a period as a servant.[63] For those who found employment in their mid-teens in another household there was both a gain and a loss in terms of their personal privacy. They might for the first and only time in their lives enjoy the seclusion of a bedroom, albeit cramped, cold, sparsely furnished and shared with another servant.[64] But they were subject to a surveillance of their conduct and communication that was legally enforceable. They were expected neither to have nor to seek close emotional, still less sexual, relations with other servants. Dismissal would follow the discovery that they had been gossiping out of doors about their employer's affairs. Both parties in the employment relationship that in so many homes complemented the marriage contract were faced with intractable problems of controlling information.[65] Few houses were large enough for the emotional and physical lives of the master and his family to be shielded from those who shared the accommodation. Servants had to go out of doors to purchase goods for the domestic enterprise, or travelled with the family as increasingly visits were made to urban centres. In the performance of their duties they encountered other servants or tradesmen, and it was physically impossible for their conversation to be continually monitored. For as long as the family functioned as a unit it could seek to police the boundaries of its information, but when it broke down and its affairs became matters of legal process, the eyewitness knowledge of servants gained lethal power, especially if they themselves had not merely witnessed but been willing or unwilling partners in adultery.[66] The sheer mobility of servants in what was generally an employee's market was a further difficulty.[67] Whilst the attempt could be made to circumscribe what they said to whom whilst they were in employment, once they had moved on and taken their archive to what might be a neighbouring household, all control was lost.

At issue were different registers of intimacy. What made the management of the household's secrets increasingly a matter for debate in eighteenth-century commentaries and advice manuals was the latent tension between contractual and emotional discipline. Dismissal was both a real threat and a last resort. Better to rely on the increasing emphasis on the household as a self-sufficient structure of moral authority, where its head taught by example and instruction how all of its members should behave in relation to each other. In this regard, as more generally, there was a diminishing expectation that external sanctions were relevant to policing the boundaries of privacy. What were needed were relations of trust which would ensure the appropriate conduct of servants when out of the sight and hearing of their superiors. This in turn required the servant to subordinate the motivation of monetary gain in their employment strategy, an increasingly difficult expectation in the expanding sector of personal services. There was a further question of the substance of the personal knowledge that was under threat. At one level the matter was an applied version of the more general exchange of sensitive information within a bounded community. The Scottish manservant John MacDonald moved regularly between employers. In one household he was particularly impressed by the capacity of the principal servant, who combined professional with listening skills: 'The housekeeper was one of the best common cooks in Scotland, and she was up to the gossip in the parlour.'[68] She had accumulated a body of information which at her discretion could be shared with fellow servants or with others outside the household. But there was a deeper level of transfer inherent in the relationship between the individuals thrown together by the demand for service and the need for an income. MacDonald recalled with pride the physical assistance he rendered a subsequent employer: 'I lived with my master one year. One day in particular my master dined out, and I waited on him, and at night we both came home merry; when I put his hair in papers, and undressed him, I took up his shoes in my left hand, and put his coat over the same arm.'[69] This was true intimacy, an unspeaking interaction involving an exposure of the person whether or not it was subsequently talked about, or, in MacDonald's case, written down.

The servant problem, as it was coming to be labelled, existed in the countryside and the city. There was a spatial consistency of experience, the more so given the increasing tendency of those with large country houses to establish satellite bases, particularly in London. It is a further reason for resisting the polarization of early-modern society between a world of strangers in the rapidly expanding urban centres and a life of face-to-face familiarity in the villages and smaller towns, from which the migrants and visitors were drawn and where most of the population still lived. Irrespective of location, there was a general strengthening of the expectations held of the household as a bounded communication arena and a corresponding weakening of the power of formal or informal communal intervention. More value was placed on the discretion of private couples and less weight on the conversation of those with whom they mixed outside the home. Paradoxically, London, the shock city of eighteenth-century Europe, could be valued as an avoidance of extremes. Those who found their way to its teeming streets escaped the intense surveillance of squires and clergymen. With time and experience, whether or not assisted by the published guides, they could learn to navigate levels of personal encounter, from the oblique glance at passers-by, to the easy conviviality of a wider range of associations, to the immediate neighbourhood of the home, and to its interior secure behind its threshold.

The guides to negotiating the boundaries between private and public life in the city reflected growth in the market for print and in the skills required to decode it. They were a product of the world they sought to describe. Urban communities in the early-modern period were more literate than those in the countryside and were the centres of local and regional book production. Signature literacy for men was passing 50 per cent in the more developed countries of Northern and Western Europe at the beginning of the eighteenth century.[70] Even amongst the labouring poor there was a scattering of capacity picked up in church or private day schools, or learned from educated family members or friends. Amongst women, books and their use had ceased to be the preserve of a tiny educated elite and had become an expectation of those in the middling and upper orders of society. Change is most apparent in the enhancement of the life of the household. The rambler through the city streets described by Ward and Gay barely had time to decipher the shop signs, let alone sit and read an extended text. The domestic interior, particularly in the towns, became the location for mental recreation and exploration. Increasing physical comfort combined with a wider availability of printed matter, permitted more time and attention to be devoted to pursuits that further accentuated the contrast between the exterior crowd and the world behind the front door. For the privileged minority who could afford to construct and furnish a closet or a study, print facilitated a further level of retreat within the household. Less prosperous but equally determined readers sought to abstract themselves amidst the noise and bustle of multi-functional interiors; it required effort and persistence to maintain concentration and a willingness to negotiate with the conversational needs of others.

For the most part however, the acquisition and consumption of print accentuated, rather than undermined, sociability, and sooner or later propelled the literary consumer out of doors. The cost of reading matter continually outran the budgets of those eager to enjoy it. In response, lending libraries proliferated in the eighteenth century, whether purely commercial operations charging a guinea a year or book collections associated with coffee shops, cathedrals, schools and other voluntary associations.[71] Out in the street, books could be bought new from specialized shops, or second-hand from market stalls. They were carried to the countryside by networks of literary pedlars, chapmen in England, colporteurs in France, and shared amongst villagers until their pages disintegrated. The scale of the trade reflected the breadth of the reading population. The middle-ranking London publisher Thomas Tias had a stock, at the time of his death in 1664, of around 90,000 bound and unbound chapbooks ready to be distributed by itinerant booksellers, enough for one family in fifteen in the kingdom.[72]

Inside the home print enlarged social intercourse. Books were exchanged between friends and relations; they were read aloud to family, servants and visitors, for entertainment or for distraction as other manual tasks such as sewing were undertaken.[73] From the process of learning to read, which until late in the nineteenth century involved the constant recitation in the classroom of syllables and whole words,[74] through to the adult consumption of the written word, moments of silent reading were the exception rather than the standard experience. Caution needs to be exercised in associating print with the emancipation of individual intellects from the influence of more immediate structures of influence and control. As John Brewer has insisted, 'Constraints are not removed by the emancipatory culture of the printed or public word; they are changed. They operate more abstractly, but the gaze of the distant reader is every bit as present (and just as constraining) as the look of the inquisitive neighbour and the scrutiny of priest and congregation.'[75] Participation in disembodied communities of readers reconfigured, rather than transcended, the task of exercising independent judgement. The consumers of print became part of a different kind of audience. Their experience was shaped both by the writer's construction of a readership and by the responses of those who shared in the process of interrogating the text.

Within the home, religious books and sermons were common-place.[76] It can be argued that the major transformation in the role of the written word in spiritual observance came, not with Luther and the printing press in the fifteenth century, but with the rise of Pietism two centuries later.[77] The emphasis, particularly in Protestantism, shifted from hearing and debating the addresses of clergy to reading not just the Bible and the Prayer Book, but an increasing range of commentaries, printed sermons and prayers, and guides to Christian living. Catholicism also came to see the household, and what was termed by the Jesuits as 'mental prayer', as important to the mainte-nance of a spiritual society,[78] but reserved a critical role for the intercession of professional clergy and the communion of saints. The believer, with her or his text, was a more self-sufficient figure in the Protestant world.[79] The role of private prayer was influenced in a number of ways by the shift in the mode of communicating religious experience. A wide range of printed aids to personal observance appeared on the market. Some, like Lancelot Andrews' pocket-sized *Manual of the Private Devotions and Meditations*, supplied ready-made prayers for different times in the day or season.[80] Others, like Thomas Brooks' *The Privie Key of Heaven*, combined practical advice with theological justification for regular withdrawal from the company of the household. Both reading and writing were integral to the activity. In his *Enter into thy closet. Or, A method and Order for Private Devotion*, Edward Wettenhall supplied instructions for furnishing the specialized room. There should be a desk and a couch, which ought not to be too comfortable: 'To these I would add a *Bible*, a *Common-prayer book*, two *Paper books* (which when filed must be supplied by two others) and a *Pen* and *Ink*.'[81] Recording the review of the soul created a literary archive which was integral to the con-tinuing conversation with God.

The manual writers were aware that they were addressing a privi-leged minority: 'Speaking therefore', wrote Brooks, 'to such who have estates and leisure, and so may have opportune privacy...'[82] Yet even servants could be encouraged to find a moment of seclusion, if only a prayer on their knees as they went to bed and rose in the morning. At one level, this was privacy at its most individualistic and asocial.[83] The principal focus of the devotional manuals was the lone penitent, wrestling with her or his conscience as a means of attaining God's blessing in this world and the next. Where private prayer was suc-cessfully undertaken, the principal beneficiary was the believer in their personal journey to salvation. The process demanded a physical and mental abstraction from the business of the household. Opening a heart to the Almighty required a level of silence on the part of both the private meditator and the surrounding company. 'Shut the door twice over,' urged Brooks, 'the door to the closet and your own lips when praying.'[84] It reflected an increasing premium in Northern and Western European educated society on what Peter Burke describes as a 'bridling of the tongue',[85] a more disciplined approach to verbal communication in all forms of polite intercourse. Those who advocated or achieved this form of privacy did not, however, see themselves as isolated or uncommunicative beings. To the contrary, the withdrawal that they sought was analogous to the conduct of a marriage or other close relationship. In each case, openness of the heart required closure to the oversight of others. Trust and transparency were at once the condition and the outcome of the protected discourse. The true believer might be seen as the Spouse of Christ, and as such, explained Brooks, faced the same challenge as a married couple in finding the physical space in which to exchange their innermost thoughts and feelings: 'As wives, when they are walking alone with their husbands in the fields, are more free to open their minds, and the secrets of their hearts, than they are when in their houses with their children and servants about them; so 'twas with the spouse.'[86]

During the seventeenth century, the 'Paper books' that Wettenhall required for the well-found closet were increasingly finding their way into print.[87] Publications such as Thomas Comber's *Companion to the Temple and Closet: Or, a Help to Publick and Private Devotion, in an Essay on the Daily Offices of the Church* were issued to assist in different modes of spiritual reflection,[88] and the record of personal self-examination was turned outwards to the community of fellow Christians as an exemplary guide. Prayer, particularly when it was focused on instrumental outcomes, could embrace the moral and physical wellbeing of family and friends.[89] Gradually its effect was broadened by writing for a wider audience. The diary and the notebook, comprised of successive observations of the struggling believer's 'state and actions, whether his heart be so steadfast in holy purposes as it has been, or ought to be',[90] were translated into an overarching narrative. The structured review of the temporal sequence of sin and repentance initially helped to instil a collective identity in newly formed sects and emerging denominations. Publication gave voice to the silent conversation between the penitent and God. It at once celebrated and reversed the process of withdrawal, connecting the self-examining individual with a broader network of believers.[91] The early Quakers, for instance, compensated for their deliberate refusal of a national institutional structure by promoting the dissemination of accounts written by their scattered membership.

The spiritual memoir retained a shape and function through to the nineteenth century, constituting a major influence over the subsequent development of working-class autobiography.[92] Its subject was only a conditional author of the contents. He, or sometimes she, was struggling towards a self-knowledge already known to God, seeking a pathway that was there to be discovered. Nonetheless the form reflected two assumptions that facilitated a transition to an essentially secular engagement with an individual's life history. Firstly it asserted that character was infused with time. There was movement in the journey from childhood to maturity that extended beyond the process of physical ageing. The personal chronology embodied a sequence of discovery and development that could only be recaptured by a survey of the life as a whole. In ways that had to be explored, the individual's narrative intersected with the collective history of the era. Secondly it assumed an interaction between inward- and outward-facing wisdom. 'The Knowledge of a Man's Self is a Key to the Knowledge of all other things', wrote the merchant Thomas Tryon in 1705.[93] Without the former, that latter was unobtainable. Learning began and ended with self-reflection. It followed from this that the intimacies of domestic relations were the proper business of both the autobiographer and the growing volume of literary biographers in the eighteenth century. Character could not be learned by a study of official behaviour alone. As with passers-by in the street, public intercourse was too partial and fleeting to deliver a rounded picture or reveal the wellsprings of ambition and achievement.[94] The challenge was to negotiate the boundaries of private life, respecting its right to closure whilst at the same time exposing the truths which it embodied.

The publication in 1791 of James Lackington's *Memoirs of the First Forty-Five Years of the Life of James Lackington* marked a turning point.[95] Its pages contained a lively account of conversion to Wesleyan Methodism, and there were echoes of the spiritual format in the depiction of a period of dissipation followed by the discovery of the true path. But Lackington's journey led not to God but to business success as a leading London bookseller. Born in poverty to a drunken shoemaker and a mother struggling to raise eleven children, Lackington constructed an account that was a forerunner of the triumph-over-circumstances genre. It celebrated his unaided endeavours, but claimed that the narrative was both demanded by and written for a particular audience. The life history was an intervention in the public debate about his qualities: 'Many friends', he wrote in the Preface, 'have frequently expressed a desire of obtaining from myself such particulars as they could rely on, of my passage through life, and many enemies...have been industrious in propagating whatever reports they thought would best tend to impede my farther progress.'[96] Like later autobiographers, Lackington sought a balance between the personal that had public meaning, and the intimate that belonged to private relationships, including, in his case, what appears to have been more than one paternity charge in his youth. The purpose of his account was essentially didactic. He drew out the elements of his biography that would improve his readership: 'Should my memoirs be attended with no other benefit to society, they will at least tend to shew what may be effected by a persevering habit of industry.'[97] His audience both was comforted by his commitment to 'a strict adherence to the truth'[98] and also constituted its guarantee. The narrative was presenting 'some well-authenticated particulars of a man, well known to have risen from an obscure origin to a degree of notice'.[99] The memoirs were in this sense as much a reminder of a life as a recreation, its validity assured by those for whom it was written.

The buoyant book trade in which Lackington made his fortune sustained the expansion of communities connected not by face-to-face contact but by the circulation of the written word. However, in terms of both volume and impact, an equally significant change in the period lay in writing which for the most part remained in manuscript. An immediate consequence of the Restoration of Charles II in 1660 was the passage at the end of the year of a Post Office Act which committed the state to the provision of 'constant posts for the carriage of letters to all places'.[100] A competently managed system was established, charging 2d for a single sheet for the first eighty miles, 3d thereafter and 4d to Scotland. Twenty years later the pressing needs of the burgeoning London population led to the introduction of a Penny Post, with as many as a dozen deliveries a day to the businesses and coffee houses in the City. It was the world's first affordable and efficient mass communication system. If conversation in the crowded streets was becoming more difficult, disembodied means of exchanging news and information were becoming more accessible. During the following century something like a national network was created by the introduction of cross posts from 1720 (avoiding the need for every letter to pass through London), accelerated by the introduction of fast post-coaches in 1784. Despite the attempts to preserve a state monopoly, the cost of postage, which was increased in 1711, promoted a range of informal means of carrying unstamped mail by friends, relatives and business associates.

The step change in the role of correspondence from the middle of the seventeenth century onwards was a function partly of the infrastructural state, partly of the expansion of commerce which multiplied the movement of people and information, and partly of the spread of functional reading and writing capacities.[101] Studies of the eighteenth-century Poor Law have shown that in an emergency, capacity reached as far down as the pauper population, which became adept at learning, or borrowing, the skills of composition in order to negotiate with the overseers.[102] What Susan Whyman terms an 'epistolary literacy' emerged, based on an ability to handle sentence structures, compose meaning, deploy sufficient accuracy in spelling and punctuation to be understood, and manage the technology of pen, ink, paper, seals and, where they were used, the Post Office's processes and timetables.[103] The consequence was a significant widening of the realm of virtual privacy, the management of intimacy in the absence of physical presence. Distance was a frequent factor. Men, and increasingly women, wrote to maintain connections with family members away on business or in search of work, at school or university, in service, or just travelling for pleasure, including the visitors to London whose relatives in the city sent them letters containing information on its geography and facilities that was far more tailored to their needs than the published guides.[104] Correspondence was also valued as an addition to the range of communication devices within a bounded community. Roger Lowe in Ashton-in-Makerfield found it more effective to make a formal, confidential statement of his feelings to the girl he was courting: 'I sent to Emme my designes and thoughts, enclosed in letters, and in short time made a conclusion of my overtyred thoughts, and upon the 23 March 1668, we consummated our grand designe of mariage att Warrington, done by Mr. Ward, minister of Warington, att my Cozen Beckeinson's house.'[105]

As the volume of correspondence increased and the proportion written by secretarial hands diminished, the act of writing a letter became more personal. It enhanced a sense of individual control of intimate information. Correspondents were giving expression on paper to their own thoughts and emotions, and through the transmission and receipt of the letter sustaining a relationship that was particular to them. They increasingly asserted a property in the letter, shielding where possible its writing, and expecting it to be opened by the addressee and not by its carrier or another member of the household.[106] During the course of the eighteenth century addresses themselves began to become more specific, with house numbering introduced in London in 1767 to facilitate the frequent deliveries. At the same time epistolary intercourse introduced new levels of stress in the management of private communication. Although the manuals on correspondence that were published in increasing numbers always recommended that the practice should be approached as a form of refined speech, writing was not the same as talking. 'I am indeed too apt to be concerned about the letters I write', confessed the young Dudley Ryder in 1715. 'The reason is because I take so much pains about them, indeed I take too much pains in them. It is not so much because I want something to say but the manner of saying it costs me most time and I am apt to turn it every way before I let it go.'[107] The challenge lay partly in the construction of prose by an unpractised hand, and partly in the task of imagining the recipient as they read the letter. The correspondent had to overcome the difficulty of bodily absence. Lacking the face-to-face presence of an interlocutor, the writer needed to find literary devices that would do the work of gesture, vocal inflection and facial expression, adumbrated by Montaigne at the end of the last chapter.[108] There was no immediate feedback as the words were read. The discourse could not be adjusted in the midst of the communication. Complexity was a challenge and error a constant threat. However many pains were taken, only the receipt of a reply, or a subsequent oral conversation, offered any kind of assurance that the letter had been received and opened by the right person, and that the intended meaning had been derived from its contents.

A further set of tensions was introduced into the conduct of the household. In one sense the growing familiarity with this mode of communication enhanced its integrity and the reach of its head. The nurturing or disciplinary role of parents could be exercised in spite of bodily absence. In 1772, the Lancashire flax merchant Thomas Langton sought to oversee the education of his son, two hundred miles away at a school in Essex: 'I should be glad to see how you improve in your writing, and to know the plan of business you pursue, what books you read and how your time is chiefly employed and what masters you have to instruct you.'[109] The tasks of offering spiritual guidance, practical advice and emotional and financial support were reshaped, rather than terminated, by a journey away from the home by either a parent or a dependant. Business actions or key life decisions were debated and determined through the mail. At the same time correspondence offered a further means of escaping surveillance. As letter-writing became more commonplace and expectations of its confidentiality increased, so new avenues of secluded discourse were created. Alongside finding odd moments of time and space inside the house, or escaping into gardens and fields, correspondence facilitated illicit or unsanctioned intimacy. In London, where more than a million items were circulating in the Penny Post annually by the early eighteenth century, liaisons could be set up and conducted in the course of a single day. The process might be slower over greater distances, but its consequences could be just as disruptive. The postal service exacerbated the long-standing problem of managing courtship. On 27 July 1685, John Evelyn's household woke up to find one of its members missing:

> This night when we were all asleep went my daughter Elizabeth away to meet a young fellow, nephew to Sir John Tippet (Surveyor of the Navy, and one of the Commissioners), whom she married the next day, being Tuesday, without in the least acquainting either her parents, or any soul in the house. I was the more afflicted and astonished at it in regard we had never given this child the least cause to be thus disobedient, and being now my eldest, might reasonably have expected a double blessing. But it afterward appeared that this intrigue had been transacted by letters long before, and when she was with my Lady Burton in Leicestershire, and by private meetings near my house... We were most of all astonished at the suddenness of this action, and the privateness of its management.[110]

Parental authority had been evaded rather than enhanced by the privacy of correspondence. Given the fragility of the seals on letters, and the familiarity of the letter carrier and the local postmaster, Elizabeth Evelyn had taken a risk. But the success of her strategy, at least on her own terms, was a harbinger of future difficulties as diversifying modes of communication multiplied the dimensions of virtual privacy.

The written message was also implicated in the emergence of the public sphere in European polite society from the seventeenth century onwards.[111] Alongside the face-to face locations of salons, clubs and coffee houses, it constituted a means by which intimate communication was translated into political agency.[112] Networks of private individuals could exchange information and generate opinion through letters to each other, and to the emerging press, which from the outset made extensive use of correspondence from its readers, whether genuine or supplied by the editors. The process reflected two aspects of the evolving character of privacy in this period. Firstly there was a growing emphasis on the validity of the enclosed household. Increasing status was claimed for values and opinions formed in close conversation with other family members and visitors, or through reflection on literature consumed within its walls.

Secondly, the trajectory was not a simple matter of written communication enhancing the individual at the expense of broader col-
lectivities of practice or expression. Nor was it a case of print and
writing everywhere undermining the spoken word. Rather the cur-
rents of change reconfigured the interaction between the personal
and the social, and between formal and informal modes of communication. Whether it was the jostled city pedestrians finding
enhanced forms of community in their urban residences and in new
kinds of enclosed social gatherings, or readers combining to obtain
and discuss literature, or relationships made, extended and undermined by epistolary intercourse, there was a constant movement
between different registers of association. There was no single arc
of experience.[113] The interaction between correspondence and the
public sphere described by Jürgen Habermas illustrated the inequality and instability of the emerging regime of privacy. As much as
the altered processes depended on the skills of literacy, the comforts
of the home, and the threats and opportunities of urban living, so
engagement with new practices of privacy was conditioned by
income, gender, education and residential location. Despite the
nominal commitment to the inclusive practice of rational discourse,
the coffee-house clientele was socially and economically exclusive,
however thirsty or well-read potential customers might be.[114] Women
and self-educated artisans were formally prevented from making the
journey from intellectual inquiry to participation in affairs of state.
Neither group, however, was excluded from the world that lay
beyond the home or the workshop. It was possible for women to
combine respectability with a wide range of public recreational and
business activities.[115] According to poll-tax records, over a fifth of
late-seventeenth-century London coffee houses were actually owned
by women.[116]

The tripartite distinction between the state, the public sphere
and the intimate household was always a provisional construct.[117]
The Post Office Act of 1660 was followed three years later by a
Proclamation which assured users of the confidentiality of their correspondence in the new system:

> no Postmasters or other officers, that shall be employed in the convey-
> ing of Letters, or distributing of the same...shall presume to open any
> Letters or Packets, not directed unto themselves, or that they, or any
> other persons whatsoever, do stop any Mayl in the passage to or from
> London, or any other place whither the same is consigned and directed,
> but shall truly and faithfully deliver the same, without any opening,
> concealing, or retarding the delivery thereof.[118]

This undertaking was enshrined in legislation in 1710 which, together with the enhanced defence of the threshold of the home to invasion by agents of the state, constituted the foundation of the meagre tradition of privacy law in the UK and in the growing colonies in North America.[119] However, the protection only covered the conduct of individual letter carriers and postmasters. The secretary of state retained the power that had been actively used since the time of the Commonwealth of issuing confidential warrants to open the mail of presumed enemies of the state. In this period there took form the two-tier approach to government surveillance that has continued with some modification to the present day. The state proclaimed and largely delivered low-level security, and concealed but actively practised political interception. Those who had good grounds for keeping their mail secret responded to the general threat by expanding their use of codes, ciphers and invisible ink. In turn the Post Office enhanced its own capacities for interception.[120] Amongst the several continuities between the Commonwealth and the restored Stuart monarchy was the employment of the mathematician John Willis, famous across Europe for his skills as a code-breaker. All governments clung to their reserve powers in the knowledge that the emerging public sphere could suddenly be transformed from a conversational partner to a subversive threat. When such a moment occurred in the French Revolutionary crisis of the 1790s, any respect for the private realm as a location beyond politics rapidly evaporated.[121] Spies were sent into neighbourhoods and places of assembly, attempts were made to control the production and consumption of subversive literature, habeas corpus was suspended, postal espionage was practised. In France, the emergent public sphere brought down the old order and was then exposed to the intrusion of the revolutionary state. Under pressure, everything was fragile, from the seal on a letter to the lock on the front door, to the secrets of the domestic archive.

3

Privacy and Prosperity 1800–1900

The turn of the century ushered in two grand narratives in the history of privacy. The first of these has framed debates about the surveillance of personal thought and behaviour until the present day. Whenever contemporary accounts of the condition of privacy seek an historical dimension for their analysis, their standard point of reference is the Panopticon – either in Jeremy Bentham's original conception, in its reformulation as George Orwell's Big Brother in *1984*, or as the organizing metaphor in Michel Foucault's *Discipline and Punish*.[1] It stands as the foretelling of privacy's ultimate fate. As Michael Froomkin writes in his 2000 article 'The Death of Privacy?', since the Panopticon, 'the image of the all-seeing eye, the Argus state, has been synonymous with the power to exercise repression.'[2] Most recently, the unbuilt prison was deployed by Glenn Greenwald to explain the effect of the surveillance practices revealed by Edward Snowden, and by Snowden himself to characterize the US National Security Agency (NSA).[3] Bentham would have accepted these epochal claims for his conception as nothing less than its due. In his writings and lobbying over more than a quarter of a century, he urged upon Parliament his practical solution for *'punishing the incorrigible, guarding the insane, reforming the vicious, confining the suspected, employing the idle, maintaining the helpless, curing the sick, instructing the willing* in any branch of industry, or *training the rising race* in the path of *education'*.[4] He had found an economical means of ordering behaviour in an era of impersonal numbers. The oversight of the governor in the curtained watchtower was made complete by his absence. Bentham's vision was Christianity's last great contribution to social theory.[5] His 1787 formulation of the Panopticon had, as an epigraph, a quote from the Psalms: 'Thou art about my path, and about my bed: and spiest out all my ways.'[6] The subsequent explication drew his readers into a shared frame of reference: 'I flatter myself there can now be little doubt of the plan's possessing the fundamental advantages I have been attributing to it; I mean, the *apparent omnipresence* of the inspector (if the divines will allow me the expression,) combined with the extreme facility of his *real presence*.'[7] Nothing was hidden. With the appropriate architecture and organization, everything could be known and judged.

The second narrative presents the era as the summit in privacy's long journey from unfulfilled aspirations in earlier centuries to increasing erosion in the more recent past. The fourth volume of *A History of Private Life* commences with the claim that 'the nineteenth century was the golden age of private life, a time when the vocabulary and reality of private life took shape.'[8] The rising bourgeoisie fused ideology and material condition. They placed the enclosed home at the centre of their vision of themselves and the society in which they lived.[9] Rather than preparing its members for union with God, the family now constituted his earthly realm.[10] 'God made the first man after a divine original,' wrote James Baldwin Brown, 'and after a divine original too, He made the first home.'[11] For those who could afford to pay for it, privacy seemed as solid and secure as the Victorian furniture with which they filled their houses. The broad question of how to protect the boundaries of intimate relations became focused on a single mode of day-to-day living. Under the governance of its male head, the household constituted a shared world of personal knowledge. Its members conversed freely with each other, constrained only by the semi-permeable membrane between the family and the servants who laboured to maintain their comforts. Neither wider society, nor the agents of political authority, had a right of access to the domestic discourse. The household communicated with the wider world solely at its own discretion. Its head and other male residents developed their qualities as moral and rational beings within the confines of the home and gave expression to their opinions and beliefs in an increasingly broad range of business, professional and political contexts.

In the short term, the second narrative was foregrounded in public debate. Bentham's long campaign to secure funding for what would have been by far the most expensive public building constructed for secular, civilian purposes was finally rejected following an inquiry by a Select Committee in 1811. Leading penal reformers attacked the project on the basic issue of surveillance. Bentham had argued that the device of the hidden governor would cause prisoners to reform themselves without exposing prison staff and visitors to contact with their noisome, infectious bodies. His critics responded that the task of influencing and monitoring the inmate's journey to repentance and rehabilitation required regular face-to-face contact, however great the risk. Bentham's technological solution of connecting the central watchtower to each cell by means of conversation tubes would not work, and if ever it did there was the danger of the prisoners using them to talk back to the governor.[12] Oversight that generated knowledge and changed behaviour could not be delivered remotely. The Select Committee insisted on 'the necessity of having persons nominated expressly for the inspection and superintendence of every part of an establishment of that nature'.[13] There was no substitute for frequent, physical contact with the taskmaster, the governor, the surgeon and in particular, the chaplain. The prison was never built, but its design lived on. In the meantime, other tasks lay ahead in defining the boundaries of the private sphere and managing the tensions within it.

In penal policy, as in social order more generally, the challenge remained that of adapting established channels of knowledge and discipline to a rapidly expanding and increasingly mobile society. The British population doubled between 1801 and 1851, and doubled again by 1911. Whereas the proportion living in towns and cities was little altered by the eighteenth-century growth, in the nineteenth it was transformed from a fifth to four-fifths. Britain became the world's first large-scale urban society. As James Vernon has argued, the sheer weight of numbers, frequently detached from their place of origin, generated an agenda for change across society, the economy and the state.[14] The private individual represented an ambiguous prospect. Either he or she constituted a self-sufficient entity with whom those in authority would have to negotiate on the basis of ultimately limited knowledge; or as a husband or wife, a parent or a child, they constituted a unit whose shared intimacy would generate the values and behaviours that would secure the stability of the emerging industrial society.

The growing preoccupation with strangers was reflected in the revival of the guides to unknown London. In 1820 Pierce Egan commenced serial publication of *Life in London; or, The Day and Night Scenes of Jerry Hawthorn, Esq. and his elegant friend Corinthian Tom, accompanied by Bob Logic, The Oxonian, in their Rambles and Sprees through the Metropolis*.[15] This once more deployed the device of an innocent countryman introduced to the pleasures and perils of the town by worldly friends. It was a direct descendant of Ward's *London Spy*, but its impact was multiplied by the subsequent growth of the consumer market. The serial was lavishly illustrated by George Cruikshank, and within months of its first appearance *Life in London* had been translated into a host of consumer products including prints, tea trays, snuff boxes, handkerchiefs, fans, screens, broadsides, songs, pirated texts and at least six adaptations playing in London theatres.[16] Tom and Jerry entered the bloodstream of popular culture. A survey of their career throughout the nineteenth century noted that the most successful of the theatrical versions 'then appeared in rapid succession at the Theatres all over England, Ireland, Scotland and Wales; likewise in most of the United States of America, the West Indies, &c.'.[17] The success of Egan's project rested in part on its claim to authenticity. The readers were taken through real streets to identifiable assembly rooms and theatres, clubs and public houses, sporting and drinking venues. They sampled the pleasures on offer around the clock and were invited to learn the lively slang language of those who patronized them. Consuming the scenes in a range of media gave residents of the city a sense of belonging. It supplied a map for incomers and temporary visitors and an entertainment for those for whom London remained a distant source of fascination.[18]

At the same time *Life in London* was a performance. It was no accident that its 'scenes' translated so successfully to the stage. Its focus, and that of later imitators, was on characters playing roles in public places. Charles Westmacott's *The English Spy* of 1825–6, which borrowed Ward's title and Egan's plot, announced that 'Life's a theatre, man the chief actor, and the source from which the dramatist must cull his choicest beauties, painting up to nature the varied scenes which mark the changeful courses of her motley group.'[19] The traveller and his guide, now given the appropriate name of 'Bob Transit', passed through the locations without fear of contamination.[20] The city was full of perils, explained Egan:

The author, in consequence, has chosen for his readers a *Camera Obscura* View of London, not only from its safety, but because it is so *snug*, and also possessing the invaluable advantages of SEEING and not being *seen*...LIFE IN LONDON will be seen without any fear or apprehension of danger either from *fire* or *water*; avoiding also breaking a limb, receiving a *black* eye, losing a pocket-book, and getting into a watch-house; picking up a *Cyprian* and being exposed next morning before a magistrate for being found *disorderly*.[21]

London was becoming not so much a place of strangers as a city whose strangeness demanded an attempt to embrace it as a single, complex entity. The more difficult it became to know the totality of streets and houses by direct experience, the more urgent it was to find an alternative means of comprehending the whole. Alongside the printed guides and their spin-offs, entertainment entrepreneurs found a market for panoramas which presented the teeming mass of buildings in a single view. The most striking of these was Thomas Horner's 'Panoramic View of London', which was displayed in the newly constructed London Colosseum in Regent's Park in 1829.[22] This depicted the metropolis for twenty miles in all directions as it would appear to a spectator looking out from the top of the dome of St Paul's Cathedral.[23] It was a marriage of form and content. The world's largest city was surveyed in the world's largest oil painting. The willingness of the public to pay to look at their own locality reflected their conviction that they lived amidst a wonder of the modern age whose identity could now only be grasped through a textual or visual medium.

These attempts to grasp the physicality of the streets without being physically present in them indicated that the boundaries between public and private were changing rather than collapsing. In his *English Spy*, Charles Westmacott distinguished between the registers of legitimate inquiry:

> From the throne to the thatched cottage, wherever there is character, 'there fly we,' and, on the wings of merry humour, draw with pen and pencil a faithful portraiture of *things* as they are; not tearing aside the hallowed veil of private life, but seizing as of public right on public character, and with a playful vein of satire proving that we are of the poet's school.[24]

Privacy was now so entrenched a concept that it was becoming a cliché. 'The hallowed veil' expressed both its moral strength and its practical vulnerability. In their legitimate form, which Westmacott in his later journalistic career was to have difficulty in observing, the depictions of London life were confined to types of individual or classes of occupation, or to named persons who through their public performance, or egregious transgression of public standards, had rendered themselves suitable candidates for commentary. In this perspective, anonymity belonged not to the streets but to the home. The right not to be known to the observing eye commenced with the closure of the front door. The German observer Max Schlesinger was fascinated by the elaborate etiquette of communicating with the interior:

It is by far easier to learn the language of Englishmen than to learn the language of the knocker; and many strangers protest that a knocker is the most difficult of all musical instruments. It requires a good ear and a skiful hand to make yourself understood and to escape remarks and ridicule. Every class of society announces itself at the gate of the fortress by means of the r[h]ythm of the knocker. The postman gives two loud taps in quick succession; and for the visitor a gentle but peremptory *tremolo* is *de rigueur*. The master of the house gives a *tremolo crescendo*, and the servant who announces his master, turns the knocker into a battering-ram, and plies it with such good-will that the house shakes to its foundations. Tradesmen, on the other hand, butchers, milkmen, bakers, and green grocers, are not allowed to touch the knockers – they ring a bell which communicates with the kitchen.[25]

Beyond the threshold, visibility was increasingly important. Gaslights first appeared in the London streets in 1807. By 1875, there were five thousand miles of gas mains, making the city the first industrially illuminated metropolis.[26] What was now sought was an appropriate balance of knowledge in any encounter. There should be no dark alleys, no concealed places. In towns and cities, planning bye-laws increasingly sought to open up closed courts.[27] Every thoroughfare should lead to another to promote mobility and diminish private space. Following the Highways Act of 1835, the width of main roads was standardized and pavements were specified to keep traffic and walkers flowing safely and separately. In the streets, contact between individuals should be free but fleeting. As the new generation of London guides was appearing, legislation was introduced to enforce pedestrian mobility. The 1822 Vagrant Act imposed a legal distinction between those passing through public thoroughfares and those associating in them for no discernible purpose.[28] Standing still long enough to engage in familiar intercourse was henceforth a suspicious activity.[29]

The growth of towns and cities with the associated revolution in transport, commencing with the turnpikes and culminating in the construction of a national railway network followed by the development of urban transit systems in the second half of the nineteenth century, reconfigured engagements between strangers in public places. Most eighteenth-century travellers were on foot, moving in loose groups with time enough to develop acquaintance. For those who could afford it, long-distance coach travel was essentially a set of interruptions to a succession of drinks, meals and beds in inns. Within the coaches there was opportunity for conversation with those of roughly similar status. As Jo Guldi writes, 'the social experiences of

travel encouraged openness among people.'[30] The subsequent increase
in speed enhanced the privacy of travel. Railway stations were less
intimate spaces than coaching inns. Trains contained more unknown
passengers, and from the 1860s, corridors relieved the claustrophobia
and forced intimacy of closed carriages. The development of com-
muter networks shortened journey times and diminished still further
the opportunity of getting to know those heading to the same destination. Accompanying the guides to the urban environment, a new
travel literature advised on how to avoid eye contact and maintain
physical distance in crowded spaces.[31] Railway book stalls spawned
their own genre of fiction, its perusal further withdrawing the traveller from the surrounding company.

At the same time the long-distance pedestrian, once an essentially
social being, became freighted with a new set of meanings. What
Anne Wallace terms 'deliberative excursive walking' celebrated the
pleasures of a mode of travel which contrasted with the increasing
speed of movement on the turnpikes and the iron road.[32] By 1800,
guidebooks were being published not just for the proliferating urban
streets but for the remoter countryside whose beauty awaited discovery. During the nineteenth century, the day's excursion or the longer
walking tour was undertaken by the educated middle classes in informal or organized groups, and also by individuals celebrating their
escape from the press of people.[33] William Hazlitt, influenced by his
friendship with Wordsworth, created the template for this expression
of romantic individualism in his 1821 essay 'On Going a Journey'.
'One of the pleasantest things in the world is going a journey,' he
wrote, 'but I like to go by myself. I can enjoy society in a room; but
out of doors, nature is company enough for me. I am then never less
alone than when alone.'[34] Solitude in motion permitted a depth of
reflection that could not be attained amidst distracting company:
'These hours are sacred to silence and to musing, to be treasured up
in the memory, and to feed the source of smiling thoughts thereafter.'[35] It was a new form of private prayer in which God was replaced
by the grandeur of the unspoilt landscape. Eventually, the urban
masses caught up with the educated escapees. In the later nineteenth
and early twentieth centuries, a combination of a shorter working
week and cheap rail travel enabled organized excursions away from
the smoky towns and cities.[36] Here the company was everything, to
the dismay of landowners and the distaste of those bent on spiritual
withdrawal. Fishing for pleasure, a parallel mode of retreat from
crowded homes and streets, described a similar parabola. The lone
fisherman in the exclusive trout stream was joined by, in several
senses, a coarser fraternity of working-class sportsmen, seeking the

nearest available river banks to engage in fiercely competitive angling matches.[37]

A basic driver of short- and long-term travel from the countryside to the town was and always had been the search for recreation. Any concentration of numbers multiplied opportunities for pleasure and created an incentive to invest in capital-intensive spectacle. The dominant form of urban entertainment in the first phase of nineteenth-century population growth was the theatre. As with mobility more generally, the trajectory of change was towards increasing social segmentation. The dramatic adaptations of Egan's *Life in London* played to mixed auditoria. The audiences were roughly segregated by price, with boxes costing three to four shillings and the second gallery one shilling, or sixpence in most theatres after half-time in the long evening's performance. It was an arena in which all social classes save the very poor could watch and be watched.[38] As *The English Spy* observed, 'The Opera, to the man of fashion, is the only *tolerable* place of public amusement in which the varied orders of society are permitted to participate. Here, lolling at his ease, in a snug box on the first circle, in dignified security from the vulgar gaze, he surveys the congregated mass who fill the arena of the house.'[39] The audiences were so large, with 4,000-seater barns on both sides of the Thames, that those in the expensive seats were always outnumbered by clerks and artisans.[40] After *Tom and Jerry*, the next metropolitan theatrical sensation was John Poole's *Paul Pry* in 1825. Its success immediately spawned at least three pirated versions. In a little over twelve months the plays together attracted around half a million spectators in a London adult population of around a million. By this time productions were touring provincial towns and already performing in New York.[41] A drama whose central theme was unwelcome intrusion into personal affairs was assembling night after night an eclectic body of spectators, united in their rowdy enjoyment of Paul Pry's misbehaviour and misfortunes. The event marked the beginning of the modern debate about privacy, but also the start of the decline of the collective consumption of urban popular culture. Already theatrical venues were opening in the East End of London catering for a much narrower clientele.[42] The process of change was accelerated by the Theatre Regulation Act of 1843, which finally removed the restrictions on performing non-musical drama and consolidated a division between a middle-class theatre-going public and the patrons of the multiplying music halls and penny gaffs.[43] At the same time the London pleasure gardens, which since the mid-eighteenth century had attracted a diverse strolling attendance, lost their cross-class appeal. Both the clientele and the attractions of Vauxhall Gardens, once the height of fashionable entertainment, were seen to be increasingly vulgar, and it was finally closed in 1859.[44] The pursuit of pleasure ceased to be the occasion of associating with those outside a known social network.

The proliferation of print was a further cause of change. In general it increased the opportunities for relaxation in the home, and in the case of drama it enabled the literate enthusiast to enjoy or recreate the experience of the theatre without venturing out of doors at all. In the second quarter of the nineteenth century, enterprising publishers began issuing reprints of plays and comedies for domestic consumption. The British Theatre series published by John Duncombe (sixty-seven volumes, 1825–52) and John Cumberland (forty-eight volumes, 1826–61) reproduced a wide range of stage productions at a cost of no more than a gallery ticket for those who wanted either to recollect an enjoyable evening or to bring family and friends together to perform the play themselves. Do-it-yourself acting manuals were available, as were costumes and make-up. In wealthier households children could also be supplied with model theatres, complete with miniature candle-lit scenery. In the larger country houses, such as the Duke of Devonshire's Chatsworth in 1833, private theatres were built to entertain house parties.[45] The domestication of what had been the quintessential collective recreational form of the early nineteenth century reflected the broader transformation of the function of the home. The rise of living standards, particularly among the urban middle class, encouraged an increasing investment in the variety of functions and activities that could be undertaken behind the closed front door.

The search for domestic comfort and seclusion had, as we have seen, a longer history than some accounts of the nineteenth-century family would suggest. Since the late Middle Ages, those who could afford to do so had sought the provision of at least partially distinct living spaces and had insisted on a differentiation of life within and beyond the threshold. What turned evolution into something like a transformation was an intersection of material and normative aspirations. For the increasingly prosperous business and professional households, it finally became possible not only to separate sleeping from living quarters, the kitchen from the dining room, the public receiving room from the private socializing space, but to envisage nurseries, schoolrooms and separate bedrooms for the children, and dressing rooms, morning rooms and sewing rooms, and studies or libraries in place of the occasional closet.[46] The words 'sitting room' and 'lounge' entered the English language in 1806 and 1881.[47] The larger country houses, which had been constructing corridors since the late seventeenth century, further separated the public hall from the family quarters, and each room from the circulation of people between them. Servants, whenever they were employed, were relegated to separate quarters, accessed in larger houses by back staircases. The late-eighteenth-century invention of the bell-pull meant that staff no longer had to linger in the company of their superiors waiting to be summoned.[48] Change was driven and in turn facilitated by a promotion of seclusion as the key objective of the home.[49] 'However small and compact the house may be,' wrote Robert Kerr, in his guide to planning English residences, 'the family must have privacy and the servants commodiousness; and the whole dwelling must display an unassuming grace.'[50] He listed twelve key characteristics of the gentleman's house. These included such desiderata as 'Spaciousness', 'Salubrity' and 'Elegance', but top of the list was 'Privacy'. This applied both to intercourse with the outside world and to the internal organization:

> It is a first principle with the better classes of English people that the Family Rooms shall be essentially private, and as much as possible the Family Thoroughfares. It becomes the foremost of all maxims, therefore, however small the establishment, that the Servants' Department shall be separated from the Main House, so that what passes on either side of the boundary shall be both invisible and inaudible on the other.[51]

What was required was a kind of willed myopia. 'Under no circumstances, of course,' wrote the architect J. J. Stevenson, 'should the servants overlook the private life of the family, while they in their servants' hall and apartments are entitled to live unobserved by the family.'[52]

The more numerous the rooms and the thicker the internal walls, the easier it was for individual members to be by themselves with their own thoughts, perhaps with a book or a pen in their hand. But given the constant presence of children, servants and visitors, this kind of peace had to be sought rather than assumed. As had always been the case, seclusion was most easily located out of doors, and a bounded garden became an essential concomitant of the well-found urban dwelling.[53] 'Fences not only define boundaries and insure security,' prescribed Beeton's *Book of Garden Management*, 'they also convey ideas of possession and seclusion, and impart a reputable or disreputable character to a property, according to the taste, or the want of it, by which they are distinguished.'[54] The enclosed space for flowers and vegetables was now an extension of rather than an alternative to the private realm of the domestic arena, sheltered from the gaze as well as the entry of neighbours and passing strangers.[55] Inside the house the occupants increasingly battled for space with their possessions. The relatively spare interiors of the early-Victorian middle-class interiors gave way to a display of wealth and a passion for accumulation.[56] Morality became associated with poor taste rather than excessive expenditure. Where once furniture was regularly moved to suit the activities of the moment, now the occupants had to navigate around heavy chairs, tables, wardrobes and beds and avoid the fragile perils of shelves and cabinets overloaded with ornaments.[57]

With increasing numbers of servants employed to keep the rooms and their contents clean and the dining table supplied with regular meals, the family and any additional relations or visitors had time to interact with each other. More books were read and more letters written, but for most of the time, most of the occupants talked. Domestic libraries were seen as sociable spaces and women in particular were encouraged to read aloud and discuss their literary experiences with each other.[58] If the nineteenth century was the golden age of anything, it was that of intimate conversation. Without the earlier distraction of remunerative work taking place in the home, or the solitary experience of engaging with electronic media in the following century in what were much smaller domestic units, members of the households connected with each other through face-to-face communication as the routines of the day unfolded. Children, who were likely to comprise half the family unit, played with each other or with visiting cousins. Their mothers entertained other mothers in sociable discourse. The paterfamilias, home from work, read and talked to his offspring, usually once they were out of infancy and particularly if they were male. Husbands and wives shared confidences in their bedroom, which was now their sole territory. When the family gathered in the evening the available means of passing the time – relaying news, discussing events and people, reading to each other, playing games, engaging in amateur theatricals – all involved the spoken word. The widespread concern that any exchanges within the family should not be overheard by servants emphasized the status of talk as a carrier of private information. These were words given meaning by the familiarity of the interlocutors and the reinforcing devices of gesture, tone and facial expression.

The increased substance of the idea and reality of the middle-class home should not, however, be confused with greater ease in the management of privacy. In every direction complexity and anxiety increased. At the outset there was the basic question of the composition of the households. Only just over a third were confined to the conjugal family. Just under half, in mid-nineteenth-century England, contained at least one other individual, either a stray relative, a servant, a lodger, a live-in apprentice or a journeyman.[59] The willingness to take in widowed grandparents, parentless kin or migrants from the countryside yet to establish their own social networks was the counterpart to the relative absence of homeless street-dwellers. The more prosperous the head of household, the more likely that the additional residents were servants. Further down the economic scale, the family lived alongside those who contributed to its economy as either subordinate workers or rent-paying lodgers. This did not mean that the home was full of strangers. Rather there were layers of familiarity that had to be negotiated and reconstituted as household members came and went. The child of a distant relative was recognized in a general sense as belonging to a distributed family and could in time be accepted into the group of conjugal children. A lodger might be a relatively unknown bird of passage or a familiar presence at the meal table. His likely fate, as Thomas Wright explained from his own experience, was a form of domestic limbo, neither without nor within the family, with many obligations and few rights: 'his every movement in the house, which by the great commercial law of payment he has a right to consider in some degree his own, is criticised and found fault with not only by his landlady, but by every gossiping acquaintance of hers.'[60] A high turnover of servants was common, but some at least were embraced in a relationship of trust and affection. For the husband and wife at the head of the protean social unit, every day brought new questions about how much was known by whom or could be told to them. Even where they could control communication in busy rooms separated by thin party walls, they had to make constant judgements about drawing the boundaries of personal information. In turn, the two household heads each had their own relations of intimacy with other members, which did not necessarily coincide.

The physical environment of the private realm itself required constant attention and decision-making. The speed and scale of construction in the expanding towns and cities meant that there was possibly a greater temporal consistency in the housing stock since the rebuilding of London after the Great Fire. It remained, however, a perpetual struggle to match aspiration with reality. Most houses were rented, which left any tenant seeking appropriate levels of comfort with the difficult task of either persuading the landlord to invest in improvements or, more commonly, transferring to new premises. For all the emphasis on personal taste, occupants were not in control of domestic architecture. As Gervase Wheeler's *The Choice of a Dwelling* pointed out, 'the erection of a London house rarely comes within the experience of a private gentleman, unless he happens to be the landlord.'[61] The physical mobility of households in nineteenth-century towns and cities, whether it was up and down streets or to and from more salubrious districts as finances waxed and waned, rendered the home closer to a caravan than the preferred image of a domestic castle complete with its drawbridge.[62] There was always a spur to find a better stage set for the drama of privacy. So much of the capacity to live in the prescribed mode depended on the detail of construction and layout. Robert Kerr was scathing about the shortcomings of much of the housing built for the new urban middle class:

> Not to mention that most unrefined arrangement whereby at one sole entrance door the visitors rub shoulders with the tradespeople, how objectionable it is we need scarcely say when a thin partition transmits the sounds of the Scullery or Coal-cellar to the Dining-room or Study; or when a Kitchen window in summer weather forms a trap to catch the conversation at the casement of the Drawing-room; or when a Kitchen doorway in the Vestibule or Staircase exposes to the view of every one the dresser or the cooking range, or fills the house with unwelcome odours. Those who are acquainted with the ordinary class of suburban speculation Villas, which, by the standard of rent, ought to be good houses, but are not, will at once recognise the unexaggerated truth of these illustrations.[63]

For all but the most secure in their income and tastes, the ideal of the private sphere generated little but constant effort and unrealized aspiration.

The gradual arrival of domestic plumbing in Britain in the final third of the nineteenth century presented a further set of difficulties. Unless the house was built from scratch with a full complement of separate lavatories and bathrooms, the occupants seeking to achieve privacy for their bodily functions had to find a way of inserting the pipes, drains and enclosed spaces into existing rooms and staircases, and determining who should be able to use them. In this regard, most of the urban and rural population lived in an earlier century. Recourse to outside lavatories and sources of water forced cooperation and conflict with groups of neighbours, even where the supplies and drains were part of a modern network. The first systematic survey of housing density in 1911 revealed that three quarters of the English population were still living in one- or two-roomed accommodation.[64]

At best, the aristocracy of labour had begun to rent houses where the sleeping and living quarters were on different floors, and where it was possible to differentiate between the functions of the downstairs spaces. They were aspiring to what was becoming a hallmark of the well-found private home: the provision of dormant space reserved for courtships, formal visits or the ceremonial agenda of weddings and funerals.[65] Whether it was an over-furnished and under-used parlour in an artisan terrace, or a more spacious and tasteful reception room in a middle-class home, such developments did not extend the private realm so much as compress it into the quarters in which the life of the household was conducted.

Finally there remained the task of managing the transition between the more sharply defined spheres of private and public. The challenge varied markedly by location, class and gender. In the countryside, the compensation for the imperceptible pace of housing improvement was the continued access to the gardens and lanes that surrounded the home. Flora Thompson, growing up in late-nineteenth-century Oxfordshire, described the cycle of discomfort and adjustment as children were raised in confined spaces.

> None of the cottages had more than two bedrooms, and when children of both sexes were entering their teens it was difficult to arrange matters, and the departure of even one small girl of twelve made a little more room for those remaining. When the older boys of a family began to grow up, the second bedroom became the boys' room. Boys, big and little were packed into it, and the girls still at home had to sleep in the parents' room. They had their own standard of decency; a screen was placed or a curtain was drawn to form a partition between the parents' and children's beds; but it was, at best, a poor makeshift arrangement, irritating, cramped, and inconvenient.[66]

Yet always there was the world outside, particularly for children for whom the walls of the home were made porous as they explored the village and surrounding fields, only half visible to the adult inhabitants: 'Of what was going on around them, not much was hidden, for the gossips talked freely before children, evidently considering them not meant to hear as well as not to be heard, and, as every house was open to them and their own home was open to most people, there was not much that escaped their sharp ears.'[67] Although the northern industrial towns were sufficiently compact to permit walking access to the surrounding countryside, a cost of urban expansion for the labouring poor was the loss of the garden attached to the home, particularly in London. Only a privileged few later in the century could aspire to terraced homes with small front plots exposed to the passing life of the neighbourhood.

Middle-class children were no longer free to play in the streets and their mothers faced increasing constraints. Recent research has qualified the absolute separation of the male and female spheres. There were still opportunities for activities outside the home other than carefully choreographed social or shopping expeditions. Women's organizational abilities and reforming zeal could find an outlet in a range of philanthropic activities, particularly those revolving around visiting the homes of the poor to advise them on managing their budgets and families.[68] These ventures rested on an assumption that poverty eroded the right to domestic privacy, but this was not a view shared by those upon whom they called, who strove to defend their thresholds and demanded real services in return for entry.[69] Home-visiting represented the social and ideological role of the respectable housewife temporarily translated to another space. Those who ran the schemes expected the volunteers to subordinate their missionary zeal to the family calendar, including annual holidays. The occupational and associational activities of their fathers and husbands, by contrast, expressed their right to an existence apart from their role in the household. Their difficulty lay in navigating between their separate personas. John Tosh's work on the nature of masculinity in this era includes a case study of a couple constructing their marriage in mid-nineteenth-century Yorkshire. The ambitious husband, travelling extensively for his business, has no sense of confining his identity to the physical location of his new home, which, with its neighbouring community, is now his wife's entire universe. Neither does he find it easy in his correspondence to adjust between the languages of commerce and affection. What in the end contains the tensions is partly the slow development of a deep emotional and physical intimacy, and partly the couple's joint immersion in evangelical Christianity which found its true expression in the domestic rather than the commercial arena.[70]

The more physically confining the private domain, the more important became the realm of virtual privacy, especially for women. As we have seen, the frail letter had been a means of binding social networks since the late Middle Ages. By the end of the eighteenth century, the use of the mails was commonplace amongst the middling orders of society.[71] Payment-on-delivery penny posts spread across the towns and cities, convincing reformers that it would be possible to create, for the first time, a national mass communication system.[72] Flat-rate pre-payment would remove both the constraints on demand

and the costs of scale. Historians concentrating on the period of reform which commenced with the Penny Post in Britain in 1840, and rapidly spread to Europe and North America, have emphasized the 'rupture', as Bernhard Siegert puts it, 'in the history of media technology'.[73] In practical terms, however, the case for innovation rested on an appeal to continuity. The appetite for correspondence had been demonstrated and the means of moving messages at comparative speed within and between communities was already in place. The capacity of the new railways to accelerate still further the rapid bulk carriage of the mail was an unexpected bonus. The innovation lay less in the machinery and more in its projected purpose. The arguments advanced for the Penny Post committed the state for the first time to the promotion of privacy. The 1837–8 Select Committee, which gave official backing to Rowland Hill's project, published evidence from a range of witnesses on the benefits of sustaining contact between the increasingly distributed networks of the labouring poor. 'I have no doubt that,' claimed a witness, 'in the course of a short time, as the poorer classes have the common affections of the human breast, they would form a taste for the pleasures to be derived from intercourse with absent friends and relations.'[74] The increasing mobility of the working classes, driven by a combination of occupational change and urbanization, was threatening to destroy their structures of moral and material support; related kin were in danger of becoming strangers to each other. Enabling them to sustain intimate relations over distance would strengthen the family as an affective and disciplinary unit, with benefits to the cohesion of society, the expansion of the economy and the maintenance of political order. There were frequent appeals to the suffering of women separated from working husbands and departed children.[75] The campaign, which resulted in a costly innovation, revolved around the axis of private intercourse and public education. The state's concurrent investment in both elementary schools and cheap postage was of a piece. Literacy would facilitate the writing and reading of letters, and in turn the awakening appetite for correspondence would create a demand for schooling.[76]

After disappointing early returns, the reformed system proved capable of sustained growth.[77] Over the course of the nineteenth century per capita letter flows expanded from eight to sixty, placing Britain at the head of the European table of postal communication, with twice the rate of its emerging rival Germany. The limited statistical evidence suggests that in spite of the initial hopes, middle-class men and women were the principal beneficiaries of state investment, either expanding their business use or sustaining relations with extended social and domestic networks. The newly educated did not begin to make habitual employment of written communication until the rules were relaxed on the design of the halfpenny postcard at the very end of the nineteenth century.[78] Until then, the receipt or composition of a letter remained a rare and usually collective event. Even before the reform, however, there were indications of how a combination of a reliable postal service, a basic command of literacy and an entrepreneurial publishing industry was capable of formalizing the face-to-face conduct of affective relations. The translation of the valentine from a hand-made to a purchased message, with the consequent distortion of the mails on 14 February, was already visible in the late-Georgian era. When the receiving inamorata or inamorato was freed of the burden of paying for her or his compliment, volumes increased still further.[79] On Valentine's Day 1850, Charles Dickens looked in through a window of the central London Post Office at Mount Pleasant and marvelled at 'those silent receptacles of countless millions of passionate words, for ever pouring through them like a Niagara of language, and leaving not a drop behind'.[80] Most of the passionate words were mass-produced doggerel.[81] The ease of purchase and the accessibility of the mail were creating a disjunction between text and emotion. The cards were not descriptors but signs of affection, their standardized form creating, or forever frustrating, the possibility of subsequent intimate discourse.

In terms of virtual privacy, the ancient technology of correspondence remained the dominant medium until well into the following century. The electric telegraph was under development as the Penny Post was introduced. Its capacity to eliminate both time and distance from communication excited commentators then and since.[82] 'Everybody knows how much letters had to do with our daily life', observed an early survey of European developments. 'But, we are fast approaching a time when all social and commercial intercourse will be carried out by telegraph, the letter sent through the Post-Office merely serving to confirm the message entrusted to the wires.'[83] A national network was in place by the late 1840s, the first international link was established to Paris in 1852, and after a series of failures, a transatlantic cable was operating by 1866.[84] The service was used by some forms of business and by newspapers and press agencies, and made possible the management of Britain's growing empire. It enabled the standardization of time within and between countries. However, despite suggestive parallels with the digital revolution, the telegraph did not become the Victorian internet.[85] At the end of the nineteenth century social intercourse was still largely the preserve of speech and the written word. Even in the United States, where the challenge of time and distance was so much greater, the telegraph, writes Richard John, 'remained a speciality service for an exclusive clientele of merchants, lawmakers, and journalists'.[86] The problem was partly cost. Whilst it was now possible to send virtually unlimited postal messages for unlimited distances within the UK, and internationally after the creation of the Universal Postal Union in 1874, the telegraph charged by the word and by the mile. In the early British network, thirteen shillings, a week's wage for a labouring man, would buy a message of just twenty words from London to Bristol. Secondly, it was a matter of confidentiality. Whereas a letter, securely sealed within the newly invented, mass-produced gummed envelope, could only be opened with the aid of a government warrant, the technology of the telegraph required the operator to read everything that was transmitted. The clerks were enjoined to 'observe the strictest secrecy in respect to all telegrams, business and other matters',[87] but governments and businessmen remained apprehensive about sensitive content. A direct consequence of the telegraph was a revival of the practice of encoding messages. The increasing effort invested in concealing messages, according to its historian, 'made cryptography what it is today'.[88]

The second electronic communication revolution of the nineteenth century, the telephone, described a similar arc of high expectations and low private usage. Expense was a yet greater deterrent, compounded by the need for both parties to be subscribers. After 1875, a combination of uncertain technology, aggressive capitalism and restricted public funding created a network that was neither efficient nor affordable. The decision was taken to charge a high flat rate for the service, with unlimited calls for the small number of subscribers able to install a line in their homes. Two decades after the first patent was taken out, a Parliamentary inquiry explained that 'persons who are rich enough to pay a fixed annual sum, and who use the phone sufficiently often to find such a payment advantageous to themselves, whose correspondents also pay a similar sum, and use the service with similar frequency, can alone, or almost alone, avail themselves of this mode of communication.'[89] Again, the role of the operators presented a threat to confidentiality, and the need in the early days to shout down crackling lines recreated the timeless problem of overheard conversations. There was a more enthusiastic take-up in the United States where Bell's invention could link isolated farmsteads, but the early dependency on party lines created a separate concern about eavesdropping.[90] Whilst the technology no longer needed the skill of functional literacy, it challenged the etiquette of managing the

privacy of the home against callers. Answering the phone was tanta-
mount to opening the front door to unannounced visitors, or still
worse, to tradesmen. Better, argued the leader of the Association for
the Protection of Telephone Subscribers, to have the servant pick up
the receiver.[91]

Rather than constituting a step change in the realm of virtual
privacy, the new technologies represented a reversal to an earlier era
when the bulk of the population only made use of the services, if at
all, in cases of extreme domestic crisis. For this reason the anxieties
associated with communication beyond the confines of the household
differed only in scale from those of earlier centuries. The Penny Post
was designed to eliminate the spoken word from the transmission of
correspondence; as post-boxes were introduced and letter-boxes cut
into front doors, it was no longer necessary to conduct conversations
with the postmaster when sending a letter or with the postman negotiating payment for delivery. Street signs and house numbers removed
the element of inquiry from the location of addressees. But the tendency for usage to outstrip functional literacy prolonged the requirement for the collective writing or reading of letters.[92] The proliferating
manuals on letter-writing amplified earlier warnings about the intrin-
sic insecurity of epistolary intercourse. 'Remember the liability of a
letter to miscarry,' wrote a guide of 1876, 'to be opened by the wrong
person, to be seen by other eyes than those for whom it is meant,
and be very careful what you write to the disadvantage of anyone.'[93]
The ease with which wives and older children could make secret use
of the post compounded the threat it posed to the authority of the
head of the household. Above all there remained the challenge of
imagining the absent interlocutor. 'The problem with correspondence', notes Lauren Berlant, 'is that it is conversation without context,
intimacy without intimation.'[94] Despite the continuing emphasis on
letter-writing as a form of polite talking, the communicative props of
speech were absent. On the one hand, there was concrete evidence
of the expansion of the realm of virtual privacy. For the first time a
nation's communication practices could be counted while the daily
presence of the uniformed postman constituted the most familiar and
welcome representative of the nineteenth-century state.[95] On the
other, there was the endless uncertainty of talking to an absent face
and managing what William Decker describes as the 'unverifiable
possibilities' of the non-reply.[96]

Privacy derived purpose from the possibility of betrayal. The protection and invasion of intimate information gained strength from each

other. The more that was hidden, the greater the appetite for exposure; the larger the threat, the thicker the walls that were erected around the domestic archive. What made privacy modern in the nineteenth century was not so much the desire for seclusion, which had a long history, but rather the dialectic between publicity and concealment. The tension was captured by the catchphrase of John Poole's play *Paul Pry*, the theatrical sensation of late-Georgian London. The double negative of 'I Hope I Don't Intrude' conveyed both the heightened sensitivity to attacks on privacy and the delight in curiosity about the affairs of others.[97] At the end of the play Paul Pry's advances to the leading female character are repelled because he is too inquisitive. 'Pooh, pooh!', he responds indignantly. 'A spirit of inquiry is the great characteristic of the age we live in.'[98] Curiosity was a subversive practice. Its increasing celebration represented an assertion of openness against closure, of reason against rank and of morality against hypocrisy.[99] It was integral to the developing liberal polity, whose subjects were expected to inquire into the circumstances of their freedom.[100] Above all, it conveyed a combination of energy and pleasure in the discovery of information, whether the unearthing of new knowledge or the revealing of existing vices.[101] The spirit infected the realms of recreation, fiction, journalism and politics, wherever satisfaction was to be found in its expression, or money made from its dissemination.

The guides to hidden London which culminated in Pierce Egan's literary and dramatic triumph at the beginning of the 1820s began to take on a new edge. It became necessary to distinguish more sharply the fields of legitimate investigation. In the first of a series of periodicals that lasted throughout the next half century, Paul Pry promised to 'establish himself in popularity, not by resorting to the defamation of private character, or private life, but by shewing up, in a bold and manly manner, the various quacks of all descriptions that inundate the overgrown metropolis'.[102] Journalism, together with its sister occupation policing, was gaining a new professional identity and influence in the second quarter of the nineteenth century.[103] However, the editors of the widening range of daily and weekly papers faced an even longer and less complete journey than the police to recognized and consistent ethical standards. If the journalistic flag-bearers of the public sphere were claiming the right to hold governments to account, their counterparts in the lower reaches of the press were courting prosecution with every issue. A succession of entrepreneurs with close connections to the burgeoning market for pornography were discovering how to monetize privacy.

The source of their profit was the substance and appeal of gossip translated from the oral to the printed medium. The proliferation of urban street communities in the nineteenth century reframed time-honoured means of enforcing group standards and feeding prurient curiosity.[104] It exposed shameful behaviour but was itself a morally compromised activity.[105] Conversing about the behaviour of neighbours was an enclosed discourse about a restricted body of knowledge. 'Gossip as a social practice', observed Ferdinand Schoeman, 'is private communication in the sense that it is not addressed to an unrestricted audience. To this extent, privacy and gossip converge in strictures on disclosure.'[106] In spite of their editorial protestations, a range of penny weeklies found that the wall between the exposure of quacks and the defamation of private life was attractively porous.[107] An 1856 *Paul Pry* commenced publication with the highest of motives:

> The time has arrived for the satirist to lay bare the falsehood and fraud, and licentiousness and chicanery, which are now unfortunately the mainsprings and incentives to action in the present day. Be ours, therefore, the task to lead the van of political, social and moral progress.[108]

It duly attacked scandals such as the adulteration of food and the behaviour of loan companies, as well as the alleged sexual harassment of women telegraph operators. However, its front-page story was the 'Secret Memoirs' of a mistress of Louis Napoleon, and attention was then turned to misbehaviour in a much more local register: 'Mrs. S-t-l-s, of Brighton Street, Argyle Square to leave off her amours with Bill, in the temporary absence of her better half. It is very unbecoming in a married woman to forsake the downy couch where virtue sleeps.'[109] Every week, the periodical carried columns of gossip drawn from named locations in different parts of the country, featuring the activities of minimally disguised individuals. Activities that could only have meaning for a specific neighbourhood held fascination for a national readership. Together with a succession of rival penny publications, this periodical found that there was a readership for obscure personal conduct that transgressed general moral standards. Providing it was written up with spirit and conviction, printed gossip could at once invade and uphold the conventions of privacy. If everything was a campaign, the audience could see themselves as ethical actors whilst enjoying the titillating detail.

There was also, it transpired, an income to be made from keeping privacy secret. Editors offered victims the option of paying to keep misbehaviour out of their columns. In turn, neighbours extorted sums for not sending anonymous letters to the local agent of the papers. Exposure turned to blackmail and journalists found themselves in court. The law was changed to offer greater protection to the domestic archive. Section 3 of the 1843 Libel Act was directly aimed at what was termed 'the Paul Pry nuisance'. It specified that

> who shall publish or threaten to publish any libel upon any other person, or shall directly or indirectly threaten to publish it, or shall directly or indirectly propose to abstain from printing or publishing, of any matter or thing touching any other person, with intent to extort any money or security for money, or any valuable thing shall be guilty of a misdemeanour and liable to three years' imprisonment.[110]

An attempt was made to separate journalism from pornography with the Obscene Publications Act of 1857. Urged on by the Society for the Suppression of Vice, the courts put a succession of periodicals out of business and their editors in jail. The courts' attention was focused on cheap publications directed at uneducated readers. With the final abolition of the newspaper stamp in 1855, it was hoped that a self-regulated industry would emerge, in which highly capitalized entrepreneurs would respect the privacy requirements of middle-class householders.

In practice, the delight in the defects of other people's lives turned out not to be confined to the lower orders. At every turn the growing demand for seclusion was challenged by the increasing appetite for news. Deborah Cohen has drawn attention to the centrality of blocked communication to the survival of the Victorian household: 'Secrecy was privacy's indispensable handmaiden, for the various sorts of shame that could be visited upon families – an illegitimate birth, a son with a propensity for "unnatural crimes", suicide, insanity, adultery, bankruptcy – were catastrophic, subject both to legal disability and to social scorn if they were known.'[111] In this struggle, the law played an ambiguous role. There were minor adjustments to the protection of the private realm, including a much-cited ruling in 1853 that prevented the unauthorized publication of etchings made by the queen and Prince Albert on the grounds that the defendant had stolen 'one attribute of property, which was often its most valuable quality, namely, privacy'.[112] Elsewhere, the courts were reluctant to extend the patchwork of judgments into anything resembling a general right, distinct from the enjoyment of physical property. Instead they upheld the freedom of the press to report in salacious detail any domestic scandal that reached the public domain, especially as a consequence of the legal process itself. Just as respectable newspapers were acquiring a mass readership the 1857 Matrimonial Causes Act created an inexhaustible new source of domestic scandal. For the first time the process of divorce was placed on a formal legal footing, and in two years more marriages were dissolved than in the preceding century. To ensure that litigants did not conspire to prevent exposure of sexual and other misconduct, a queen's proctor was appointed to force the detail into the open, and into the columns of *The Times* and the *Daily Telegraph*.[113]

The essence of the public interest in marital breakdown was the irreducible complexity of private life. Adultery was a single act with an infinite variety of forms. This kind of curiosity contrasted sharply with the most salient engagement of the state with the behaviour of its citizens in the nineteenth century. Beginning with the 1801 census and accelerating with the rise of the statistical movement in the 1830s, governments began to collect and publish information on how the population lived and died.[114] Activities that lay at the heart of the enclosed domestic realm, such as marriage and childbirth, were systematically examined. The political justification for investment in the General Register Office and other data-collecting exercises was the preparation of evidence-based legislation.[115] It was a means by which the multiple challenges of an industrializing and urbanizing society might be translated into appropriate interventions whose impact could in turn be measured.[116] The statisticians and the audience for their reports were fascinated by the discovery that complex conditions, such as, for instance, the reading and writing capacities of the nation, could be expressed in a single table of numbers which in turn became a consistent time series.[117] This could then be linked with similar exercises in other advanced countries. From the outset, the enterprise generated international conventions and comparative studies. As with the reformed postal system, which itself became a source of statistical information, the process was a tribute to the possibilities of the low and slow technology of manual transactions. Using a minimum of mechanical devices, small numbers of well-organized clerks generated a mass of reports about the burgeoning population whose accuracy has rarely been challenged.

The 'avalanche of numbers' was driven by the conviction that counting transcended opinion.[118] A host of accurately recorded details could be summed into objective facts which stood above the competing arguments about the future of the economy and society.[119] But the subjects of the exercise, particularly the dispossessed, the criminal and the illiterate, had no control over the categories in which they were placed. The binary divides in the tables between paupers and the deserving poor, the law-abiding and the law-breaking, the ignorant and the educated, bore little relation to the makeshift cultures of getting by in which the majority of the population lived. In this sense numbers, and the legislative reforms that they sustained, were a fictive, ideologically informed intervention in the management of family economies and behaviours.[120] Nonetheless, care should be taken in applying the catch-all term 'surveillance' to the growth of this infrastructural professionalism.[121] The officials were not interested in persons with individual identities and histories. The census forms required names and addresses only to check the accuracy of the temporary enumerators.[122] The under-staffed General Register Office lacked the capacity, as well as the will, to track households and their members through serial data-sets or to link their presence in separate categories of public records.[123] Its enterprise rested on the construction of society as a body of strangers, about whom nothing was known except specific, standardized attributes. Only by this means could the tables be compiled, and only on these grounds could the latent conflict between public inquiry and household privacy be contained.

Throughout the nineteenth century, law-abiding adult householders remained unnamed and secure behind their front doors. The police required warrants, philanthropic visitors had to negotiate entry. The only exceptions were for children. The 1853 Vaccination Extension Act prescribed a register of names of vaccinated infants, and the 1889 Prevention of Cruelty to, and Protection of, Children Act gave the authorities right of access to the home where it was suspected that a child was in danger of ill-treatment.[124] Liberal governmentality derived its authority from a deliberate act of withdrawal from the private sphere.[125] The balance was sustained in the nineteenth century by the established practice of denying publicity to the state's latent powers of direct surveillance. An era that began with the war with revolutionary France and the emergence of the first class-conscious protest movements was too dangerous for security to be entrusted wholly to the rational discourse of the public domain. Governments continued to deploy spies and open correspondence until Peel's home secretary, Sir James Graham, became the centre of a political scandal in 1844, when he was found to be opening the mail of Italian exiles in London at the behest of the Austrian government.[126] What Graham's biographer described as a 'paroxysm of public anger'[127] was partly a matter of timing. An intended consequence of the Penny Post in 1840 was a reassertion of the state monopoly in communication, which since the seventeenth century had increasingly been diluted by private networks of carriers seeking to avoid the high costs of the official system. Now every letter was to pass through the Post Office, and the revelation that each was vulnerable to interception if national security was claimed to be at risk suddenly focused attention on the vulnerability of virtual privacy and the limits to liberal restraint.

More generally, the paroxysm was a function of secrecy itself. In Parliament, Graham rehearsed the doctrine, which in Britain has remained largely intact to the present day, of declining to discuss official security. By refusing to admit what it had done, the government was also unable to deny what it had not done. Graham's biographer described the outcome:

> It was like a match struck for a moment amid profound darkness, revealing to the startled crowd vague forms of terror, of which they had never previously had a glimpse, and about which they forthwith began to talk at random, until a gigantic system of espionage had been conjured up, which no mere general assurances of its unreality could dispel.[128]

The fictional sensation of the moment, G. W. M. Reynolds' serial *The Mysteries of London*, adapted its plot to include the figure of 'The Examiner', an unnamed, all-powerful official, opening correspondence in the 'Black Chamber' in the Post Office headquarters and thereby gaining access to the hidden domestic archive of polite society: 'There were few, either men or women, of rank and name, of whom he knew not something which they would wish to remain unknown.'[129] If Bentham's reform agenda found its fullest expression in the great machine of postal communication, his vision of surveillance was re-awakened in the 'gigantic system of espionage' conjured up in 1844. Reynolds' 'Examiner' was a re-working of the prison governor, hidden in his watchtower. The modern debate over the invasion of privacy by information technology was infused with the notion of the network and the vision of an all-seeing mind at its heart. The shadow of omniscience, a function of a secular apprehension mediated by a religious sensibility, was a constant presence in the unfolding debate.

The single most influential article on privacy was published as the nineteenth century drew to a close. In the *Harvard Law Review* of 1890, Warren and Brandeis sought to establish a new legal right amidst the prevailing confusion of judgments and legislation. In doing so they exposed a fault line in the conception of the subject that was to become increasingly salient as public concern about privacy grew during the twentieth and early twenty-first centuries.

On the one hand, they were protesting about the offspring of the 'Paul Pry nuisance', the aggressive invasion by modern media of the domestic realm. 'The press is overstepping in every direction the obvious bounds of propriety and decency', they wrote. 'Gossip is no longer the resource of the idle and the vicious, but has become a trade which is pursued with industry as well as effrontery. To satisfy a prurient taste the details of sexual relations are broadcast in the columns of the daily papers.'[130] The problem of print was being compounded by the new technology of cheap photography. There was more than an element of prejudice in the protest. The market was driven by those without purpose in their lives: 'To occupy the indolent, column upon column is filled with idle gossip, which can only be procured by intrusion upon the domestic circle.'[131] The central concern, however, was with the widespread and long-standing defence of what Warren and Brandeis termed 'the sacred precincts of private and domestic life'. Their article had been provoked by the unwelcome invasion of the *Boston Saturday Evening Gazette* into the wedding breakfast arranged by Warren for his daughter.[132] This was a family occasion, given meaning by the intimate relations of those involved, and trivialized and misrepresented by its translation into popular entertainment.

By contrast, the second dimension of their protest constituted a rejection of all forms of personal interaction. The article proclaimed 'the right to be let alone', a phrase whose journey will be traced in the remaining chapters.[133] 'The intensity and complexity of life,' wrote Warren and Brandeis, 'attendant upon advancing civilization, have rendered necessary some retreat from the world, and man, under the refining influence of culture, has become more sensitive to publicity, so that solitude and privacy have become more essential to the individual.'[134] The roots of this response lay in the tradition of private prayer and reflection; however, now there was no divine interlocutor. Prominence was given instead to a form of romantic individualism, the possibility of finding the true self through withdrawal from the company of others. It was a matter of balance. William Hazlitt, the prophet of ambulatory solitude, was seeking to replenish rather than reject his social existence. He continued to spend a good part of his working life in that most boisterous gathering, the late-Georgian theatre. The nineteenth-century family was a means of containing the latent conflict in the practice of privacy. The individual found his or her identity in the context of marriage, and the family itself was foregrounded as the basic unit of religious observance. For the more prosperous, the pressures of teeming households were relieved, but not removed, by the provision of libraries, dressing rooms and eventually lockable bathrooms and lavatories. However difficult it was to maintain the confidentiality of conversation and correspondence amidst the press of people and the expansion of mass media, the body of knowledge that defined privacy was largely social. Proclaiming the 'right to be let alone' challenged this compromise. It implied that the noisy world of domestic relations, which for the poor so often spilled out into the open spaces of the street, was not the location but the enemy of the most valued core of private life. The archive that needed protection was an attribute not of intimacy but of isolation.

4

Privacy and Modernity 1900–1970

In 2013, the former cabinet minister Alan Johnson wrote an account of his childhood in the slums of Notting Hill.[1] It stood in a long tradition of autobiographies by members of Parliament tracing their path from humble beginnings to political office. The *Crow-Scaring to Westminster* genre celebrated the upward mobility made possible by the emergence of the trade unions and the Labour Party.[2] For the most part such life-stories were dutifully written and respectfully received. *This Boy*, however, became one of the non-fiction publishing events of the year, garnering large sales, critical acclaim and literary prizes. Its success reflected the state of British political culture in the second decade of the twenty-first century. There was an appetite for an authentic and affirmative reconnection of the public and private spheres. Too often senior figures were seen to have no lives outside politics or to be in denial about their back-stories. There was the appeal of the careful artlessness of the writing, and the moving depiction of two exceptionally tough and compassionate women, his mother and his older sister, who together raised him in great poverty following the desertion of his feckless father. But above all there was a striking collapse of historical perspective. Here was a man still in the middle of his life, until lately home secretary, seen by many as a potential leader of his party (the more so following the book), recounting a Dickensian childhood. Although he started life just after the creation of the welfare state in 1948, he endured an upbringing in a series of damp, urine-smelling, vermin-infested rooms, with shared plumbing and cooking facilities, following the carts of coal merchants to scavenge for fuel, negotiating credit with local shopkeepers for basic supplies. 'I was constantly hungry', he wrote. 'I've never forgotten that emptiness and craving for food.'[3] Dickens himself would have been proud to have written the story of Johnson's Christmas day in 1957. After his mother had been taken into hospital and his father had gone off on a drinking spree, his ten-year-old sister tried for the first time to cook a chicken and failed, leaving the two children alone with a few sweets and the vegetables from what was left of their Christmas dinner.[4]

There is a collision between the physical immediacy of Johnson's life-story and the normative framework in which it is embedded. From the early years of the twentieth century, privacy had increasingly become the subject of official definition and promotion. Following the 1908 Children's Act and the Maternity and Child Welfare Act of 1918, neglect of children justified intervention by the state and its health visitors. The sexual abuse of children in their own homes, which had been excluded from public debate until late in the nineteenth century, was addressed by the Punishment of Incest Act of 1908.[5] The built environment of private life was the target of legislation, beginning with Addison's Housing and Town Planning Act of 1919, and Chamberlain's and Wheatley's Housing Acts of 1923 and 1924. Elsewhere in Europe, housing conditions became the subject of growing debate, though less often of public intervention.[6] In the aftermath of World War II, all the combatants embarked on social reform programmes that centred on the promotion of what were held to be healthy domestic surroundings. Privacy was translated from an unofficial aspiration to a fundamental expectation. The 1948 Universal Declaration of Human Rights asserted that 'No one shall be subjected to arbitrary interference with his privacy', and a few months after Johnson was born, Article 8 of the European Convention on Human Rights declared that 'Everyone has the right to respect for his private and family life, his home and his correspondence.'[7] The question that arises is how far in the first two thirds of the twentieth century did privacy become modern. The public narrative of welfare states rested on a contrast with the inability of the mass of the population in previous centuries to attain the basic standards of domestic civilization. In the epochal conflict between dictatorships and liberal democracies, privacy was deployed by both sides as a measure of progress and its absence. It is a matter of striking a balance between the differences and continuities over time and within and between societies.

In the first instance, *This Boy* served as a reminder of the uneven development endemic in the long-run history of privacy. At one level, the combination of slum clearance, wartime bomb damage and large-scale public and private housing schemes compressed the range of circumstances across the population. It was increasingly unacceptable for the bulk of the labouring poor to be living in radically different conditions from their middle- and upper-class superiors. Official definitions of minimum housing design were set out in the Tudor Walters Report of 1918, and revised in the Parker Morris standards of 1961. Four million new homes were built in Britain between the world wars and nearly seven million between 1945 and 1969.[8] The proliferation of sanitary and health inspectors reflected a growing official intolerance of significant deviations from twentieth-century norms of domestic circumstances and conduct within given communities. Yet there remained immense variations in provision and experience. About half the interwar working-class population remained unaffected by the building programme.[9] When Johnson began his life, a third of the housing stock in Britain was more than eighty years old, and the subsequent construction programme still left a third of homes built before 1918.[10] Thirty-seven per cent of the population shared his experience of no fixed bath and a fifth either had no internal water closet or had to use it with others. Deprivation was not spread evenly across the urban communities. The housing estates that were being constructed on the edge of the towns and cities were generally supplied with electricity, indoor sanitation and as many as three bedrooms. But there were substantial areas of nineteenth-century stock that lacked all of these amenities. In Shoreditch just one in seven of homes had an indoor bath in 1938.[11] The 1951 census revealed that two fifths of homes in Manchester did not have exclusive use of a bath and only 56 per cent enjoyed what was by this time seen as the basic right of private access to a WC, piped water, a cooking stove and a kitchen sink.[12] Only two thirds of dwellings in London County had their own water supply and their own WC. As late as 1971, over half a million Greater London homes had use of either a shared bathroom or no facilities at all.[13] Near-universal enjoyment of basic sanitary provision was not achieved until the final quarter of the twentieth century. In rural areas beyond the reach of municipal housing schemes, where it was expensive to attach residences to water supplies, sewerage systems and the national grid, there was no consistent programme of improvement. Across Europe the more rural the society the less likely was the provision of basic amenities.[14]

The Johnson family was abreast of the present only in the sense that its accommodation was officially registered as unfit for habitation, together with nearly a million other homes in the early 1950s.

Ever since the middling orders of society began to invest in their accommodation in the early-modern period, the experience of privacy had been conditioned by wealth. By the nineteenth century, there was a chasm in domestic space and comfort between the middle class and much of the working class.[15] It can be argued, however, that the scale of inequality was never greater than in the interwar and immediate post-war periods, when the fault lines ran through the mass of the population. For all the variation in the Victorian era, internal sanitation did not become commonplace in respectable households until late in the century, and electricity was only installed in 2 per cent of homes by 1910. After 1918, both water supply and electric light became the expectation, but not the experience, of society as a whole. As working-class families shrank to the new middle-class model of two children, it was possible to prescribe rooms used only for sleeping, with parents separated from their offspring and adolescent girls and boys from each other. In practice, as a consequence of income, persisting demographic variations or the accident of geographical location, some working-class families were living in the twentieth century and others were enduring conditions little changed in half a millennium.[16] They had no access to the increasing range of domestic appliances which required an electrical supply; their sanitary arrangements would have been familiar to Tudor labourers. It was still impossible to keep the seasons at bay by artificial light and effective heating. Dedicated interior spaces and beds specific to particular users remained unobtainable. Maud Pember Reeves surveyed conditions in 1913:

> Supposing the family to consist of eight persons, most people would be inclined to prescribe four beds. As a matter of fact, there will probably be two. In a double bed in one room will sleep father, mother, baby, and ex-baby, while in another bed in another room will sleep the four elder children. Sometimes the lodger granny will take a child into her bed, or the lodger uncle will take a boy into his; but the four in a bed arrangement is common enough to need attention.[17]

Two decades later Margery Spring Rice recorded a beleaguered housewife still failing to achieve the long-sought-for specialization of domestic spaces and functions: 'I have a bed in the back for the two girls, a bed for the boy which I take down every day and put up at night to make more room, we have our food in this room I do all my cooking here; in the other room is my bed a bed I make up for the other little boy on the sette[e] and the pram the baby sleeps in.'[18]

Homes and neighbourhoods were increasingly subject to academic study. Sociologists were fascinated by the range of conditions they uncovered in particular communities. In the late 1950s, Margaret Stacey undertook a detailed study of Banbury, a transitional community in the south Midlands, lacking the heritage of urban squalor found in London or the northern industrial towns and cities. It possessed areas of older middle-class housing, new owner-occupied estates (in one of which the present author began his life), council estates on the outskirts with the full range of domestic amenities, and, left behind by progress, 'tight-packed terraces in the narrow streets and alleys that lie behind the shops in the town centre'.[19] These houses, built before 1914, and rented from private landlords, contained nearly a third of the town's population. Stacey described their condition:

> The front doors, which open straight into the room, open straight on to the street. In some there is no access except through the house to the back-yard, which may be common to several houses...The houses themselves are small: one or two rooms upstairs and down. In them family life is lived in a crowd, overcrowded in cases like that of the couple with three children who were interviewed in one such one-bedroomed house. The houses have no bathrooms and no indoor lavatories.[20]

Their occupants were not the poorest of the poor, but often skilled working-class families, older than those who had moved out to the new estates with their plumbing and gardens. The radical but fractured process of change after 1918 created a laboratory of privacy. The increased emphasis on the right to an enclosed domestic realm, combined with similar families living in what amounted to different centuries at the same moment in adjacent locations, demanded comparative analysis. By examining the contrast in aspiration and experience, it might be possible to identify for the first time the underlying continuities and changes in the pursuit of privacy. Further, as we shall see later in this chapter, the rise of totalitarian regimes in Fascist and communist Europe brought into focus as never before the role of the state as an upholder or enemy of private life.

The first conclusion reached by these studies was that the significance of the front door transcended time and class. 'In England,' wrote Margery Spring Rice in 1939, 'side by side with the passionate wish to preserve the integrity of the family, there is found the determination to keep it as a whole as *separate* as possible from other families and from any outside intrusion.'[21] The prosperity of the family influenced merely the extent to which a common ambition could be achieved:

> This is not a prejudice only of the poor. There is hardly a garden in England which is not surrounded by wall or hedge or railing, the obscurer the better. There is hardly a London Square garden which is not protected from the public by padlock and key. There is hardly a window in any family house which is not curtained effectively to obscure the view of the inquisitive passer-by.[22]

As Edwin Heathcote notes in his 2012 study of the home and its meanings, crossing the threshold was at all times a 'profoundly symbolic moment'.[23]

No matter how cramped the home, no matter how much of the family's business had to be conducted in the street and in view of the neighbours, there was a sharp sense of the difference between the interior and the exterior, and of the importance of the physical boundary between them. Kathleen Dayus grew up in a Birmingham slum in the early years of the century. Beds were shared inside the house, and in the yard there were stinking lavatories and two wash-houses where everyone did their weekly wash. The neighbours looked out for each other, particularly when officialdom came calling.[24] Nevertheless, her mother kept the outside world at bay, refusing to 'have any neighbours in our house unless it was essential', and after the turmoil of the day, 'we always put the bolt on the door when we were alone.'[25] In its compendious survey of living conditions in the early 1940s, Mass Observation found no variation in a common aspiration:

> The desire for privacy, for keeping oneself to oneself, is a powerful motive in modern society. One of the three most important reasons that people gave in the present survey for liking their houses was that it was 'all on our own like' or gave them their own street door. Whatever people may think of their neighbours in the street or the people they meet shopping or going down town, they definitely like to have their home to themselves. Any idea of having to share a home or even to share a gateway or a front-porch is repugnant to a great many people, and this applies also to being overlooked, either while sitting in the garden or when in the house.[26]

There was general agreement that the provision of semi-detached homes on the new council estates, together with fenced gardens to the front and the rear, represented not a new privilege but the realization of an ingrained demand. Alan Johnson's second volume of memoirs commenced with the escape of his new young family from Notting Hill to a council estate in Slough. He was acutely aware that his new housing conditions were nothing less than his mother had always wanted:

> My mother had spent her entire adult life on the council waiting list, bringing up her children in barely habitable, multi-occupied slums. Her dream had been to have her own front door to a house like this. She had died, aged forty-two, still waiting. The offer of a council house came two weeks after her funeral. Now here we were, Judy and me, at the beginning of our married lives, with the chance to move straight into this solid, modern, well-appointed house.[27]

The problem for the mostly left-leaning social investigators was how to reconcile the unquestionable gain of the escape from the slums with the implications of what Mass Observation had termed 'keeping oneself to oneself'. In 1959, Mark Abrams wrote an article entitled 'The home-centred society' for the *Listener*, the weekly noticeboard of the intellectual middle class, in which he drew attention to the extensive improvements in domestic comfort caused by housing programmes and the post-war consumer boom. 'The outcome', he concluded, 'is a working-class way of life which is decreasingly concerned with activities outside the house or with values other than those of the family.'[28] The theme was addressed by Michael Young and Peter Willmott in their influential comparative study of inner-city Bethnal Green and the new estate of 'Greenleigh'. They accepted that the desire for a separate domestic space was a given in both communities. 'The proper thing in Bethnal Green', they wrote, is 'to have a "home of your own"; for most people anything else is a second best.'[29] And they understood the longing to escape overcrowded accommodation and shared facilities. Nonetheless their account of the move to the estate was informed by a sense of loss. There was a unilinear decline in the quality of social relations. 'The newcomers', they observed, 'are surrounded by strangers instead of kin. Their lives outside the family are no longer centred on people; their lives are centred on the house. This change from a people-centred to a house-centred existence is one of the fundamental changes resulting from the migration.'[30] It was not just a matter of personal interactions shrinking as households were less exposed to the intrusion or support of neighbours and as migrants lost contact with relatives. Rather it was a displacement of people by material objects:

> Their relationships are window-to-window, not face-to-face. Their need for respect is just as strong as it ever was, but instead of being

able to find satisfaction in actual living relationships, through the
personal respect that accompanies almost any steady human interaction, they have to turn to the other kind of respect which is awarded,
by some strange sort of common understanding, for the quantity and
quality of possessions with which the person surrounds himself.[31]

In Young and Willmott's account, privacy stood opposed to a
newly endorsed conception of community. Their verdict reflected a
more general concern that in meeting the needs of the working class
for decent living conditions, reformers were destroying the culture of
mutuality that had sustained the electoral drive towards social justice.
Family and Kinship in East London was published in the middle of
the long period of Conservative rule that followed Labour's post-war
creation of the welfare state. It is possible, however, to argue that the
investigators were misinterpreting the threat to established forms of
private life and in doing so overstating the scale of change in the era.
The key to privacy was not the substance of interpersonal relations
but the capacity to control what was known of them. The attraction
of what were now widely termed 'traditional' working-class communities was their time-infused familiarity. By the standard of inner-
London neighbourhoods, Bethnal Green was unusually stable.[32] Here
it was possible to establish an association between long-term occupation of a particular set of streets and the capacity of the inhabitants
to maintain and continually update a social and economic map of
the terrain, with its patterns of friendship and enmity, threats and
assistance.[33] Investigators found that when the opportunity of a house
on a new estate arose, it was the younger families who were prepared
to take the risk of forming new networks in an unfamiliar setting,
whilst the old preferred to stay with what they knew, for all its
discomforts. Young and Willmott accepted that for this reason
'Greenleigh' might in future decades come to seem much more like
Bethnal Green than it did at the time of their survey, but nonetheless
persisted with their account of the contrasts between the settlements.
What they failed to emphasize was the distinction between resource-
fulness and power.

The slum dwellers were adept at making the most of their conditions, but there remained basic limitations on their capacity to
manage the exposure of their domestic circumstances. In terms of
consumption, for instance, the move to the estates, combined with
the sharp rise in general living standards in the 1950s, changed the
pattern of shopping. Instead of every street possessing a retail outlet
whose owners were barely more prosperous than their customers,
there were fewer, larger shops, less dependent on personal relations

between providers and users.[34] With better weekly wages, the spread of refrigerators and more domestic storage space, there was no longer a need to leave the home every day in search of basic necessities. Above all, it was possible to diminish the continual negotiation of credit or the weekly visit to the pawnbroker.[35] The history of borrowing was closely associated with the history of privacy. It was and has remained a key interface between the family economy and external scrutiny. Robert Roberts, whose family ran a corner shop in Salford, watched the process from the inside as his parents minutely cross-questioned customers on the state of their family economies in order to determine how much to advance, acutely aware that a succession of ill-informed judgements could in turn imperil their fragile business.[36] Directly or indirectly, intelligence had to be gathered on such matters as the number and health of children, whether and how much either parent drank, how secure was the father's income, how much was owed elsewhere. By the same measure, the street would discern the difficulties of a particular family by the frequency of the visits to the pawnbroker and its inability to redeem basic household items.[37]

As the micro-economy of credit declined, an alternative form of borrowing – hire purchase – expanded, assisted by the relaxation of restrictions in 1954. It was increasingly used to purchase the characteristic consumer items of the post-war period: cars, televisions and domestic appliances. Contemporaries registered concern at what Selina Todd has described as the 'mounting levels of debt' in the 1950s and 1960s.[38] In purely quantitative terms it is difficult to measure the scale of change. So much of the local borrowing lay beyond official statistics, including recourse to elderly female street lenders operating outside the 1900 Moneylenders Act and charging a penny in the shilling or two shillings in the pound (8–10 per cent) per week.[39] Only from the 1970s onwards was it possible to calculate the changing ratio of debt to income. In terms of personal surveillance, the direction of travel was from intense investigation of all aspects of character and income towards a reliance on standardized indicators of a capacity to repay a loan.[40] On both sides of the Atlantic, national networks supplying companies with information on the creditworthiness of customers had been in existence since the second quarter of the nineteenth century.[41] Their growth was a function of the growing complexity of the commercial economy and the greater mobility of debtors. It became easier to escape the multi-level scrutiny of neighbours, making it more difficult for potential creditors to predict future ability to repay on the basis of current and past behaviour. As social units became larger, a premium was placed on information that was centrally recorded and accessible to those paying a subscription for the service. The nineteenth-century guardian societies and the American credit bureaus struggled to manage the tension between the boundless descriptors of personal integrity and the limited facilities for storing and reproducing knowledge. They increasingly relied on external signs of character, such as dress, known family associations, affinities with reputable organizations, together with more formal indicators of probity or its absence, particularly court records of non-payment and bankruptcy.

The essence of the process was the translation of an oral archive to paper, which could then be reproduced by further written or verbal reports. Year by year the ledgers became more extensive. In 1926, a century after its foundation, the Manchester Guardian Society for the Protection of Trade claimed that 'over 40,000 written reports are supplied every year, and about 13,000 verbal reports given over the counter.'[42] Some use was made of modern communication systems, particularly the telegraph, which could deliver rapid responses to firms anxious not to delay decisions and lose business. The high cost of transmission down the wires placed a premium on the economy of the information. As early as 1885 the National Association of Trade Protection Societies, in an attempt to link the databases of its forty-seven members, experimented with a 'telegraphic code' which condensed the creditworthiness of potential debtors into a set of categories, each with a keyword which the operator could send to an inquiring subscriber.[43] It was a preview of the future, but until the arrival of computers and companies covering the whole of national markets from the 1970s onwards, the predominant medium of this form of surveillance was the paper file, updated from time to time and summarized for an inquiry. The London Association for the Protection of Trade used the same form to describe each potential debtor from 1842 to 1964.[44] Even in the United States, which by the middle of the twentieth century possessed a more comprehensive network of credit bureaus, the geographical scope of most firms was confined to a particular locality, from which a haphazard body of information was abstracted and stored in folders.[45] Data linkage rarely extended further than connecting basic demographic information with local court records. In Britain the alternative forms of bureaucratized credit and debt in working-class neighbourhoods were the large-scale suppliers of goods through club or check trading. Companies such as the Provident Clothing and Supply Company sought to supply the intelligence previously available to corner-shop owners and street moneylenders by employing centrally supervised local agents to generate business and collect payments.[46]

For the bulk of the population living on the margins, there were transitions in this period from intense neighbourhood oversight to modes of collecting and deploying information that were more systematic and impersonal. A combination of rising living standards and declining street surveillance made it easier to keep private the day-to-day, week-to-week stresses and strains of the family finances. New paper-based archives were being created but they were limited in their range both substantively and spatially. At the end of the 1960s, only just over a quarter of adults possessed a bank account. The remainder lived in an economy of cash, which had no history, no records, and no links to any other databases. Where required, recourse was made to credit extended on terms that were largely comprehensible and where the worst that could happen was the confiscation of relative luxuries. It was now less often necessary to manage unpayable debt by uprooting the family from a known address and moving it to a neighbourhood where there was safety amongst strangers.

During the interwar and post-war periods the combination of better housing, larger real incomes, shorter working hours and technological innovation increased choice as to how time was spent and with whom. There were more options for finding leisure, and a better chance of enjoying it with people of similar age or inclinations. The most striking change significantly expanded the space in which individuals could withdraw from each other's company, or conduct relationships in seclusion. As we have seen, the out-of-doors, whether in the form of fenced gardens or lanes and fields, had always served as an extension of the walled interior. The rapid urbanization of the nineteenth century made it difficult for the urban poor to cultivate anything more ambitious than window boxes, and they faced an ever-extending walk to open countryside. The new century transformed opportunity. Trams, buses and excursion train tickets made it easier to reach the edge of towns and cities. The Smallholdings and Allotment Act of 1908 required local authorities to purchase or lease land upon which their communities could grow food. The reform unleashed a pent-up demand. By 1914 there were between 450,000 and 600,000 allotments, rising to over 800,000 by 1939.[47] At the same time the house-building programme, based on a watered-down version of the garden city movement, responded to public expectations by supplying as standard front and back gardens, whether in council estates or middle-class suburbs.[48] Despite the introduction of high-rise flats surrounded by shared space, two thirds of public housing built between 1945 and 1969 was on the cottage model with its own gardens.[49] By the end of the 1960s, four fifths of all homes had their own demarcated lawns and flower beds.[50] For those moving out of the slums gardening became a formal duty, with post-1945 rent books stipulating that weeds be kept down and hedges trimmed.[51]

In 1955, Geoffrey Gorer reported that 'gardening is far and away the most popular leisure occupation of Englishmen (to a lesser extent English women)'.[52] A decade later just under half of all male householders were gardening regularly, and about half as many women.[53] With the reduction in the length of the working week that had been taking place since the end of the previous century, there was more time to spend outside in evenings and at weekends, and an increasing range of magazines, plant nurseries and packaged seeds to support the activities. The cultivated land performed a range of functions. The allotments in peacetime and particularly during the two world wars were a significant source of food. The flower beds allowed expression of a personal aesthetic, with a strong preference for scaled-down versions of the colourful herbaceous borders prevalent in Victorian and Edwardian country houses.[54] Growing vegetables and flowers supplied an outlet, particularly for men, for the urge to compete in the community, encouraged by municipal authorities awarding prizes for best-kept gardens. Clothing could be hung out to dry without exposing the state of the household's wardrobe to the gaze of the neighbours. For children the lawns reached through front or back doors were a compromise between parental supervision and free playing. No two gardens were exactly alike, or used in precisely the same way. The common condition was that access to the space, whether rented or owned, was controlled by the user, and as far as fencing or hedges would permit, was concealed from sight. In one sense, it increased the household arena at the expense of the shared life on the streets. In another, it supplied for the bulk of the urban population a long-sought-for alternative to the confines of domestic rooms and the life that was led in them. Although smaller nuclear families were now occupying larger houses, their members remained in close physical proximity as they went about their business. Outside they could labour, or talk, or merely sit quietly, away from those with whom they shared their daily existence.

Next to gardens, the second significant revolution in the dimensions of privacy was the spread of the motor car. What had been the privilege of the elite before 1914 became the possession of the commercial and professional middle class between the world wars, and from the 1950s was affordable by the upper reaches of the working class. Between 1950 and 1970, the number of cars on the road increased from 2 million to nearly 10 million.[55] Like gardens, motoring was at once an alternative to and extension of domestic privacy. Once cars had attained a degree of mechanical reliability they permitted a new form of engagement with the countryside by urban dwellers. By the late 1930s, as many families were taking a 'Sunday drive' to a beauty spot as were attending church.[56] The post-war spread of ownership broadened this form of escape from the home, and at the same time increased the enjoyment of private space. The new housing estates had originally been planned as walking communities, but as their occupants began buying cars it became possible for people to enjoy their new homes whilst at the same time commuting to former jobs or ranging more widely in search of alternative employment.[57] Amongst the new owners was Alan Johnson in Slough, who acquired a second-hand 1959 Ford Anglia through connections in the trade. 'Having a car (and a licence) revolutionized family life', he recalled, making it much easier to maintain contact with relatives left behind by the move from the Notting Hill slums.[58] Moreover, as observers began to realize, the car was quite unlike any alternative form of transport in its impact on enclosed space. Its function was independent of the journey, as Mark Abrams explained:

> It might be argued that the widening ownership of motor-cars constitutes a check to the growing British appetite for home-centred privacy, since it takes people away from their own immediate neighbourhood. In fact, the opposite seems to be true. Most owners treat their car as a detachable extra room to their house. They use it on week-days to travel to and from work in privacy – that is, without having recourse to public transport where they would be thrown into contact with other people. And they use it at the weekend as a small mobile room that can be taken to the seaside or the country, and in which they can sit in isolation when they have arrived at their destination.[59]

The home had gained wheels, literally so in the case of those who could afford a caravan.

The third revolution was in the realm of domestic entertainment. In the post-war consumer boom, the ownership of cars and televisions marched in tandem. Between 1951 and 1955, the number of motorists increased by almost a half, whilst possession of television sets increased from 1 million to 5 million.[60] Ten years later there were televisions in over 90 per cent of homes.[61] However, the triumph of domestic viewing was late in coming. Only two fifths of the audience for the 1953 coronation of Queen Elizabeth II watched it on their own sets. The remainder saw it on the sets of neighbours or in public spaces including cinemas. Until the late 1950s, the dominant broadcasting medium was radio. Between the world wars, ownership of radio licences had increased from one in ten to seven in ten of the population. Access to the airwaves was widespread though not universal. A combination of poverty and lack of an electricity supply meant that over 13 million people were without a radio in 1939.[62] In Jerry White's 'Campbell Bunk', the slum dwellers were still dependent on conversation and occasional reading.[63]

For those who could afford a set, listening to the BBC supplied a new focus for home life, enabling different family members to share in the same activity. The heavy, valve-driven radio, as later the television in its cabinet, was too large and expensive to be a personal possession. In this sense the electronic media both sheltered recreation from the involvement of neighbours and promoted greater intimacy within the domestic unit. It would be misleading, however, to view patterns of leisure in this period as leading exclusively to greater privacy. The coming of the radio was accompanied by the development of dance halls and the cinema as major sources of entertainment, particularly for the young. Instead of a handful of people in the streets or public houses, those seeking a release from work were regularly associating in groups of some thousands, the more so if they went to a football match, where attendance at first division matches increased from 6 million to 14 million between the world wars. After 1945, there was a general reduction in collective recreation, and in Britain, though not elsewhere in Europe, cinema audiences began to decline. Visits to the seaside and other tourist destinations continued to grow, however, at least partly as a consequence of car ownership. And around 1960, a development in radio technology merged transport and broadcasting, initiating a new era of personalized recreation. The 1962 Pilkington Report celebrated the transistor with uncharacteristic levity:

> The advent of the car radio and the light portable, particularly the ultra-light transistorised portable set, has added a new audience for sound broadcasting, an audience of those who travel and are out of doors. It is evidently not only the car driver who finds companionship in the radio, for truly,
>
> > The set in her handbag, as everyone knows
> > Provides all with music wherever she goes.[64]

There were two underlying trajectories of change in the impact of leisure on privacy. In the first instance radio and then television expanded the mental universe of the consumer. Where once only the printed or written word invaded the local information environment, it was now easier to be alone, or in a small group, and at the same time engaged with a spectrum of news, knowledge and entertainment. Compared with the marginal increases in the number and size of rooms in this period, this was much the larger transformation in personal space. The radio (unlike the later television) gave users access to international news and culture. The *Radio Times* in the early 1950s listed not only the domestic channels but the frequencies of sixty-two other European broadcasters ranging from Vatican City to Moscow, and offered weekly summaries of their highlights. Secondly, it increased apprehension about the negative implications of domestic privacy. At one level, the broadcast media, as also the cinema, permitted state control and censorship of communication on a scale that had long been abandoned in the realm of the printed word. Not since the era of mass church attendance could those in authority be so certain about what was being seen and heard, and when. The problem was how it was received. A combination of comfort and seclusion, combined with the regular association of older and younger generations, was thought to undermine the capacity to resist indoctrination, particularly by more vulgar or sensational forms of entertainment. The 1960 Pilkington Committee on Broadcasting endorsed a concern that was shared by both left- and right-wing commentators: 'Sitting at home, people are relaxed, less consciously critical, and, therefore, more exposed. Further, audiences are often family groups and include children who are normally protected from outside influences, and therefore especially vulnerable.'[65] Withdrawn from the crowd and enclosed in a tight social circle, there was no certainty about what the all-too-receptive audience was thinking. Privacy was the primrose path to infantilism.

The increasing ease with which individuals could conceal their behaviour from scrutiny was causing anxiety in different contexts. The car was blamed for both facilitating illicit trysts and itself being a location for unsupervised misconduct. All forms of mass communication at once strengthened and transgressed the bonds of domestic intimacy. Although the telephone had been introduced during the final quarter of the preceding century, the ancient technology of correspondence long remained the most widely deployed means of extending the realm of physical privacy. Perhaps its peak usage in terms of both volume and value was in the great wars of the twentieth century, when in spite of military censorship it played a crucial role in keeping lovers in touch with lovers, parents with children, across the global span of hostilities. As Claire Langhamer writes of World War II, 'The love letter was not a wartime innovation but during this conflict it became an ordinary means of communicating extraordinary experiences.'[66] In Britain, the volume of phone calls did not overtake that of letters until 1970. By 1975, the telephone had decisively replaced correspondence as the leading mode of communication, with 16 billion calls to 9.9 billion letters.[67] The Victorian paraphernalia of paper, envelopes and stamps, still collected, sorted and posted entirely by hand as Alan Johnson discovered when he became a postman in 1968,[68] was for the bulk of the population long the most familiar means of connecting over a distance in times of family celebration or crisis.[69] In North America and Scandinavia, where distance was a major obstacle to any kind of human interaction, the adoption of the phone was much more rapid. Party lines connecting isolated rural homesteads were widely adopted in the United States early in the twentieth century.[70] But in the relatively compact and crowded British Isles, a device that initially had been intended principally for the use of business and the middle class remained an expensive and optional investment. Young and Willmott found that there were seven times more phones per head in the new council estate than in Bethnal Green, where in the 1950s walking down the street was still the most efficient means of exchanging greetings and information with friends and relatives.[71]

Those who have focused on the coming of the phone have tended to overstate the discontinuity in the transition from written to electrical communication. Carolyn Marvin writes of the introduction of the new invention that it

> threatened a delicately balanced order of private secrets and public knowledge, in particular that boundary between what was to be kept privileged and what could be shared between oneself and society, oneself and one's family, parents, servants, spouse or sweetheart. Electrical communication made families, courtships, class identities, and other arenas of interaction suddenly strange, with consequences that were tirelessly spun out in electrical literature.[72]

As we have seen, the post had long challenged the information boundaries of the home, connecting in what was hoped was confidence individuals inside and outside the family circle. To take one example, courtship conducted by correspondence had for centuries undermined the authority of parents in the critical moment of family formation. Equally the letter had posed the challenge of the disembodied voice, lacking the reinforcing devices of tone and gesture and the instant correction of misinterpreted meaning. The synchronous device of the telephone both qualified and accentuated the problems of virtual privacy. On the one hand it reduced the uncertainty of the absent recipient, who might never have received the message, and indeed might no longer be alive. An answered call supplied immediate reassurance. The telephone introduced the prospect of dialogue transcending the physical boundaries of the home. Whilst the quality of penmanship always had the capacity to convey more than the words alone, the transmission of the voice together with any background noises in the room generated new forms of long-distance intimacy. The conversation contained its own feedback loop, increasing the prospect of reciprocal intimacy. On the other hand Bell's invention compounded the problem of secrecy. There were more threats to the confidentiality of communication. Until the introduction of Subscriber Trunk Dialling (STD) in 1958, the operator was a latent third party to the exchange. Most domestic premises had only a single, wired handset, making it more difficult to speak without being overheard than write without being overseen. At the same time the home lost its privileged status as a bounded speech community. Callers no longer had to use the front door. The channels of private intercourse became less visible and less controllable.

The second general trajectory was the slow, uneven growth of what came to be termed the companionate marriage.[73] At the centre of the range of meanings associated with the new family form was a combination of intimacy and seclusion. Husband and wife spent more of their leisure time in each other's company, and less in gender-specific gatherings outside the home. They valued the privacy of their domestic unit and their enhanced capacity to manage the flow of information across its boundaries. They had more space in which to live together, and few children or other co-residing relatives to share it. The roles between the household members were not interchangeable although there was more shared involvement in the day-to-day business of raising children. Men retained their identity as breadwinners despite the beginning of the growth in married women's employment from the 1950s onwards. They were more likely to manage the garden and carry out repairs around the house. The car remained largely a male preserve as ownership spread: 56 per cent of men held a driving licence in the mid-1960s, compared with just 13 per cent of women.[74] Many men found it difficult to negotiate between the camaraderie of what were still mostly women-free workplaces and the duties now expected of them in the home.[75] Alan Johnson was embarrassed by the recollection of his performance as a paterfamilias in the late 1960s. He was working long hours in an entirely male sorting office and doing little but spending some time with his young children when he came home:

> I'm conscious that this creates a fair impression of Andy Capp; of a bloke with a self-centred social life that left his wife to look after the kids, cook, wash and make a comfortable home. And that was pretty much the division of labour back then... I was...perpetuating the male lifestyle adopted by my father, if not the excesses to which he took it.[76]

Escaping his cultural heritage was proving difficult but he also knew that many of his contemporaries were now playing a more energetic part in the 'Do It Yourself' boom (or 'Don't Involve Yourself', as his exasperated wife defined it).

The greater possibility of a couple managing their lives out of the sight and hearing of neighbours and other family members raised the expectations of emotional and sexual fulfilment.[77] The generation reaching adulthood after World War II married in larger numbers and for longer periods than any before or since.[78] Privacy was at once a condition and a consequence of the increased intimacy between husband and wife and parents and children. The more the outside world was kept at bay, the greater the prospects of open and affective discourse within the home; the more that was invested in the relationships, the less need for exposure to those beyond the front door. There were, however, two growing tensions in the forms of closure inherent in the companionate marriage. The first was its conservative sexual morality. The home-based society represented the final, but short-lived triumph of heterosexual monogamy. There was no place for other forms of partnership or casual relationship. Towards the end of the period there was a growing tolerance of pre-marital sex, but adultery was stigmatized, and homosexual acts were a crime in England and Wales until 1967, in Scotland until 1980 and in Northern Ireland until 1982. It was less easy to tidy away deviant behaviour in the tight nuclear families of the mid-twentieth century than it had been in the sprawling Victorian households. Now secrets proliferated as other kinds of intimacy were pursued, facilitated, as we have seen, by the communication technologies of the era. On the one hand, the letter, the phone and the car promoted illicit behaviour. On the other, as in the previous century, secrecy generated curiosity and sold newspapers. There was an appetite for stories about activities that simultaneously evoked fascination and censure. The nineteenth-century diet of divorce cases was widened to include the exposure of sexual misconduct by the rich and famous.[79]

Blocking information became privacy's shame rather than its defensive virtue. The second tension lay within the heart of the enclosed household. The hermetically sealed interior was increasingly seen as a breeding ground of emotional or sexual pathology. There was growing concern between the world wars about the mistreatment within the curtained home of its more vulnerable members, no longer offered protection by the haphazard surveillance and rough justice of the street. Questions were raised about the capacity of the family to deal with its problems in isolation. The absence of conversation beyond the domestic unit was seen as destructive of the relationships it was designed to nurture. Value was invested in the process of talking to outsiders, whether eager journalists or trained volunteers and professionals. Tabloid newspapers encouraged readers to send in their stories, offering, in the case of the *Daily Mirror*, a 'pledge of secrecy' in return for anonymized accounts of private suffering and discontent.[80] Beginning with Leonora Eyles in *Woman's Own* in 1932, the agony aunt dispensed advice that was now less easily available from a nearby neighbour or relative. Eyles, 'the woman who understands', was particularly concerned with communication itself, who should share what confidences with whom within the family circle.[81] The confession's spiritual function of exorcising guilt was translated into a range of psychotherapies based on the curative effect of talking through traumatic experiences. The National Marriage Guidance Council was founded in 1946, with a mission to strengthen the institution by offering advice and providing a place in which unhappy partners could share their griefs and grievances with trained and sympathetic listeners.

For most families, day-to-day living was a complex mixture of words and silences. As in the previous century, increasing levels of space and comfort provided an arena for endless conversation. 'Almost as important as the freedom and relaxation aspect', noted Mass Observation in 1943, 'is the home as a background to family life. There the family meets over breakfast and dinner, there they talk, quarrel, play, live.'[82] 'There was no day-time TV,' recalled a child growing up in the 1950s, 'and we played cards and board games and TALKED to each other and our friends.'[83] In the early days, BBC television was nothing if not deferential to domestic routines. Until 1957, it began showing programmes for children at 5.00 p.m. but then went off the air for an hour at 6.00 p.m. while they were put to bed. Deep inside the household, discourse took place far from the gaze of concerned investigators. In Alan Johnson's Notting Hill slum, the twin problems of lack of sleeping space and his mother's distress at the desertion of her feckless husband were resolved by his sister's decision to move into her mother's bed. In the dark, words flowed:

> At night, I'd hear them talking in the bedroom next to mine. Linda's sacrifice of her own room had had the desired effect and there were now more conversations than tears emanating from the big double bed. They talked of the past, of Lily's childhood, of her hopes and dreams, of her illness, and of how she might meet a man who would care for her.[84]

Here privacy served its core function of sustaining intimacy. The young Alan Johnson might listen to the rise and fall of the conversation, but in essence its meaning and purpose were for the mother and daughter, lying in close bodily and emotional proximity.

Outsiders for the most part paid little attention to what was said in these secluded spaces, and worried instead about the gaps in communication. In particular, they were increasingly concerned about the apparent absence of a discourse about sex. Marie Stopes' *Married Love* of 1918 was accurately titled. Her concern was with the monogamous, heterosexual partnership. She would not countenance sex outside marriage, but neither could she conceive of a successful relationship without a mutually satisfying physical relationship. In too many cases this was rendered impossible from the outset by the mutual ignorance of the couple. 'In the first joy of their union,' she wrote, 'it is hidden from the two young people that they know little or nothing about the fundamental laws of each other's being.... there is no firm foundation of real mutual knowledge beneath their feet.'[85] They did not know how to talk to each other or to any informed friend or relative about the mechanics of sex and contraception; neither did they have access to plain, accurate, written information. *Married Love* was an immediate success, selling three quarters of a million copies over the next two decades, and provoking an avalanche of correspondence seeking further advice from its author.[86] The letters, which Marie Stopes later edited for publication, stressed the ignorance of couples before their wedding. 'I married knowing practically nothing of what married life would be', wrote one wife, '– no one ever talked to me and told me things I ought to have known – and I had a rude awakening.'[87] They also were fiercely critical of the medical profession for withholding information on contraception, or failing to learn about modern techniques.[88]

Subsequent memoirs and oral histories have amplified the account of ill-informed newly married couples.[89] From the 1920s onwards, there was growing public debate about the need for more transparency but little evidence that it was reaching the mass of the population. The first British investigation of sexual practices, the post-war 'Little Kinsey' report, reiterated Stopes' basic argument: 'The fact that so little is said on these subjects, that a wall of secrecy is built up around sex, adds to the confusion and makes simple explanation more difficult...If any single result emerges from this survey it is the need for education.'[90] However as Szreter and Fisher have argued in their groundbreaking study *Sex Before the Sexual Revolution*, it is possible to take a radically different view of the consequences of this register of privacy. Their witnesses confirm the point of departure of earlier studies. Before and during their marriage they were excluded from any kind of discourse about sex. They lacked even the vocabulary for such discussion, and were only able to contribute to the subsequent academic inquiry because they had lived long enough to share in more recent openness about the practices in question. In their own time they were not told about, and made little or no attempt to discover, techniques of achieving sexual pleasure and avoiding unwanted pregnancy. If anything, their ignorance was deeper than that of earlier generations. Married couples were more likely to have exclusive use of bedrooms, and adolescent boys and girls less likely to share a bed. Most households were now far removed from the reproductive panorama of the countryside. The chances of an inadvertent education declined, and with the increasing provision of internal, lockable, lavatories and bathrooms, expectations of complete bodily privacy became more entrenched. Many of the consequent difficulties are rehearsed in Szreter and Fisher's study, including initial embarrassment and disappointments. But the overall conclusion challenges the assumption that silence and intimacy were mutually opposed. To the contrary, it was common for married couples to value their sex-life precisely because it was so private. It was neither exposed to commentary nor measured against some general norm. From their first fumblings onwards they taught each other. Experiment and empathy took the place of language and education. For all the error amidst the trials, the outcome could be more satisfying because it was their own course of learning, pursued on the basis of trust and adjustment rather than an external curriculum. The study cites the inarticulate account of 'Frank': 'It were never, it were never discussed...you could, er, tell...by her reaction...we had that understanding, you know, you, you didn't need to say anything...We had [it] worked to a fine art, whereby we knew by just looking at one another...just how deeply you were involved and, what really was wanted.'[91] This intimate communication was modern in that more was expected of sex in this period, and the increasing seclusion and comfort of the marital bed made the prospects of achieving it greater. But however limited their chances, earlier generations will have travelled along the same wordless path, and achieved something of the mutual affection and satisfaction at the end of it.

The early years of the twentieth century witnessed the beginning of the surveillance state. The large-scale government systems for collecting information about the population in the Victorian era were not designed to engage with the behaviour of most individuals and their families. Only those who broke the law or were rich enough to pay taxes found themselves on a database. Three factors transformed the deployment of official documentation of private citizens: communications, welfare and total war. The 1903 Motor Car Act and the 1904 Wireless Telegraphy Act required users to apply for a licence for the new technologies. The 1908 Old Age Pensions Act and the 1911 National Insurance Act established central bureaucracies to ascertain eligibility and manage payments. World War I finally created a system of national registration and for the first time made it compulsory for Britons travelling abroad to possess a passport.

The initial motive of change was fear of anonymity. The early motor-car drivers, swathed in leathers and goggles, crossing police jurisdictions at will, had to be identified as they threatened life and limb on roads built for horses and pedestrians.[92] Radio communication was at first seen as a military device, particularly for signalling between naval ships and shore-bases, and a central record was demanded on grounds of national security. The licences did not become a means of funding a broadcasting service until the BBC was established in 1922.[93] The second factor was the displacement of local judgement by formal records as a determinant of receipt of welfare. The New Poor Law was subject to central regulation but the application was in the hands of Boards which were held to possess the knowledge of local conditions necessary for the economical administration of relief. State pensions merely required proof of age and marital condition, and insurance benefits evidence of contributions and current health or employment status. Finally the conditions of war foregrounded the importance of a comprehensive record of the entire population, at least as long as hostilities continued.

Critical to the process of change in an emerging liberal democracy was the issue of consent. The dispossessed had a long tradition of extracting benefit from intrusion. 'It is impossible to deny that the poor demand a price for admission to their homes', began Martha Loane's 1909 study, *An Englishman's Castle*.[94] For middle-class visitors to cross the threshold, a price was exacted: 'They must pay their footing, must "bring their welcome with them"; and the worst part of it was that there was no fixed scale of charges…they were asked for a milk pudding one week, five hundredweight of coal the next, and so on, the terms increasing at a geometric rate.'[95] The demise of the Poor Law over the period between 1908 and 1948 was caused not just by the humiliation of officials entering a home and demanding that possessions be sold, but also by the sense that the resulting benefits were too insubstantial to justify the loss of dignity.[96] For all the rhetoric of fortification, householders were in the last resort willing to parlay with their enemies. What changed in the new century was the nature of the negotiation. There was an exchange of rights for professionalism. Entry to the house was more willingly conceded where there was a specific service on offer, delivered by trained employees armed with statutory responsibilities. By 1918, 2,500 health visitors were calling on mothers and children, and 6,000 by the late 1940s.[97] Public health inspectors came to the door to examine damp and sanitation, with powers to compel landlords to make improvements which their tenants were themselves powerless to achieve.[98] Those escaping to municipal estates had to accept constraints on their autonomy as officials inspected their upkeep of the new house and garden. There remained ample scope for conflict over competing standards and expectations, but with the growth of maternity and child welfare services such invasions were no longer exclusively the experience of the poor and those in rented accommodation.

The contested boundary between privacy and surveillance was particularly apparent in the case of national registration, which was introduced in both world wars. In neither case was there significant resistance to the argument that national security and the need to allocate scarce resources in a war economy required an unprecedented extension of the state's supervisory powers. Nevertheless politicians and their electorate were not prepared to countenance the continuation of the system in peacetime. Registration survived longer after the second conflict only because of the extension of wartime rationing. The scheme was finally abandoned in 1952, once the identity cards were no longer necessary to obtain food and clothing.[99] Striking a lasting balance between rights and benefits proved more intractable in the case of welfare payments. At one level, the early-twentieth-century reforms forced a working population that was only just achieving universal literacy to make an irreversible embrace of writing and documents. There was no application form to enter the nineteenth-century workhouse and negligible paperwork in the process of recruiting and dismissing the industrial workforce; but employees in occupations covered by the expanding national insurance system had to give their employers an unemployment insurance card to be filled with stamps and returned at the end of the job. The card was submitted to the labour exchange in return for a receipt, and the worker then completed two forms for benefit: one for himself and a second for his dependents. Printed guidance was available for all stages of the process, and should a claim fail, a written explanation would be made.[100] The bureaucratic burden was an acceptable alternative to more invasive and open-ended forms of inquiry into past employment and current circumstances. The difficulty lay in the inability of the state in the interwar period to deliver relief without falling back on some form of household inquiry. Under pressure of mass unemployment the 1931 means test required those who had exhausted their twenty-six-week insurance benefit to complete a detailed questionnaire on their family economy and submit to a home visit from an investigating officer to check the answers and value the family's resources

What prevented history from repeating itself was the scale of the reaction against the means test. There were spontaneous and sometimes physically violent protests at labour exchanges. The Labour Party, both locally and nationally, campaigned against the invasive surveillance of household economies. The National Unemployed Workers' Movement, largely shunned by the Parliamentary left, sought to mobilize the victims and to represent them in appeals against the system. In the short term only the gradual recovery of the economy diminished the tensions; but the memory of the assault on privacy lay at the heart of the Beveridge Report of 1942 on social insurance and allied services, and the landslide victory of the Labour Party at the 1945 general election. The subsequent introduction of a comprehensive national insurance system in 1948 was designed to both extend and minimize the state's interaction with what was now the entire population. All forms of need, including health, were covered on the basis of a single system of weekly contributions. There was a residual discretionary element, termed national assistance, for those, particularly the elderly, whose needs were not fully covered by insurance benefits. In the late 1950s, as many as 8 million home visits a year were being made under the new system, but in an era of full employment these were mostly to women pensioners and rarely resulted in withdrawal of benefit.[101]

Two characteristics of the post-war compromise generated acceptance. The first was a new balance between coverage and intervention. National insurance echoed wartime registration in that the whole nation was included. Only leaving the territorial boundary of the country would permit exclusion. Membership of the scheme was coextensive with citizenship and required nothing more intrusive than a record of weekly payments. Resources for combating fraud by various forms of labour-intensive investigation were concentrated on a small number of cases. As John Rule pointed out in his pioneering study of 1970, the narrow focus of inquiry into personal circumstances both generated and reflected a broad consent by the participants. Widespread evasion of the regulations would have rendered the scheme's operation unaffordable.[102] The second characteristic was the information technology underpinning the scheme. The operation of national insurance stands as a demonstration that the digital revolution was not a necessary pre-condition of scale, speed and accuracy in large bureaucracies. Well into the era of mainframe computers the entire operation was still based on manually maintained ledger sheets. At the end of the 1960s, over 10,000 staff in the largest clerical office in Europe were dealing with 15 million claims a year using materials and processes Dickens would have recognized. Almost a century after the telephone was invented, the bulk of the traffic between the centre in Newcastle-upon-Tyne and the local offices which made the decisions on individual cases was transacted by post. The principal limitation of the reliance on paper was also its greatest strength in terms of popular acceptability. Record linkage was a cumbersome process. Basic demographic data was readily obtained from the General Register Office, but otherwise the national insurance system, in common with most official databases of the era, was sufficient unto itself. It is probable that local investigating officers made greater use of community archives than was formally acknowledged, but for the bulk of the insured population, personal information was not transferable. This also applied to the proliferating agencies now intervening in the conduct or conditions of domestic life. Apprehension about the growth of surveillance was constrained by the evident fragmentation of the official endeavour, as Elizabeth Bott recognized in her 1957 study of families and networks: 'In brief, social control of the family is split up among so many agencies that no one of them has continuous, complete, governing power, and within broad limits, a family can make its own decisions and regulate its own affairs.'[103]

The national insurance system was created by an Act of Parliament and governed by an immense rule book covering 130 different operations. By contrast, the national security surveillance programme which took on its modern form in this period was notable for the almost complete absence of public authorization or oversight. Under the Official Secrets Act of 1911, which was rushed through Parliament in a single afternoon, the definition of what was a secret and who was allowed to disclose it was left to the discretion of senior civil servants and their political masters.[104] The security agencies were created before and during World War I without any legislative basis, and expanded their scope in the interwar period to cover internal threats including the Communist Party and organizations of the unemployed, without further Parliamentary debate.[105] For two decades after World War II the very existence of what became the centre for the interception of telecommunications, the Government Communications Headquarters (GCHQ), was itself an official secret. The secrecy about secrecy was not a negation of the more transparent systems of welfare surveillance, but rather an alternative means of securing the same end. From the postal espionage controversy of 1844 onwards, it was an article of faith of successive governments of every political hue that consent to the surveillance of private communications was best secured by keeping the issue as far from public debate as possible.

In the period covered by this chapter the only extended official discussion of the legal basis for interception was the inquiry made in 1957 by three privy councillors, chaired by the judge Lord Birkett, following a controversy over the tapping of the phone of a barrister acting for a London gangster. The inquiry began by noting that, 'In the year 1844, a great agitation arose in the country, because the Secretary of State, Sir James Graham, had issued a warrant to open the letters of Joseph Mazzini', and concluded that the issue remained no less sensitive a century later:

> There is no doubt that the interception of communications, whether by the opening or reading of letters or telegrams, or by listening to and recording telephone conversations, is regarded with general disfavour...Whether practised by unauthorised individuals or by officials purporting to act under authority, the feeling still persists that such interceptions offend against the usual and proper standards of behaviour as being an invasion of privacy and an interference with the liberty of the individual in his right to be 'let alone when lawfully engaged in his own affairs'.[106]

The problem was that since 1844, no new legislative basis had been created either for the subsequent growth of postal espionage or for the new technology of the telephone, which, as the Report accepted, had been subject to interception since its introduction.[107] In this circumstance, the 1844 event, and the resulting Secret Select Committee inquiry into legal history, became both a warning and a source of comfort. The examples disinterred from earlier eras gave assurance that the surveillance of communication was, if not formally legal, then at least not contrary to any known statute. The objection that such precedence might not cover a technology only invented in the later nineteenth century was addressed: 'If it be said that a prerogative right could not extend to the interception of telephone conversations, because telephones were undreamt of when the power was first taken and exercised, reference should be made to the case of In re a Petition of Right, 1915 3 K.B 659 in the Court of Appeal', which, it transpired, was concerned with fishing nets made of materials not envisaged in the reign of Richard I.[108] Thus the twelfth century was deployed to justify the use of surveillance by what was now a nuclear power.

On its own terms, the tradition that took form under Queen Victoria served its purpose. It proved possible to adapt to new technologies and extend state interception of communications in the face of unpredictable threats ranging from the Fenians to international communism, at short notice and without public debate. Transparency presented a double threat to this achievement. The British breaking of the German Enigma code at Bletchley Park during World War II entrenched the view that a condition of successful surveillance was ignorance by the target of the methods and successes of the security services. The wartime achievement was kept secret at the time and for the succeeding half century in the hope that Britain's enemies would invest misplaced confidence in their own communication networks. Thus Birkett advised that keeping of a record of phone-tapping and letter-opening should recommence, but that not even the global figures should be regularly published. 'We are in particular aware', wrote the privy councillors, 'of the danger of disclosing even on a single occasion the extent of interception for security purposes...It would greatly aid the operation of agencies hostile to the State if they were able to estimate even approximately the extent of the interceptions of communications for security purposes.'[109] This view has withstood every subsequent challenge. The Intelligence and Security Committee's *Privacy and Security* report of March 2015, the most recent parliamentary inquiry into this world at the time of writing, advised that: 'While the Committee has been provided with the exact figures relating the number of authorisations and warrants held by the Agencies, we have agreed that publishing that level of detail would be damaging to national security.'[110]

Any level of informed public debate would threaten such caution, and in turn would endanger the contract at the heart of the embattled liberal democracy. Power was ceded to the state on condition that it refrained from intrusion into the private sphere unless a crime had been committed. The process of legislation, debate and periodic review would force government to define the limits of virtual privacy, whose range has been expanding with the increasing use of communication systems. It would further require a new distinction to be drawn between behaviours that lay beyond the reach of the state and those that justified intervention. The system of vetting civil servants which was introduced in 1947 rested on the assumption that a range of common character flaws including alcoholism and homosexuality constituted a threat to national security. Since the 1844 scandal, which was a constant point of reference in the Birkett Report, the silence about surveillance had done nothing to reduce the potentially explosive consequences of exposing the issue to Parliament and the press. Better not to run the risk and to settle for an *ex cathedra* assurance that all was well. 'The interference with the privacy of the ordinary law-abiding citizen or with his individual liberty is infinitesimal,' concluded Birkett, 'and only arises as an inevitable incident of intercepting the communications of some wrong-doer. It has produced no harmful consequences.'[111]

The Birkett Report was published as the battle lines of the Cold War were being drawn. For the West, privacy was placed at the centre of the conflict between progressive democracies and their enemies. Hannah Arendt's *The Origins of Totalitarianism* of 1951 described how that form of government was innovative not only in its attack on the public realm but in that it 'destroys private life as well'. Society was atomized, and replaced by 'loneliness...the experience of not belonging to the world at all, which is among the most radical and desperate experiences of man.'[112] In the absence of detailed contemporary sociological analysis, by far the most influential account of the onslaught on privacy was a work of fiction. George Orwell's *1984* presented a bleak vision of a world in which the fundamental drivers of private life had been subverted:

> The family could not actually be abolished, and, indeed, people were encouraged to be fond of their children in almost the old-fashioned way. The children, on the other hand, were systematically turned against their parents and taught to spy on them and report their deviations. The family had become in effect an extension of the Thought Police. It was a device by means of which everyone could be surrounded night and day by informers who knew him intimately.[113]

The longevity of Orwell's dystopia was assured by its engagement with the technology of surveillance, which connected him back to the Panopticon and its speaking tubes and forward to the devices of the digital age. As in Bentham's blueprint, the population never knew whether they were being watched at any one moment, and thus ordered their lives on the assumption that they were always under inspection. The hidden prison governor in the watchtower was updated to embrace a medium that was soon to become the possession of every household on both sides of the iron curtain: 'With the development of the television, and the technical advance which made it possible to receive and transmit simultaneously on the same instrument, private life came to an end.'[114]

There are, however, two essential qualifications to be made to Orwell's vision. The first concerns the limits to surveillance, however technically sophisticated, as a self-sufficient device for ensuring obedience and conformity. Big Brother did not rely on the telescreen alone, nor on the other mechanisms for invading the privacy of his subjects. Those who cite *1984* as a shorthand for all that is threatening in modern surveillance systems tend to overlook the bloody horror show in Part Three of the novel. With his direct experience of fighting Fascism, and a range of literary influences including Koestler's *Darkness at Noon* on the Stalin show trials, Orwell was fully aware that behind the technology lay terror at its most direct and physical. The text is unsparing in its description of Winston Smith's experience in room 101:

> All he had eyes for was the truncheon in the guard's hand. It might fall anywhere: on the crown, on the tip of the ear, on the upper arm, on the elbow – The elbow! He had slumped to his knees, almost paralysed, clasping the stricken elbow with his other hand. Everything had exploded into yellow light. Inconceivable, inconceivable that the blow could cause such pain![115]

In Nazi Germany, as in Stalin's Russia, the systems of spying, eavesdropping and denunciation operated within structures of judicial torture and murder. The immense bureaucracy of the German Democratic Republic's Stasi used threats of punishment in its recruitment of agents and consigned its victims to broken careers, imprisonment and execution. Everyone knew the consequences of challenging the practice and rationale of surveillance. The attack on privacy was, in the last resort, a function of the closure of reflection and debate. It was not spying by itself, but the attempt to prevent any critical awareness and response. The central drama of *1984* is the protagonist's ultimately vain attempt to meditate on his condition and react against it.

The second observation is that, however informed by the sufferings of his age, Orwell's novel was a warning, not a description. The surveillance technology did not yet exist, and neither did the inevitable, pitiless destruction of every reasoning subject. Furthermore, historical scholarship has recently called into question the extent to which the Fascist and communist regimes either desired or achieved the overthrow of the modern family. Rather than privacy's destruction standing as the hallmark of the totalitarian endeavour, its survival calls into question the ambition and achievement of the dictatorships. The persecution, imprisonment and murder on a vast scale of those whose families belonged to stigmatized racial groups, or whose sexual relationships contravened narrow heterosexual standards, were a fundamental reality. Yet there was also a narrative of permitting and promoting conventional forms of domesticity. Ideologues of the early Russian Revolution denounced the family as antithetical to the communist project, but by the early 1930s, encouragement was being given to a personal life apart from, though accessible to, the state.[116] In Nazi Germany and subsequently in the German Democratic Republic, the home as a locus of leisure and procreation was endorsed as a measure of the civilization created by the regimes. There developed a dialectic of mistrust and withdrawal. The controlling authorities glorified the family but at the same time regarded it as the last bastion of disloyalty, requiring ever-greater efforts to penetrate its secrets. In turn its members reacted to the pervasive presence of the state by retreating further into the routines and rituals of privacy. It can be argued that in this sense, the liberal achievement of a private sphere was nowhere more valued than in those societies where it was most under threat.[117]

Within the dictatorships, surveillance represented a terrain of mutual exploitation. For the secret police, the archives of personal information constituted by private relations were an inexhaustible source of intelligence. At the same time, there was a practice across centuries and societies of otherwise powerless individuals appropriating concentrations of power to achieve personal ends.[118] Where the church, whether Catholic or Protestant, had been a locus of privilege and punishment, believers had denounced each other in pursuit of private gain or the resolution of domestic or community conflicts. The rise of the twentieth-century welfare states provided a new avenue for accessing external authority as neighbours wrote, usually anonymously, to complain of abuses of means test or insurance payments.[119] If the consequences were less lethal than in contemporary tyrannies, the loss of benefits could be devastating within family economies. In Germany, the Nazis enhanced a long-established tradition of civilians acting as conduits of information to the police.[120] The Gestapo, which at its peak had only 7,000 members in a population of 66 million, was more a clearing house than an instigator of written complaints about illegal activities and sentiments. Government officials in Stalin's Russia were in receipt of an avalanche of correspondence criticizing both apparatchiks for mistreating comrades, and other comrades for betraying the Soviet project. After 1945, the Stasi in East Germany played an increasingly active role in recruiting spies from the population but was itself used as a means of achieving better housing and other material benefits controlled by the state and municipality, or of prevailing in domestic and neighbourhood disputes. Although there were examples of Orwellian betrayals by spouses and children, it appears that the bulk of reports came from those in second-level networks where advantage was sought by work colleagues or by nearby dwellers in the crowded urban apartments.

Many of the day-to-day stresses which provoked the denunciations were more acute manifestations of those in modernizing societies in the West, particularly chronic overcrowding and shared sanitation in housing stock built in the previous century. But after 1945, the countries behind the iron curtain also began to enjoy a version of the consumer revolution that was transforming family life in capitalist societies.[121] Standards of living rose and the working week shortened, allowing more resources and time for pastimes and holidays. However inferior their quality, motor cars created a new era of private transport. And however illegal, in those countries along the borders with the West, it proved increasingly possible to listen to or watch programmes broadcast from what termed itself the Free World.[122] The most striking example of a shared but intensified extension of private life was gardening. The long-established tradition of the dacha was enlarged throughout the history of the Soviet Union. Although technically communal property, the summer cottage and the land that surrounded it were experienced as a realm of private withdrawal in which families could enjoy their own rituals of sociability and recreation away from the prying eyes of the state and neighbours in the next apartment.[123] Here, as in the allotments in other East European countries, food could be grown to compensate for shortages in the towns. Not for nothing were a guide to gardening and a sex manual the two best-selling books in the four decades of the German Democratic Republic.[124]

Privacy in these societies was always an imperilled condition. The constant threat of exposure by lovers, friends and colleagues eroded trust and commitment at all levels of personal relationships.[125] At every moment there was the apprehension that embarrassment and indignity would slide into arrest and punishment. Yet there remained the possibility of enclosed communication which was a value and a source of resistance. As Paul Betts has written of East Germany, 'for the overwhelming majority the private sphere was neither a place nor experience of isolation but rather was closely connected to a profound sense of shared intimacy.'[126] Here, as elsewhere in this history, what mattered most was what need not be said out loud. No matter how sophisticated the listening devices and how careful the official eavesdropping, the time-infused, multi-layered exchanges offered protection to the most private of relationships. 'In the garrets of Berlin during the Nazi regime,' concludes Paul Ginsborg's study, 'whispered, dissenting conversations were possible. So too were mere glances of exasperation, exchanged by one member of a family with another. Codes, secrets, memories, strategies, solidarities – these were all things that families were expert at.'[127] Ever alert to the trajectory of history, George Orwell, whose novel was of course banned by the communist regimes, endowed Big Brother with the means of dealing with non-verbal communication: 'to wear an improper expression on your face (to look incredulous when a victory was announced, for example) was itself a punishable offence. There was even a word for it in Newspeak: *facecrime*, it was called.'[128] But like other aspects of his dystopia, the technology for reading countenances was not yet a reality.

5

Privacy and the Digital Age 1970–2015

The end of privacy began in the mid-1960s. Its death was foretold in an increasing range of debates and publications. Myron Brenton's *The Privacy Invaders* of 1964 drew attention to the threats facing the control of personal information.[1] In the same year Vance Packard's *The Naked Society* identified 'Five Forces undermining our privacy' which together 'have accounted for an immense growth of surveillance over individual citizens and a massive invasion of their privacy'.[2] Congressional hearings took place in the United States from the mid-1960s, in response to rising public concern. In Britain, Parliament for the first time began to take an interest in the topic, with Bills to protect what was increasingly referred to as 'the right to privacy' sponsored by Lord Mancroft in 1961, Alex Lyon in 1967 and Brian Walden in 1969.[3] Eventually, in order to assert some control over the political discourse, the Labour government set up a committee under Sir Kenneth Younger to consider the case for legislation.[4]

The alarm was generated principally by technology in the form of surveillance devices such as increasingly sophisticated cameras and listening devices, or the widening use by government and commerce of mainframe computers. The first book to proclaim the end of privacy in its title was published in 1969. 'At present,' wrote Jerry Rosenberg, 'a national computer system is planned that will have an almost limitless capability to store, intermingle and, at the push of a button, retrieve information on persons, organizations and a variety of their activities, all without the knowledge of those involved.'[5] A review of the implications of digitized data banks sponsored by the

National Council of Civil Liberties concluded 'society is on "the brink of a precipice".'[6] Its authors described themselves as 'provisional catastrophists', foreseeing the end unless immediate, radical action was taken. The capacity of computers to process and store information was such, warned Arthur R. Miller in 1971, that they 'may become the heart of a surveillance system that will turn society into a transparent world in which our homes, our finances, and our associations will be bared to a wide range of casual observers, including the morbidly curious and the maliciously or commercially intrusive'.[7]

At this stage, critics were responding more to the perceived potential than the actual operation of computers. IBM had started selling devices to large-scale public and private users in the 1950s, but during the following decade, their deployment in fields such as the census, banking, taxation, credit-rating, criminal records, the railways and national insurance was still mostly at the developmental stage.[8] In the 1970s, the initial phase of apocalyptic predictions was translated into a growing body of legal protections, beginning with the first national data protection law in Sweden, passed in 1973, in response to fears about its census.[9] The second phase commenced in the closing years of the century following the introduction of the internet in 1983, the worldwide web in 1993, and the concomitant spread of personal computers.[10] In reaction to the unlimited potential of information both describing and available to ordinary citizens, the eschatology of privacy, the doctrine of last things, burst forth with renewed energy.[11] In every channel of communication, from daily print and digital journalism to full-length studies, privacy gained a kind of zombie status, repeatedly killed but rising once more to be destroyed again.[12] Publishers responded to a seemingly limitless market for titles such as *The End of Privacy: How Total Surveillance Is Becoming a Reality*, and *Database Nation: The Death of Privacy in the 21st Century*, and *The Spy in the Coffee Machine: The End of Privacy as We Know It*.[13] The proliferating body of national and international legislation was widely seen to be failing to keep pace with computers and their applications. 'The rapid deployment of privacy-destroying technologies by governments and businesses', wrote Michael Froomkin in the *Stanford Law Review* in 2000, 'threatens to make informational privacy obsolete.'[14] 'Our privacy is shrinking quicker than the polar ice cap', warned David Holtzman's *Privacy Lost* in 2006; 'technology is eroding it faster than the legal system can protect it. This trend cannot be reversed in any obvious way. Privacy, as we know it today, is lost.'[15] Every succeeding year brought new obsequies. 'So is Privacy dead?', asked Jacob Morgan in August 2014: 'It sure seems that way, and we are the ones who killed it without even knowing it.'[16]

Alongside those deploring the destruction of privacy there was a growing body of opinion that advocated the overthrow of traditional practices. In 1975, Malcolm Bradbury published *The History Man*, a widely read zeitgeist novel which later became a successful television series. Its hero, Howard Kirk, is a radical sociology lecturer at a new university, a self-promoting commentator on all that is liberating in his time. The book opens at the end of the summer vacation, during which another book has been completed. Bradbury gives it a title which captures the progressive agenda of the moment. Howard explains the project to his wife, Barbara, and Myra, a colleague's wife (and former lover):

> 'It's called *The Defeat of Privacy*,' says Howard. 'It's about the fact that there are no more private selves, no more private corners in society, no more private properties, no more private acts.' 'No more private parts,' says Barbara. 'Mankind is making everything open and accessible.' 'Even me?' asks Myra. 'Oh, we know all about you,' says Howard. 'You see, sociological and psychological understanding is now giving us a total view of man, and democratic society is giving us total access to everything. There's nothing that's not confrontable. There are no concealments any longer, no mysterious dark places of the soul. We're all right there in front of the entire audience of the universe, in a state of exposure. We're all nude and available.'[17]

The representation of secluded intimacy as the site of distorted personal development was now sufficiently widespread to become the subject of satire. In 1967, the anthropologist Edmund Leach, speaking not from Bradbury's Watermouth University but with all the establishment authority of Provost of King's College, Cambridge, and a Reith Lecturer, claimed that 'Today the domestic household is isolated. The family looks inward upon itself; there is an intensification of emotional stress between husband and wife, and parents and children. The strain is greater than most of us can bear. Far from being the basis of the good society, the family, with its narrow privacy and tawdry secrets, is the source of all our discontents.'[18] A flourishing industry of marriage guidance was growing up, based on the therapeutic benefit of talking to strangers about the innermost details of personal relationships. For the emerging profession of psychotherapy, the more successful the blocking of communication with outsiders, the longer the road to full emotional and mental health. As Lily Pincus and Christopher Dare wrote in their *Secrets in the Family* of 1978, 'if we can let ourselves know about our responses to these

events and become aware of the experiences and feelings connected
with them, then our lives need not be dominated by some of the
damaging effects of secrets and myths in the family.'[19]

The History Man was not about technology, except in the form of
the traditional device of a camera with which a vengeful student
stalks Howard Kirk as he goes about his multiple infidelities. However,
its unashamed celebration of personal transparency found a more
recent counterpart in Facebook's Mark Zuckerberg, who, with the
same uneasy mixture of insight and self-interest, told the world in
2010: 'You already have zero privacy. Get over it!'[20] As a fictional
satire, *The History Man*'s latest successor is Dave Eggers' dystopian
novel of 2013, *The Circle,* in which a global social networking
company persuades its followers to divest themselves of every vestige
of personal privacy in the name of truth and virtue. The joint head
of The Circle condenses his message into three Orwellian slogans:
'Secrets Are Lies. Sharing is Caring. Privacy is Theft.'[21] Whatever the
position taken on this vision, commentators shared a growing preoccupation with information as a personal possession, over which the
holders held a form of copyright which they might choose or be
forced to make available to others. It was around the beginning of
the final third of the twentieth century that latent tensions in the
concept of privacy began to pull it apart. 'In the 1970s', writes
Deborah Cohen, 'privacy was being redefined to emphasize the
autonomy of the individual rather than the unbearable sanctity of the
familial sphere.'[22] The distinction was captured in the opening section
of the 1972 *Report of the Committee on Privacy,* which explored the
contemporary meanings attached to the term. It resisted the temptation to find its own formulation, but instead summarized what
appeared to be a growing bifurcation in popular understanding:

> we have conceived of the right of privacy as having two main aspects.
> The first of these is freedom from intrusion upon oneself, one's home,
> family and relationships. The second is privacy of information, that is
> the right to determine for oneself how and to what extent information
> about oneself is communicated to others.[23]

It was the latter category – what in subsequent decades came to
be termed 'information privacy' – which occupied most of the
Committee's attention. Matters relating to issues such as the seclusion
of the family within the neighbourhood could be dealt with by 'the
varied pressures, educational, cultural and social, employed in a
democratic society to persuade particular sections of the community
to behave in an acceptable manner.'[24] In any case, as it observed, 'the

peeping Tom' can be 'bound over to keep the peace under a stat[ut]e of Edward III'. [25] The agenda of legislative reform, which it tackled with some hesitation, belonged to the realm of personal information as it was threatened by new technologies. Proposals were made for legislation in such matters as information held by credit-rating agencies, licensing private detectives and the use of electronic surveillance devices. As for the technology that was driving public concern, the Committee recommended 'the immediate voluntary adoption by computer users of certain principles for handling personal information on computers'. [26]

The proclamation of the end of privacy, whether deplored or welcomed, was an historical judgement. It implied that there was, in practice or in prospect, a radical discontinuity with the past. Earlier generations had experienced conditions or rights that were now under terminal threat. As this survey has indicated, such a view of the long-term nature of change was itself a departure from former times. The capacity to control information about one's affairs had never been viewed as an absolute privilege that was either held or lost. Rather, from the plaintiffs at the fourteenth-century Assize of Nuisance onwards, privacy was a business of transient victories and daily defeats. At every level of society in every era, aspirations had to be traded against other wants and asserted against a host of material and normative pressures. Outcomes were informed by the physical environment, communication systems, legal structures and the texture of intimate relations. The common thread connecting the different campaigns was the sheer labour involved. In more recent scholarship there is a vein of analysis that has kept this perspective in view. Christena Nippert-Eng's classic study of the Chicago middle class pursues her topic through a myriad of domestic pressures and opportunities. It contains no history but reaches a truth which talks to the past. 'Achieving privacy in daily lives', she concludes, 'is work.' [27] An underlying cause of the tendency to misconstrue the dynamic of change was the prevailing state of knowledge about the past. 'No one, as far as we can discover,' wrote the Younger Report, 'has ever studied the history of privacy as such.' [28] As it happened, the first detailed monograph, David Flaherty's *Privacy in Colonial New England*, appeared on the other side of the Atlantic in the same year as Younger. Together with Alan Westin's seminal study, *Privacy and Freedom*, published in the United States in 1967 and Britain in 1970, the field was beginning to acquire a much-needed temporal and conceptual clarity.

These advances were not sufficient, however, to dispel what Alan Westin characterized as 'the heavy fog of concerned rhetoric'. [29] Three

factors conspired to obscure the landscape. The first was the association between information privacy and individualism. As we have
seen, during the nineteenth century conversation with God began to
be replaced with communion with the self as the means of ensuring
inner development and spiritual health. The pressures of urbanizing
societies made Hazlitt's 'out of doors' philosophy, where nature
is 'company enough', increasingly attractive.[30] At the same time,
progress in the rapidly expanding economy and professions became
more than ever dependent on personal reputation, as traditional
guarantees of capacity and character, such as family connection,
weakened their hold. What individuals knew about themselves, and
what their society knew about them and their history, required new
levels of protection from intrusive company and inquiry. The consequence of the embodiment of this sensibility in a proposed 'right to
be let alone' was tested in 1960, in an influential review by Dean
Prosser of the cases that had been brought before the American courts
since Warren and Brandeis' seminal article. Prosser identified four
elements: invasion of the seclusion of another; disclosing embarrassing facts; placing an individual in a false light; and theft of identity.[31]
Although they specifically related to the American law of torts and
the interpretation of Constitutional amendments, the categories were
widely influential, and were carefully summarized by Younger. Of the
elements, only the first was remotely concerned with the privacy of
intimate relationships. The remainder related to the individual's right
to control what was known about them.[32] Younger was doubtful
whether the bald 'right to be let alone' could be used as the basis of
a new legal structure in Britain, but the Report's specific recommendations for reform were all couched in terms of the discrete personality struggling to evade surveillance and to oversee the use being made
of details of his or her life.

The second factor was the broader political and ideological context.
The sense that privacy was involved in a struggle against extinction
in part reflected the state of international relations; the first death
was proclaimed two years after the Cuban Missile Crisis. The Cold
War, as the previous chapter discussed, was projected as a conflict
between the totalitarian destruction of personal privacy and its
embattled survival in the West. The language of Armageddon made
an easy transition between the bomb and the fragile personal archive.
The language of incremental growth or decline was overwhelmed by
visions of imminent disaster. A separate set of conflicts emerged
within the 'free' world, centred on the assertion of personal autonomy and the right to resist accumulations of power by the state
or large-scale capitalism. By the end of the 1960s, the high tide of

confidence in the capacity of governments to replace informal local support with comprehensive, centralized welfare services was beginning to recede. One of the most influential television films ever made, Ken Loach's *Cathy Come Home* of 1966, explored how various forms of impersonal bureaucracy were wreaking as much destruction on family life as older, piecemeal failings in the economy and community. The face-to-face encounters in the drama engender neither communication nor compassion; all is determined by institutional regulation, which by the end of the film has destroyed a family unit. Two years later the insubordinate confidence of a new generation of university students found a focus for its grievances in the files allegedly held by university administrations on their beliefs and behaviour.

The final factor was (and has remained) what Westin described as the 'over-selling and blue-sky promises of computer scientists and commercial interests...and frightened, over-credulous reactions to these shimmering visions of computer power on the part of many civil libertarians'.[33] Every communication revolution, from the invention of printing onward, has generated inflated hopes and fears; the difference on this occasion was partly the speed of change. The telephone took a century to become widespread; the postal system developed from the late Middle Ages; the paper file and card index, as they evolved from bound ledgers in the nineteenth century, were a technology of data storage and retrieval that went back to early civilization. The mainframe computer, on the other hand, promised a sudden and irreversible shift in the means of manipulating and storing information. The second difference was cost. The debate in this period was taking place as government departments and commercial firms weighed up the options for making major investments which would either transform their efficiency or ruin their economies. Many decided to wait and see as others were successfully courted by the rapidly growing national and international computer companies.

In this febrile atmosphere, the future was misunderstood and the past was forgotten. Many of the features that were claimed for the digital technology and protested by its critics were integral to classic Weberian, paper-based bureaucracies. Where they were rigorously organized, the systems were inherently scalable. The doubling and redoubling of the British population in the nineteenth century was counted with the aid of nothing more than primitive calculating devices. Insurance companies, national post offices, railway networks and, from the early twentieth century, state welfare systems dealt with millions of users and tens of millions of hand-written annual transactions without generating unmanageable inefficiencies or unacceptable levels of inaccuracy.[34] Features of computers that alarmed libertarian critics, including the impersonality of the record and its permanence, were built into the card indexes. The National Insurance centre at Newcastle-upon-Tyne, discussed in the previous chapter, was designed not to forget anybody in the working population over the whole of their adult lives and to manage information critical to the wellbeing of citizens with minimal opportunity for correction and appeal. There was, however, one fundamental limitation of the manual record, and it was the prospect of its removal that caused the greatest concern. The larger the operation, the more costly it was to link one system to another and to trace a given individual through different archives. The subjects retained the integrity of their identity; the bureaucracies only manipulated dissociated fragments. Now connection seemed feasible and imminent. 'There is little doubt', warned Warner and Stone in 1970,

> that technically the State *could* maintain an integrated dossier file on every man, woman and child...in these isles, using computer equipment which is in existence now...a number of specialized computer information centres are already in existence, and many more are being planned. Almost inadvertently, a massive integrated 'data bank' could come into being, merely by linking the existing smaller centres together.[35]

As was the case in the first privacy panic in 1844, the energizing fear was the prospect of an all-embracing network managed by a single agency.[36] In reality, the best contemporary example of such comprehensive, record-based surveillance was East Germany's Stasi, which until its abolition in 1989 was a monument to what could be achieved by the hand- or type-written file, given sufficient will and manpower. The impact of technology was conditional on the political system. What was, and would remain, uncertain was whether citizens and consumers would be equipped with sufficient understanding and control of the new mechanisms to calibrate their effects and manage their outcomes.

The 1970s were a double watershed in the history of Britain and other Western societies. The decade marked the end of the beginning of the computer, and the beginning of the end of marriage as the universal experience and expectation. In 1970, only 8 per cent of British women aged 45–9 had never been married. The post-war generation wed in larger numbers and lived longer together as couples than any cohort before or since.[37] Across Western Europe, the third quarter of the twentieth century was, in Göran Therborn's words, the 'Marriage Age'.[38] Thereafter conventions began to change. In the UK, the peak of marriages since records began in 1862 was reached in 1972. The rate per thousand for men had varied in the 50s until after World War II, when it rose to 78.4 before falling continuously, passing the historic norm by the early 1980s and reaching 22 at the beginning of the second decade of the twenty-first century. The rate per thousand for women fell from 60.5 to 20 in the same period. In 2009, weddings in Britain had reached their lowest recorded level.

There were three decisive shifts in the patterns of private lives. The first was that the relevance of income diminished. Since the middling orders began to invest in their accommodation in the sixteenth century, wealth had conditioned the capacity to protect the personal archive. It had shaped the physical constraints on privacy and, particularly during the demographic transition that began in the later nineteenth century, the size of the domestic units. By the final quarter of the twentieth century, the lag between middle- and working-class family structures was no longer visible. More than two children were becoming uncommon at any income level. In one-family households, the proportion containing three or more dependent children fell from 9 per cent in 1971 to just 3 per cent in 2010.[39] The continuing decline of live-in servants at the upper end of society and lodgers or stray children and relatives at the other meant that the small household became the standard form. The proportion of units containing more than four people dropped from one in seven to one in seventeen in the four decades after 1971.[40] Partly as a consequence, overcrowding almost disappeared. Two centuries of debate about unhealthy sleeping arrangements were resolved into an official 'bedroom standard': 'a separate bedroom is allowed for each married or cohabiting couple, any other person aged 21 or over, each pair of adolescents aged 10–20 of the same sex, and each pair of children under 10.'[41] Against these criteria, just 3 per cent of the English population were living in overcrowded conditions in 2014. By contrast, more than twelve times as many were technically under-occupying their homes.[42]

At the same time the experience of nineteenth-century standards of discomfort became increasingly uncommon. The physical persistence of the housing stock meant that as in earlier eras, the majority of the population were living in dwellings constructed at some distance from the present. In 1970, about three-quarters of dwellings dated from before World War II. The modest housing programme in subsequent decades did little to narrow the distribution. In 2014, a fifth of the English stock had been built before 1919, and more than half before 1965, whereas only one in seven homes dated from after 1990.[43] However, a combination of technological innovation, municipal building programmes, improved official standards and increasing household prosperity meant that in terms of basic amenities, the interiors came to resemble each other. The proportion of households without a bath or a shower fell from nearly two-fifths in 1951 to less than a tenth in 1971, and to negligible levels two decades later. Dwellings lacking indoor sanitation dropped from a fifth in 1951 to 1 per cent by 1991.[44] With electricity now taken for granted, with basic household appliances including refrigerators and televisions in most homes, and with access to at least a small garden widespread, the need for the life of the household to spill out into the streets virtually disappeared. Even at the level of the most visible symbol of privacy, distinctions by class were eroded; Amongst the consequences of the 1980 decision by the Conservative government to start selling council houses to tenants was the escape from municipal regulations about the design and colour of the houses' outward appearance. 'Front doors tell the story of the right-to-buy', observed Paul Barker:

> The council's doors have been removed. From Newcastle to Plymouth, from Cardiff to Ipswich, the suburbanite replacements vary between Costa Brava (the heavy Spanish style, with bright varnished panels) and Barbara Cartland (neo-Regency, with glazed fanlight). Both versions are tougher than the old doors. There is glass you can easily knock in. The woodwork is stronger. But the main point [is] to say: this is my house, not anybody else's... The message is rubbed in by the carriage lamps, the new paint, and even (sometimes) a little oriel window above the front door.[45]

In 1972, the Younger Report sought to quell the rising tide of panic about the future of privacy by stressing the countervailing forces at work in society:

> As a result of these developments the modern middle class family of two parents and their children, relatively soundproofed in their semi-detached house, relatively unseen behind their privet hedge and rose trellis, travelling with determined reserve on public transport or insulated in the family car, shopping in the super-market and entertained by television, are probably more private in the sense of being unnoticed in all their everyday doings than any sizeable section of the population in any other time or place.[46]

In its assumption that such conditions were essentially class-based, the Report was looking backwards rather than forwards. It reflected the long-standing assumption that privacy in any form was neither an aspiration nor a possibility for those who worked with their hands, and it misread the dynamics of change in the 1970s. Most of the key measures of privacy to which it drew attention were becoming commonplace. Not only demography and housing but a range of consumption practices were no longer the preserve of the salaried home-maker. Supermarkets were slower to take root in Britain than in the United States, but by the start of the fourth quarter of the twentieth century they were beginning their final move to almost complete control of the retail food industry. Televisions were already to be found in virtually every household and continued their increasing domination of all home entertainment; at the end of the first decade of the twenty-first century, watching programmes was the most frequent free-time activity reported by adults aged sixteen and over, who spent an average of three and a half hours a day in front of their sets.[47] The family car, which had ceased to be the privilege of the middle class in the 1950s and 1960s, continued its takeover of personal transport. In the early 1950s, cars and vans accounted for only a quarter of passenger miles. By 1970, they were covering four and a half times the distance of buses and coaches, and by the first decade of the following century fourteen times. Despite the recovery of rail transport since its nadir in 1982, it still accounted for only 7 per cent of the total mileage travelled in 2010.[48] The growth in the number of vehicles was propelled by second-car ownership, finally freeing this mode of transport from control by the male head of the household. By 2011, four-fifths of the population had access to their own vehicle, although income was still a factor. Only one in ten households in the top fifth of the income distribution had no car, compared with just over a half in the bottom fifth.[49] Wherever it could be afforded, the car became a mobile castle, combining the comfort and the seclusion of the domestic interior with the freedom to escape its confines without any further dependency on routes and timetables or any engagement with another individual.[50] Pedestrians in the street, passengers on buses, trains and planes and in the places of embarkation and arrival, were still required to practise what Erving Goffman described as 'civil inattention', at once recognizing and withdrawing attention from the passing company.[51]

The second change was in the growth in those conducting their private lives in physical isolation.[52] In 2013, 7.7 million people in Britain lived alone. Since 1971, the proportion of single-person households had risen from one in six to close to the current European average of 30 per cent.[53] This transition to a way of living that was almost unknown a century earlier was driven by a combination of demographic, financial and behavioural changes. More women than men lived by themselves in old age as life expectancy increased. More men than women looked after themselves in the middle reach of life as a consequence of lower marriage rates. Young people in the first flush of financial independence moved into flats before or between periods of cohabitation. In the recent past, however, there has been a reversal in the long-term growth of this sector as men and women in their twenties and early thirties cling to their parental home in the face of rising housing costs and the increasing difficulty of finding a niche in the labour market. For most of the population, the era of cooking for one was transitional. As is always the case in demographic history, the distribution of household types at any one age or period conceals the trajectory individuals follow during their life-course. Once they had finally left the parental nest, few individuals took a deliberate decision to live alone for the rest of their lives. Most, from choice or circumstance, moved between different social arrangements until old age reduced their options.

The third change lay in the power of convention in forming relationships. It is here that the notion of revolution is mostly widely deployed in histories of private lives over the last half century. At the high-water mark of the married population, deviation from monogamous, heterosexual family life was either illegal or stigmatized. Young men and women growing up found it hard to imagine an alternative to marriage and more difficult still to construct their own pathway through adult relationships. Yet during the twentieth century and particularly after World War II, they were learning to expect greater romantic and sexual satisfaction in an increasingly rigid institutional setting. A 2013 account of the resulting transition to a more varied landscape of family forms argues that the post-war regime contained the seeds of its own destruction. 'The end of the century decline of life-long marriage', writes Claire Langhamer, 'was rooted in the contradictions, tensions, and illogicalities that lay at the heart of mid-century intimacy.'[54] Taught to follow their feelings, the baby-boomers broke out of the structures in which they had been raised, and began to explore alternative routes to personal and physical content. They were able to exploit the medical developments of their age, particularly the introduction of the contraceptive pill in 1961, and the increasing effectiveness of treatments for sexually transmitted diseases. The continuing increase in women's employment, which in turn fuelled the growth in household incomes, generated a wider range of choices about how marriages should be formed, managed and terminated. The necessary legal reforms were more a consequence than a cause of changing aspirations. Following the legalization of abortion and of homosexual acts in 1967, a long debate over the meaning of marriage culminated in the 1969 Divorce Reform Act, which finally introduced a no-fault clause into court cases. In addition to specific misdemeanours such as adultery or cruelty, couples could now gain a decree simply on the basis of two years' separation (or five if the case was contested). No external judgement was sought on the quality of the relationship or the behaviour of the couple. Further reform in 1996 was designed to keep judicial intervention still more at bay. Couples were now required to go through a process of conciliation and practical negotiation prior to coming to court. They were expected to be capable of managing the break-up as rational, morally self-sufficient individuals.

It is important to define the arena of significant transformation. Over the twentieth century as a whole, household structure has the appearance less of a discontinuity and more of a cycle. By the 1990s, periods of informal cohabitation by couples in their twenties represented the pattern of deferred marriage and extra-marital sex common in the eighteenth and nineteenth centuries.[55] As had been the case in times of dearth in earlier eras, it has become uncommon for men or women to marry before twenty-five, and with the divorced reaching the altar as frequently as was once the case with the widowed, the average age of marriage reached 36.2 for men and 33.6 for women by 2010. The trajectory and the scale of change should not be confused. Divorce, for instance, which had been increasing in the 1960s, doubled with the implementation of the 1969 Divorce Reform Act in 1971, but thereafter grew slowly until the mid-1990s and then began to fall, partly because of the smaller number of couples entering into marriage. In 2013, legally defined couples, with or without children, were still by far the most common family type, accounting for almost two-thirds of households in the UK.[56] If those in long-term cohabitation are added, four-fifths of units still have the outward appearance of the families that dominated the landscape in the 1950s and 1960s. The key legislation of the early twenty-first century – the Civil Partnership Act of 2004 and the introduction of same-sex marriages in 2013 – has had a marginal impact on the range of forms. In the 2014 survey, less than 1 per cent of all units were civil-partner or same-sex cohabiting families.[57] However great the tensions that had been building up in the post-war decades, the resulting explosion has left many of the buildings still standing.

Structural change and the surrounding regulatory context were significant less for the actions that they permitted and more for the attitudes that they sanctioned. There was a turning away from outward form to inward purpose. Personal judgement about the nature of private lives was foregrounded at the expense of external constraint, whether normative or legal. In part this reflected a general desacralization across Western societies, investing greater meaning in individual commitment in preference to public ritual.[58] More generally, the morality of conforming to collective standards, whether imposed through religious or governmental authority or embodied in community or family tradition, was replaced by the virtue of personal choice.[59] Just as the lovers looked to themselves in determining how to live together, so also they refrained from passing judgement on the decisions made by others. A widening range of sexual scripts was permitted, none claiming sovereignty over another. It was calculated that by the 1990s, there were around two hundred arrangements that were regarded by Europeans and Americans as an acceptable family.[60] Except where the abuse of children or violence between adults was involved, all practices became options. The debates about legal reform in the 1960s had not been about Christian morality versus free love, but rather about the role of external scaffolding in sustaining long-term, loving relationships. With much hesitation and long-term compromise, a new orthodoxy emerged, which set the virtue of individual decisions against the distorting pressure of imposed discipline and the culture of secrecy and evasion which it engendered. Intimacy, which had coexisted with and struggled against so many material and structural pressures in the past, was now both the end and the justification of personal choice. In this sense, the quality of protected communication within a relationship gained added significance. In a notably enthusiastic endorsement of this brave new world, Anthony Giddens stressed how the individual's journey to fulfilment with another began before speech: 'The "first glance" is a communicative gesture, an intuitive grasp of the qualities of the other.'[61] Once the relationship was formed, everything depended on the couple's ability to exchange meaning without the pressure of external surveillance: 'The imperative of free and open communication is the sine qua non of the pure relationship; the relationship is its own forum.'[62]

The fundamental physical boundaries of privacy were still in place. Whether alone or in small family units, the great majority of the population conducted their domestic lives behind closed doors and within sound-insulated walls. Living accommodation with ground-level access remained by far the most popular choice. In 2012, high-rise flats accounted for less than 2 per cent of English dwellings.[63] Most of the accommodation had access to some kind of controlled space. Front gardens were never used for sitting in, back gardens were always fenced. It remained as unacceptable as it had been four centuries earlier to peer in through windows or listen beneath the eaves. Visitors had to approach the residence with caution and respect. The incumbents deployed a range of tactics to decide whether to open the door to an outsider, and what part of the house to let them enter.[64] Until the digital revolution began to facilitate working away from the office, the physical distance between the public and private realms had never been wider. The medicalization of childbirth, illness and dying, and the rapid expansion since the 1970s of residential holidays not only away from home but out of the country, diminished the collective rituals and rites of passage.[65] At the same time, each enclosed household had to manage its relations with adjacent units. On the overcrowded island, the nineteenth-century move towards detached residences has been curtailed. Almost three quarters of present-day dwellings in England are conjoined to another, as terraces, semi-detached houses or flats. The shift that has taken place is in the growing indifference to those living next door or in the same street.[66] A recent survey found that only a fifth of households reported regular visits from a neighbour, and more than a third confessed to seeing neighbours only by accident. The one service that was performed on a large scale, irrespective of age, class or gender, was taking in mail or parcels.[67]

A subsequent survey asked, 'how certain do you feel that, if domestic violence or other abuse was regularly taking place in the five homes or apartments closest to yours, you would know about it?'[68] Only 6 per cent replied 'definitely' and more than half either 'probably not' or 'definitely not'. With less community or official control, more was now expected of the compass by which individuals steered a course in their intimate lives. The risk register of privacy increased its complexity. Permitting more latitude in the conduct of enclosed relationships did not of itself prevent the assertion of self-interest and the abuse of power. For instance, the increase in women's employment contributed to the dissolution of the dominant post-war model of marriage, but women's income usually remained lower and less regular than that of their male partners. At key moments of debate and decision, women still had fewer options, particularly as both in law and in collective expectation, they were likely to be left responsible for any children of a relationship. Children were no less vulnerable to neglect or abuse. As a consequence, the dismantling of controls over how adults lived together was accompanied by far from successful attempts to protect the rights of their offspring and enhance systems of external surveillance and intervention. The 1989 Children

Act required parents to make agreed plans with outside professionals to ensure not only that no immediate harm was caused to children of troubled families but also that the children's long-term health or development was not impaired.[69] With the gaze of neighbours now turned inwards, efforts were made to increase the legal support given to women vulnerable to assault by their partners. In all the centuries covered by this survey, women had no recourse in law for rape in marriage. Finally, in 1991, England and Wales, in line with other developed countries, determined that there should be no marital immunity in the crime of rape.

Reform was generated by the collision between continuing structural discrimination on the basis of gender, age and ethnicity, on the one hand, and the celebration of the enclosed arena increasingly out of reach of external inspection and regulation, on the other. At its most vigorous the critique generated a full-scale attack on the separation of the public and private spheres that had been the cornerstone of the liberal enterprise since the nineteenth century. It was argued, most vocally by Catharine MacKinnon, that privacy was an illusion which systemically disempowered subordinate groups. As nominally private beings, women were denied standing in public discourse, and the increasingly inaccessible domestic sphere allowed violence and other forms of discrimination to persist unchecked.[70] The attack was associated with celebrations of the death of privacy noted earlier in the chapter. Other critics sharing the same point of departure drew attention to the gains generated by the increased choice in how relationships were formed and ended, and to the continuing importance for women as well as men of protecting their intimate discourse from external surveillance. Treating the categories of private and public as inherently oppositional was unnecessarily reductive. These critics argued instead that the boundary between the spheres should take the form not of a castle wall but of a semi-permeable membrane, through which appropriate knowledge and action could pass and full equality of condition and expectation could be pursued.[71] It was a bet on the continuation of change. The hope was that the break-up of the post-war certainties was the beginning, not the end, of how individuals should conduct themselves when trust and mutual respect were at a premium.

As the twentieth century drew to an end there was a reaction against the liberalization of private conduct. The AIDS epidemic and the end of the post-war economic boom challenged the optimism of the reformers and generated a counter-movement from the Christian right. But in spite of the increasingly vocal attacks on issues such as abortion and gay rights, governments refrained from re-entering the bedroom. The main legislation remained in place, and there is little evidence that sexual practices or household formation were affected by the often bitter public debates.[72] Instead, the growing pace of the digital revolution ushered in a new era of state intervention in private communication. As a key Organisation for Economic Co-operation and Development (OECD) document put it, 'the 1970s may be described as a period of intensified investigative and legislative activities concerning the protection of privacy with respect to the collection and use of personal data.'[73] In the process, the defence of personal information became an international event. For much of the modern era, the relationship between privacy and the state had been a matter of contrast rather than consistency. In the nineteenth century, countries defined their path towards liberal democracy by comparing their respect for the private sphere to its supposed wholesale invasion by dynastic *anciens régimes* such as Russia or Austria. Allowing the free flow of information, declining to employ agents to spy on the domestic population, and respecting the sanctity of the home were held to be defining characteristics of modernity, however uncertain the progress of some countries to that destination. The tradition, as we have seen, gained added force during the long struggle between totalitarianism and democracy that was initiated by the Russian Revolution. Now consistency became a virtue, irrespective of frontiers or regimes. Urged on by a range of international organizations, the same legislative interventions took place across much of the Western world. The problem was constructed on a common basis, defined in similar language, and embodied in largely standardized machinery.

There were two drivers of convergence. The first was the emergence of privacy not as a contested household aspiration but as an unquestioned human right, whose force was only qualified when it collided with another cherished value such as freedom of speech. The post-war declarations by the United Nations and Europe embodied a defence of the home and personal communication that was invoked as a matter of course by all those advocating intervention in the last quarter of the twentieth century and beyond.[74] The right was given force by the European Convention on Human Rights in 1950, and the subsequent creation of a European Court to uphold it. The incorporation of the Convention into British law in 1998 has been associated with much of the more recent domestic legislation in this field.[75] The second driver was the digital revolution, whose impact was widely, if vaguely, grasped from the outset. In their way, the earlier revolutions had similarly internationalized the management of personal information. In the nineteenth century, the invention of the telegraph and the rapid growth of correspondence led to the creation of the International Telegraph Union in 1865, and the Universal Postal Union in 1874, which in their structure and aspirations were forerunners of the League of Nations and the United Nations.[76] Both bodies survived into the computer era and played a continuing role in defining and implementing global communication standards.

Such developments were not, however, sufficient to achieve a single, comprehensive outcome. A co-ordinated programme of legislation required a narrowing of ambition and a redefinition of the networks in need of protection. The post-war human rights declarations specified the home or the family as the vulnerable unit. In common law jurisdictions, such as England and Wales, it remained very difficult to embrace so broad an aspiration in a single statute. It was more feasible where there was a written constitution embodying general principles. For instance, the 1949 Basic Law of the German Federal Republic stated that 'marriage and the family shall enjoy the special protection of the state', and that 'the privacy of correspondence, posts and telecommunications shall be inviolable.'[77] When the Netherlands re-wrote its nineteenth-century constitution in 1983, it prescribed that 'everyone shall have the right to respect for his privacy.'[78] Even the USSR included the right in its 1977 constitution. Further, its criminal code specified punishment by 'correctional tasks for a term not exceeding six months, or by a fine not exceeding 30 roubles, or by social censure' for those breaching 'the secrecy of citizen's correspondence'.[79] However, progress in translating general rights into national law remained piecemeal. The concept of data protection, on the other hand, offered a more manageable field of concerted action. Despite its broad title, the US Privacy Act of 1974 was restricted to the manipulation of citizens' data, and then only by the state, not by the private sector.[80] What came to be termed 'informational self-determination' became the basis of a new wave of legislation across the developed world.[81] A year after the OECD report, the Council of Europe issued the 'Convention for the Protection of Individuals with regard to Automatic Processing of Personal Data', which subsequently became a binding European Union Directive.[82] National laws were passed, in the words of the UK's Act of 1984, 'to regulate the use of automatically processed information relating to individuals'. [83] The standard form was a set of common, legally embedded principles that were sufficiently broad to be adapted to the administrative and political conventions of particular countries, even those, such as the UK, which were initially reluctant to become involved at all.[84] The structure of regulation and machinery embodied the claim that identifiable persons had ownership of any data relating to them. They had a right to ensure that it should not be collected by an agency except for a specified reason, that it was accurately recorded, and that it should not be passed to a third party without their consent.[85]

The prescription envisaged a universe comprised of autonomous subjects who wished to connect with each other within and across national boundaries. There was no reference to communication inside domestic or social units, or to knowledge that was held in common by intimate parties. Where the networks were specified, it was in terms of economic transactions. The intervention by the OECD and the European bodies was driven by a concern not to initiate but to control the process of reform. By 1980, half the members of the OECD had already passed or formulated data protection laws. In the context of the digital revolution, the rhetoric of privacy threatened to collide with the project of deregulation and open markets. 'It is necessary', advised the European Convention, 'to reconcile the fundamental values of the respect for privacy and the free flow of information between peoples.'[86] By unsystematically responding to the fears generated by information technology, countries were liable to forgo its benefits.[87] 'There is a danger', warned the OECD, 'that disparities in national legislation could hamper the free flow of personal data across frontiers; these flows have greatly increased in recent years and are bound to grow further with the widespread introduction of new computer and communications technology.'[88] European policy-makers suspected that states were using the policing of data as a means of erecting non-tariff trade barriers at just the moment that they were being dismantled. The prospect of global software or internet companies performing a similar function had yet to be envisaged.

Despite its limitations, the data protection movement represented a transnational intervention in the management of information on a scale not seen since the papacy lost its battle to control the consequences of Gutenberg's invention. Legislation to protect private communication from surveillance by governments and private companies armed with increasingly powerful information technologies was much less consistent and effective. Regulations that had grown up since the seventeenth century to protect the security of correspondence and subsequently the telegraph and the telephone had to be adapted to meet the threat of the digital revolution. At the outset there was the problem of the role of governments in protecting their populations. Except in the case of the US telephone system, communication networks had generally been public monopolies. It became part of the contract of liberal democracy that states supplied the infrastructure of non-face-to-face interactions but refrained from using the expanding networks to enhance their capacity to spy on the intimate lives of their citizens. Just as the police required a search warrant to enter a house, so the security services needed some kind of case-specific judicial authority to breach the sanctity of the mails or electronic conversations. In practice, governments retained reserve powers in case of a perceived threat to national security, which were widely deployed during the global conflicts of the twentieth century, and less overtly in response to peacetime tensions.

Once the scale and complexity of the internet and the worldwide web became apparent, governments divested themselves of the task of investment and control. The networks of virtual privacy were everywhere privatized. At the same time politicians glimpsed unprecedented possibilities of accessing the thoughts and opinions of their subjects. As the endgame of the Cold War was succeeded by an era of international terrorism, there was renewed enthusiasm for hidden surveillance of potential security threats. Attempts were made to generate a framework of privacy protection along the lines of the Data Protection movement. In 1999, the European Parliament passed the 'Lawful Interception of Communications Resolution on New Technologies' (Enfopol), which proposed a regulatory agenda for the law enforcement community.[89] It was designed to make transparent and consistent the processes by which governments obtained data from global internet providers. In reality, the landscape displayed neither of these virtues. The patchwork of national regulations was further confused by the growing terrorist threat, with Britain passing the 2000 Regulation of Investigatory Powers Act (RIPA) and the United States rushing through the Patriot Act following the 9/11 attack in 2001.[90] Such legislation was at once obsolescent and evasive. It was rapidly overtaken by the growth of social networking and failed to comprehend the range of activities in which the security services were already involved. As far back as 1967, the journalist Chapman Pincher revealed that the NSA was collaborating with GCHQ in securing intercepts from American telephone corporations.[91] In 2013, Edward Snowden reminded the public of what it once knew.[92] What had changed in the intervening half-century were both the scale of the data that was now available and the alleged willingness of the security agencies to bypass formal agreements with the internet companies and tap directly into their fibre-optic cables.

As in the first modern privacy panic in 1844, it is difficult to establish a sense of proportion in the practice of steaming open electronic envelopes. Now, as then, politicians, especially in the UK, have compounded the problem by seeking to hide behind the 'neither confirm nor deny' firewall, which has the unintended but predictable effect of promoting limitless conspiracy theories. Now, as then, the shadow of omniscience hangs over the event, the willingness to assume that at the centre of the web of surveillance there exists a single all-comprehending mind. It is no surprise that Edward Snowden characterized the NSA as 'the panopticon' as he explained his actions.[93] As we have seen, there is a similar atmosphere of overheated hopes and fears generated by a major communications revolution.

Above all, there is continuing uncertainty about the nature of the threat that the abuses present. In much of the debate the issue is one of privacy at its most sacred and vulnerable. Snowden explained himself by saying that he did not want to live in a world 'where everything that I say, everything that I do, everyone that I talk to, every expression of love or friendship is recorded'.[94] There are two reasons for arguing that this was a misplaced fear. The crisis of digital surveillance on the grounds of national security has more to do with the relation between the private and governmental spheres in the liberal polity than with the protection of private communication. In *Citizenfour*, the film about Snowden, one of the leading digital activists, Jacob Appelbaum, captured the slide in terminology: 'what people used to call liberty and freedom we now call privacy. And we say, in the same breath, that privacy is dead...When we lose privacy we lose agency, we lose liberty itself, because we no longer feel free to express what we think.'[95] The existence, if not the legitimacy, of this argument was accepted by the post-Snowden report of Britain's Parliamentary Intelligence and Security Committee: 'For many, the free and open nature of the internet represents liberty and democracy, and they consider that these values should not be compromised for the sake of detecting a minority who wish to use it for harmful purposes.'[96] As this book is completed, there are some signs of a movement in the official position. The USA Freedom Act was passed by Congress at the beginning of June 2015, partially curbing the bulk collection of telecommunication records by government agencies, although only within the United States. Later in the same month, a report by David Anderson, the UK Independent Reviewer of Terrorist Legislation, concluded that

RIPA, obscure since its inception, has been patched up so many times as to make it incomprehensible to all but a tiny band of initiates. A multitude of alternative powers, some of them without statutory safeguards, confuse the picture further. This state of affairs is undemocratic, unnecessary and – in the long run – intolerable.[97]

How the new Conservative government will respond to the recommendations for legislative streamlining, and for the transfer of powers to authorize interception from ministers to judges, remains to be seen.

The settlement that took form in the nineteenth century demanded that governments only sought to discover what their citizens were saying, thinking or doing if a demonstrable breach of the law was suspected. Otherwise the state was content to withhold its gaze from the interior of households and the minds of their inhabitants. The rise of welfare systems in the following century weakened that convention as central bureaucracies began to collect, store and manipulate information about classes of individuals and in some cases aspects of their personal relationships. However, the surveillance was for an accepted purpose, and except in wartime was not amalgamated into a full profile of the subject. The sheer scale of web-based communication, in terms of both the volume of users and the range of personal information being transmitted, appears to represent a decisive discontinuity in relations between the governments and the governed. If everything is collected in case an offence might be planned or executed, the balance between access and withdrawal is reversed. Rather than surveillance taking place only when suspicion is aroused, information is collected because all might be capable of thinking or acting in ways which threaten national security. The liberal distinction between the private and governmental spheres represented a judgement that states could govern in the absence of wide areas of information about their electors. In the early twenty-first century, seduced by the boundless possibilities of digital communication and unsettled by the unlimited threat of terrorism, governments no longer know what they do not need to know.

The second caution about the impact of digital surveillance arises from the nature of intimate communication. Since the 1970s, there has been a continual tendency to over-estimate the surveillance capacities of new technologies. In the sense of the physical invasion of privacy, surveillance comprises five sequential events: the capacity to observe; the act of observation; comprehension of what is seen; intervention on the basis of that knowledge; and a consequent change of behaviour by the subject.[98] Too often the final four have been assumed from the possibility of the first. Much anxiety was generated, for instance, by the arrival of CCTV cameras in public spaces and interiors. Britain led the way in Europe, setting up over four million devices. By the end of the twentieth century it had more cameras per head of population than any other country, including totalitarian regimes.[99] Jeremy Bentham would have been entranced by the disembodied eye looking down over an unsuspecting population, and in contrast to the fate of the Panopticon, substantial public funds, amounting to an estimated half a billion pounds by the late 1990s, were allocated to their installation.[100] Evidence-based academic study followed, rather than preceded, this investment. It suggested that for the most part the screens were watched by redundant non-professionals with little commitment to their new task and working with notably weak codes of practice.[101] The cameras were frequently in the wrong place; the quality of the images was rarely sufficient to play a decisive role in the prevention or solution of crime. The only consistent impact on behaviour was in the use of car parks. Further doubt has been cast on the current capacity of visual recognition software to overcome the problem of the volume of unintelligible images that were being generated.[102] In turn the opposition to such surveillance was deeply a-historical. Until the motor car became a common possession in the final third of the twentieth century, it was accepted that once individuals left their house, they were, to a greater or lesser extent, in the public gaze, unless they were deliberately seeking further seclusion in open spaces. If they were taking a journey, they did so in the company of others or in view of passers-by. At any point before the recent past, the notion that the mass of the population should have total control of their personal image as they proceeded about their business or pleasure was inconceivable.

Accessing emails, mobile phone calls and, most recently, social media appears to offer a richer source of information about private intercourse. As earlier chapters have argued, all those committing their thoughts and feelings to communication technologies have run a more or less conscious risk of the messages falling into the wrong hands. 'Epistolary anxiety' was recognizable as early as the fifteenth-century Paston Letters, and was succeeded by related fears over the use of the telegraph and the telephone. The nineteenth-century electronic innovations introduced the threat of invisible interception, and with it an increasing resort to coded texts. The conflict between those using some kind of encryption to protect their messages and those employed by the state to break them goes back at least as far as John Willis in the mid-seventeenth century. The difference in the digital era has been one of scale. Privacy-enhancing technology has been seen by the security agencies as a fundamental threat to their surveillance

capacities, and by users as the best alternative to the uncertain prospect of legislative protection.[103]

A frame of reference for the new anxieties also has to be informed
by a sense of the complexity of the process of change in the introduction of new media. For most of the period covered by this chapter,
most people communicated through devices familiar to the Victorians.
After 1450, print added to, but did not supplant, the communicative
functions of speech.[104] In the same way the successive waves of digital
innovation from the mainframe computer to the mobile, from emails
to Facebook, enriched what John Naughton refers to as the media
'ecosystem', in which older technologies formed new patterns of use
with newer arrivals.[105] Digital networks represented the direction of
change, not the entire reality at any one moment. As late as 2007,
for instance, for UK women engaging on a daily basis in a basic form
of private communication – 'catching up with close friends or relatives' – the most common channel was 'face-to-face conversation' at
51 per cent, followed at 47 per cent by the telephone, a technology
by then into its second century. Text messaging was third, followed
at a distance by emails. The victim of this kind of frequent contact
was the letter. Whereas in late-Victorian cities up to twelve deliveries
a day facilitated interactions not far distant from text messages and
emails in speed and frequency, now only 1 per cent of regular catch-
ups used this medium. It was still, however, by far the most widely
used channel where contact with friends and relatives was only maintained 'less than once or twice a month'.[106]

Since the first decade of the twenty-first century, the use of social
media has risen very rapidly, raising fears that exhibitionist privacy
is destroying all established defences of personal information and
ceding control of its use to global corporations, whether or not in
collusion with government agencies. It is perhaps best to see the
phenomenon not as a radical disjuncture but as an intensification of
several long-standing characteristics of managing privacy. In the first
place, aspirations and capacities have always been conditioned by the
life-cycle. At all times in the past, what an individual could feasibly
expect was related to age and family condition.[107] A growing child
gradually asserted more rights to their own information, and as an
adult formed new bodies of intimate knowledge with members of the
households it created and larger circles of friends. In old age there
were fewer threats to the personal archive but a reduced sphere of
intimacy. The rise of digital media offered connectivity to the increasing numbers of people living alone, although there was no simple
trade-off between solitude and the internet. In general, the old were
more likely to be in single-person households, and less likely to be

using the social media. Most of those using the new networking opportunities were seeking an enrichment of rather than a substitute for personal networks formed in the neighbourhood, school or the home. A 2013 study of American teenagers found that 'Facebook was seen as an extension of offline interactions and the social negotiation and maneuvering inherent to teenage life.'[108] During the nineteenth and twentieth centuries, increasing numbers of adolescent children had been able to lay claim to their own space, and embarked on a complex struggle to protect it from siblings and parents. Writing letters, making telephone calls, texting friends were all means of escaping the physical confines of the home. As with Elizabeth Evelyn's secret epistolary courtship in the late seventeenth century, the technology of virtual privacy was a resource of concealment and evasion.[109] The channels of communication challenged the authority of parents seeking to oversee the moral development of their children. They were an alternative to closing the door of your room to the gaze of others. With all media, there was an exchange of risk. The inescapable prospect of exposure had to be balanced against the feared impoverishment of social networks.

Absolute privacy in personal communication had rarely been an option at any level of society or period of time.[110] Walls were too thin, rooms too crowded, envelopes too frail, social media too unconfined. The issue was the relative level of control that could be exercised, and above all the power of those who might intercept the transmission. There might be a concern in principle that a distant agency or individual could know that a message had been sent and in some circumstances what it contained. What really mattered was whether the unsanctioned reader had the capacity to move through all the five stages of surveillance, and at the end intervene to affect adversely the present or future of the subject. For this reason studies report a hierarchy of anxiety amongst teenage social media users that has at the summit not national security bodies or global corporations, but mothers, followed by teachers and potential employers.[111] The challenge therefore was one of manipulating the often less than transparent privacy settings of a rapidly evolving array of platforms, and managing a pathway between the opportunities and threats that they were seen to offer. In this task, practitioners exercised discretion in how they presented themselves to whom, what they chose to reveal, and how they encoded their messages. The key variable was not the content of a message, but its context.[112] Information was released in a form and language that made sense to its intended audience but was more or less opaque to others who might see it. 'Through such encoded language,' writes Dana Boyd, 'teens can exclude people who are not part of the cycle of gossip at school, including parents, teachers, and peers outside their immediate social sphere.'[113] Pew researchers found that a majority of teenage social media users 'will obscure some of their updates and posts, sharing inside jokes and other coded messages that only certain friends will understand'.[114] It was a matter of nuanced vocabulary, of shared cultural references, of prior knowledge of persons, events and experiences. 'All the stuff I put up on Facebook', explained a user, 'goes to people who know me therefore they understand what I'm talking about.'[115]

Despite the apparently alarming exposure of personal details and feelings there was a conscious sense of reticence and focus amongst the consumers of social media. Different texts were fashioned for specific audiences as teenagers explored the possibilities of relationships and experimented with a range of identities. No one channel, no one set of messages, contained all that the user thought themselves to be. Reading the signs embedded in digital intercourse required an expertise which surveillance systems have struggled to match, despite the investment in semantic recognition. It was one thing to automate the process of selecting key words in a billion intercepted emails; it was quite another to reconstruct the range of meanings contained in the most casual exchange between bored teenagers. The best protection that privacy always had was the complexity of the communication process. Whether it was all the variety of facial signs that Montaigne catalogued in the sixteenth century, or the distinction that Niklas Luhmann drew between content, utterance and comprehension in all kinds of verbal intercourse,[116] there was a cumulative loss of understanding the further the witness was from the context of an exchange embedded in some form of social network.[117]

Viewing information as a species of personal property has both overstated and understated the value of privacy. The autonomous owner of every thought, fact and feeling, past and present, has become a more salient figure amidst the pressures of modern industrial societies and communication systems. The data protection legislation generated in response to the digital revolution has foregrounded networks of discrete subjects in command of their own archive of personal detail. As enclosed intimacy has been emphasized at the expense of looser and more varied emotional arrangements, greater stress has been placed on the need for physical and emotional escape from the over-pressing company of others.[118] These forms of lonely self-sufficiency have shallow roots. Solitude has its own history, stretching back, as we have seen, at least as far as the secret prayers of the late-medieval period. However, in its spiritual forms it was a reaction against a preoccupation with the isolated self, and as a practice it was integrated with other categories of collective observance. In its later, more secular manifestations, it was for the most part a means of replenishing social relations rather than escaping from them altogether.

The case for protecting privacy is embedded in what Helen Nissenbaum terms 'contextual integrity', the rules and expectations surrounding the transmission of information within a particular social process, whether with other individuals or with providers of services such as banks, doctors or commercial vendors.[119] Whether a particular personal fact should be withheld or transmitted depends on a perceived balance of gain in a given transaction. Consent to that exchange can be rendered meaningless by the necessity of obtaining what has become a basic good in the modern economy, such as credit.[120] Where there is a critical asymmetry of power in the relationship or fundamental obscurity in the rules that govern it, there will be a need for intervention, but the demand arises from the specific context rather than the category of information or the absolute claim to possession. The focus on individual rights has weakened the argument for protection. As Priscilla Regan observes, 'the philosophical basis of privacy policy overemphasises the importance of privacy to the individual and fails to recognize the broader social importance of privacy.'[121] By the same measure it has underemphasized the importance of privacy to the functioning of democracy and its associated freedoms.[122] The polarity between personal gratification and public good has compromised the argument with agencies of the state. 'Protecting individual privacy', writes Daniel Solove, 'need not be at society's expense – in fact, the value of safeguarding people's privacy should be justified by its social benefits.'[123] Placing too much emphasis on protecting the personal archive has made it more difficult to define a 'reasonable expectation of privacy'. It has set up aspirations to anonymity and informational autarky which in the past have been neither feasible nor attainable. At the same time it has deflected attention from the complexity and the subtlety of the communication process in any given context, and the challenge facing those who would intercept it. The threat posed by old or new forms of surveillance has been less the destruction of privacy and more its distortion through the misinterpretation of the meanings that are exchanged.[124]

At the beginning of the period covered by this chapter, Francis Ford Coppola, fresh from his triumph with *The Godfather*, was able to find the funds to make *The Conversation*, a personal project that addressed the rising concern about eavesdropping. 'The movie will say something significant about the nightmarish situation that has

developed in our society', he told the *New York Times*: 'A system
that employs all the sophisticated electronic tools that are available
to intrude upon our private lives.'[125] *The Conversation* was, however,
not just a witness to the paranoia of its times. It had additional preoccupations which together created a much more nuanced account
of the topic. A central theme was the distinction between a positive
privacy as the deepest form of intimacy and a negative privacy as a
desolate isolation. The principal character, a legendary professional
eavesdropper, is preoccupied with his work, which demands a deliberate absence of curiosity about the lives he records, and so protective
of his own privacy that he is unable to form any meaningful human
contact, even with his own staff. The only possession that he really
values is his own door key. Coppola names him 'Harry Caul', evoking
the image of a face covered by a membrane, unable clearly to see or
be seen in his contact with other people, and dresses him throughout
the film in an opaque plastic raincoat.[126] Harry Caul is heading for
a breakdown, propelled by a critical failure of understanding. The
tension in the drama arises from his repeated attempts to make sense
of the exchange between two lovers that his devices have recorded.
When he finally clarifies the words, he fundamentally misconstrues
them. He mis-locates an intonation in the key sentence which reverses
its meaning.[127] The lovers' communication between themselves
remains concealed from him. Those he assumes to be the potential
victims of murder turn out to be the bloody perpetrators. The last
scene cuts between Harry Caul tearing his apartment to pieces search-
ing for the bugs that he believes have now been planted on him, and
a tender moment in the lovers' original conversation, with the woman
removing something from the man's eye.[128] What they were to each
other, no amount of surveillance had been able to discover.

Notes

ᓚᓯ

Chapter 1 Privacy before Privacy 1300–1650

1 All the cases are reported in Helena M. Chew and William Kellaway (eds.), *London Assize of Nuisance, 1301–1431*. London Record Society Publications, vol. X (London: London Record Society, 1973), p. 88.

2 Georges Duby, 'Introduction: Private Power, Public Power', in *A History of Private Life. II: Revelations of the Medieval World*, edited by Georges Duby (Cambridge, MA: Belknap Press, 1988), pp. 4–6.

3 See, *inter alia*, Emily Cockayne, *Cheek by Jowl: A History of Neighbours* (London: Bodley Head, 2012), p. 14; Judith Flanders, *The Making of Home* (London: Atlantic Books, 2014), p. 67; Edwin Heathcote, *The Meaning of Home* (London: Frances Lincoln, 2012), p. 155; Thomas O'Connor, 'The Right to Privacy in Historical Perspective', *Massachusetts Law Quarterly*, 53 (June 1968), p. 102; Lawrence Stone, *The Family, Sex and Marriage in England 1500–1800* (Harmondsworth: Penguin, 1979), p. 170; Peter Earle, *A City Full of People: Men and Women of London 1650–1750* (London: Methuen, 1994), p. 211; Edward Shils, 'Privacy and Power', in *Center and Periphery: Essays in Macrosociology*, by Edward Shils (Chicago: University of Chicago Press, 1975), p. 323.

4 Samuel D. Warren and Louis D. Brandeis, 'The Right to Privacy', *Harvard Law Review*, 4, 5 (1890), pp. 193–220. On the article, see pp. 2, 76–7, 116.

5 Alan F. Westin, *Privacy and Freedom* (London: Bodley Head, 1970), p. 7.

6 Diane Shaw, 'The Construction of the Private in Medieval London', *Journal of Medieval and Early Modern Studies*, 26 (1996), p. 450.

7   William Reddy, *The Navigation of Feeling.: A Framework for the History of Emotions* (Cambridge: Cambridge University Press, 2001), p. 45.

8   Diana Webb, *Privacy and Solitude in the Middle Ages* (London and New York: Hambledon Continuum, 2007), p. ix. Also, Irwin Altman, 'Privacy Regulation: Culturally Universal or Culturally Specific?', *Journal of Social Issues*, 33, 3 (1977), pp. 81–2.

9   David Gibbons, *A Treatise on the Law of Dilapidations and Nuisances* (2nd edn, London: John Weale, 1849), p. xxv; C. C. Knowles and P. H. Pitt, *The History of Building Regulation in London 1189–1972* (London: Architectural Press, 1972), pp. 6–14.

10 Cockayne, *Cheek by Jowl*, p. 30.

11 Chew and Kellaway, *London Assize of Nuisance*, p. 100.

12 Chew and Kellaway, *London Assize of Nuisance*, p. 103.

13 John R. Gillis, *A World of Their Own Making: Myth, Ritual and the Quest for Family Values* (Cambridge, MA: Harvard University Press, 1996), p. 33.

14 Barbara H. Rosenwein, *Emotional Communities in the Early Middle Ages* (Ithaca: Cornell University Press, 2006), p. 191.

15 Christena Nippert-Eng, *Islands of Privacy* (Chicago: University of Chicago Press, 2010).

16 David H. Flaherty, 'Visions of Privacy: Past, Present, and Future', in *Visions of Privacy: Policy Choices for the Digital Age*, edited by Colin J. Bennett and Rebecca Grant (Toronto: University of Toronto Press, 1999), p. 26.

17 Jane Grenville, *Medieval Housing* (Leicester: Leicester University Press, 1999), pp. 127–32.

18 Flanders, *The Making of Home*, pp. 56–7.

19 Christopher Dyer, *Everyday Life in Medieval England* (London: Hambledon, 1994), pp. 133–65.

20 R. Machin, 'The Great Rebuilding: A Reassessment', *Past Present*, 77 (November 1977), pp. 33–56.

21 N. W. Alcock, *People at Home: Living in a Warwickshire Village, 1500–1800* (Chichester: Phillimore, 1993), pp. 54–93.

22 Nicholas Cooper, *Houses of the Gentry 1480–1680* (New Haven: Yale University Press, 1999), pp. 275–7.

23 Raffaella Sarti, *Europe at Home: Family and Material Culture 1500–1800* (New Haven: Yale University Press, 2002), pp. 129–30.

24 Bill Bryson, *At Home: A Short History of Private Life* (London: Doubleday, 2010), p. 65.

25 Henry Wotton, *The Elements of Architecture* (London: John Bill, 1624), p. 8.

26 Lena Cowen Orlin, *Locating Privacy in Tudor London* (Oxford: Oxford University Press, 2007), p. 300.

27 W. G. Hoskins, 'The Rebuilding of Rural England, 1570–1640', *Past & Present*, 4 (November 1953), p. 54.

28   Tim Meldrum, 'Domestic Service, Privacy and the Eighteenth-Century Metropolitan Household', *Urban History*, 26, 1 (1999), p. 33. Also, Linda A. Pollock, 'Living on the Stage of the World: The Concept of Privacy among the Elite of Early Modern England', in *Rethinking Social History: English Society 1570–1920 and its Interpretation*, edited by Adrian Wilson (Manchester: Manchester University Press, 1993), p. 82; Orest Ranum, 'The Refuges of Intimacy', in *A History of Private Life. III: Passions of the Renaissance*, edited by Roger Chartier (Cambridge, MA: Belknap Press, 1989), p. 211.

29   Nicole Castan, 'The Public and the Private', in Chartier, *A History of Private Life. III: Passions of the Renaissance*, p. 412.

30   J. H. Baker, *An Introduction to English Legal History* (London: Butterworths, 1971), p. 284. By 1500 the crime had become associated with entry at night. Daytime entry came under the offence of housebreaking, which was codified during the early sixteenth century.

31   Grenville, *Medieval Housing*, p. 126.

32   Virginia Smith, *Clean: A History of Personal Hygiene and Purity* (Oxford: Oxford University Press, 2007), pp. 156–7.

33   D. J. H. Clifford (ed.), *The Diaries of Lady Anne Clifford* (Stroud: Alan Sutton, 1991), pp. 25–7.

34   Bryson, *At Home*, p. 55.

35   Alice T. Friedman, *House and Household in Elizabethan England: Wollaton Hall and the Willoughby Family* (Chicago: University of Chicago Press, 1989), pp. 146–7.

36   Orlin, *Locating Privacy in Tudor London*, p. 299.

37   Anne Laurence, 'The Closed Disclosed: The Ambiguous Privacy of Women's Closets in Seventeenth-Century England', unpublished paper; Andrew Cambers, *Godly Reading: Print, Manuscript and Puritanism in England, 1580–1720* (Cambridge: Cambridge University Press, 2011), pp. 43–54.

38   Sarti, *Europe at Home*, p. 131.

39   Ronald Huebert, 'The Gendering of Privacy', *Seventeenth Century*, 16 (2001), pp. 37–67.

40   Sasha Roberts, 'Shakespeare "Creepes into the Womens Closets about Bedtime": Women Reading in a Room of Their Own', in *Renaissance Configurations: Voices/Bodies/Spaces, 1580–1690*, edited by Gordon McMullen (Basingstoke: Palgrave, 1998), pp. 35–7; Philippe Braunstein, 'Towards Intimacy: The Fourteenth and Fifteenth Centuries', in Duby, *A History of Private Life. II: Revelations of the Medieval World*, p. 538; Cambers, *Godly Reading*, p. 73.

41   Alan Stewart, 'The Early Modern Closet Discovered', *Representations*, 50 (Spring 1995), p. 83.

42   Gillis, *A World of Their Own Making*, p. 32.

43   Duby, *A History of Private Life. II: Revelations of the Medieval World*, p. 510.

44   John Harvey, *Mediaeval Gardens* (London: B. T. Batsford, 1981), pp. 74–112.

45 Webb, *Privacy and Solitude*, p. 192.
46 Dyer, *Everyday Life in Medieval England*, pp. 113–31.
47 Charles Chenevix Trench, *A History of Angling* (London: Hart-Davis, MacGibbon, 1974), p. 28.
48 F. R. Raines (ed.), *The Journal of Nicholas Assheton of Downham, in the County of Lancaster, Esq.: For the Part of the Year 1617, and Part of the Year Following*. Chetham Society Publications, o.s. 14 (Manchester: Chetham Society, 1848), pp. 15–96.
49 Rebecca Solnit, *Wanderlust: A History of Walking* (London: Verso, 2001), p. 87.
50 Clifford, *The Diaries of Lady Anne Clifford*, p. 27.
51 Cambers, *Godly Reading*, pp. 110–15.
52 Clifford, *The Diaries of Lady Anne Clifford*, pp. 50, 52.
53 Francis Bacon, *Of Gardens: An Essay* (1625; London and New York: John Lane, 1902), p. 26.
54 Orlin, *Locating Privacy in Tudor London*, pp. 171, 231–6.
55 Steven Ozment, *Magdalena and Balthasar* (New York: Simon and Schuster, 1986), p. 32.
56 Dorothy M. Meads (ed.), *Diary of Lady Margaret Hoby 1599–1605* (London: George Routledge, 1930), p. 66.
57 Meads, *Diary of Lady Margaret Hoby*, p. 62. Entry for Friday 10 August 1599.
58 Samuel Slater, *A Discourse of Closet (or Secret Prayer)* (London: Jonathan Robinson and Tho. Cockerill, 1691), p. 19.
59 Ian Green, 'New for Old? Clerical and Lay Attitudes to Domestic Prayer in Early Modern England', *Reformation and Renaissance Review*, 10, 2 (2008), p. 198.
60 Patricia Crawford, *Women and Religion in England 1500–1720* (London: Routledge, 1993), p. 77.
61 Slater, *A Discourse of Closet (or Secret Prayer)*, p. 40.
62 Alan Macfarlane (ed.), *The Diary of Ralph Josselin 1616–1683* (London: Oxford University Press, 1976), p. 134.
63 Daniel Featley, *Ancilla Pietatis, or, The Hand-Maid to Private Devotion* (London: Nicholas Bourne, 1626), p. 111.
64 Isaac Archer, *The Diary of Isaac Archer 1641–1700*, in *Two East Anglian Diaries 1641–1729*, edited by Matthew Storey (Woodbridge: Boydell Press, 1994), p. 43.
65 Germaine Fry Murray (ed.), *A Critical Edition of John Beadle's A Journall or Diary of a Thankfull Christian* [1656]. The Renaissance Imagination series, edited by Stephen Orgel (New York: Garland, 1996), p. 63.
66 John Fielding (ed.), *The Diary of Robert Woodford, 1637–1641* (Cambridge: Cambridge University Press, 2012), p. 96.
67 Cambers, *Godly Reading*, p. 54.
68 Murray, *John Beadle's A Journall or Diary of a Thankfull Christian*, pp. 137–8. The second half of the second sentence is a quote from the

Sermon on the Mount (Matthew ch. 6, v. 6, Authorized Version). For a discussion of the popularity of the text in this period see Diarmaid MacCulloch, *Silence: A Christian History* (London: Allen Lane, 2013), p. 131.

69 Peter Burke, 'Notes for a Social History of Silence in Early Modern Europe', in *The Art of Conversation*, by Peter Burke (Cambridge: Polity: 1993), p. 127.

70 Eamon Duffy, *Marking the Hours: English People and their Prayers, 1240–1570* (New Haven: Yale University Press, 2006), pp. 3–5.

71 Murray, *John Beadle's A Journall or Diary of a Thankfull Christian*, p. 148.

72 Michael Mascuch, *Origins of the Individualist Self: Autobiography and Self-Identity in England, 1591–1791* (Cambridge: Polity, 1997), pp. 72–3.

73 Ralph Houlbrooke, *English Family Life, 1576–1716: An Anthology from Diaries* (Oxford: Blackwell, 1988), pp. 2–5; Braunstein, 'Towards Intimacy, p. 553–4.

74 Fielding, *The Diary of Robert Woodford*, p. 96.

75 Philippe Ariés, 'Introduction', in Chartier, *A History of Private Life. III: Passions of the Renaissance*, p. 5.

76 David Cressy, 'Levels of Illiteracy in England 1530–1730', *Historical Journal*, 20, 1 (1977), pp. 5–11.

77 R. A. Houston, *Literacy in Early Modern Europe: Culture and Education 1500–1800* (London: Longman, 1988), p. 130.

78 Andrew Taylor, 'Into his Secret Chamber: Reading and Privacy in Late Medieval England', in *The Practice and Representation of Reading in England*, edited by James Raven, Helen Small and Naomi Tadmor (Cambridge: Cambridge University Press, 1996), pp. 41–61.

79 Jessica Brantley, *Reading in the Wilderness: Private Devotion and Public Performance in Late Medieval England* (Chicago: University of Chicago Press, 2007), p. 12.

80 Mary C. Erler, *Women, Reading, and Piety in Late Medieval England* (Cambridge: Cambridge University Press, 2002), p. 136.

81 Karen Cherewatuk and Ulrike Wiethaus, 'Introduction', in *Dear Sister: Medieval Women and the Epistolary Genre*, edited by Karen Cherewatuk and Ulrike Wiethaus (Philadelphia: University of Pennsylvania Press, 1993), p. 4.

82 William Fulwood, *The Enemie of Idlenesse. Teaching the Manner and Stile how to Endite, Compose, and Wryte all Sortes of Epistles and Letters: As Wel by Answer* (London: Augustine Lawton, 1571), p. iii. See also, Angel Day, *The English Secretorie, or Methode of Writing of Epistles and Letters* (London: Thomas Snodham, [1625]).

83 Ozment, *Magdalena and Balthasar*, p. 27.

84 Stephen Ozment, *Flesh and Spirit: Private Life in Early Modern Germany* (New York: Viking, 1999), p. 17.

85 Linda A. Pollock, 'Parent–Child Relations', in *The History of the European Family. 1: Family Life in Early Modern Times 1500–1750*, edited by David I. Kertzer and Marzio Barbagli (New Haven: Yale University Press, 2001), p. 207.

86 Gemma Allen, *The Cooke Sisters: Education, Piety and Politics in Early Modern England* (Manchester: Manchester University Press, 2013), pp. 8–9.

87 Rebecca Krug, *Reading Families: Women's Literate Practice in Late Medieval England* (Ithaca: Cornell University Press, 2002), p. 18.

88 Norman Davis, *Paston Letters and Papers of the Fifteenth Century, Part 1* (Oxford: Clarendon Press, 1971).

89 Colin Richmond, *The Paston Family in the Fifteenth Century: Endings* (Manchester: Manchester University Press, 2000), p. 92.

90 Duncan Campbell-Smith, *Masters of the Post: The Authorized History of the Royal Mail* (London: Allen Lane, 2011), pp. 8–25.

91 Howard Robinson, *Britain's Post Office* (London: Oxford University Press, 1953), p. 2.

92 Diane Watt, *The Paston Women: Selected Letters* (Cambridge: D. S. Brewer, 2004), p. 83.

93 Pollock, 'Living on the Stage of the World', p. 85.

94 James Daybell, *The Material Letter in Early Modern England: Manuscript Letters and the Culture and Practices of Letter-Writing, 1512–1625* (London: Palgrave Macmillan, 2012), pp. 148–74.

95 James Daybell, ' "I Wold Wyshe My Doings Myght Be...Secret": Privacy and the Social Practices of Reading Women's Letters in Sixteenth-Century England', in *Women's Letters Across Europe, 1400–1700: Form and Persuasion*, edited by Jane Couchman and Ann Crabb (Aldershot: Ashgate, 2005), p. 157.

96 Ozment, *Magdalena and Balthasar*, p. 43.

97 Fulwood, *The Enemie of Idlenesse*, p. iii.

98 John Dod and Robert Clever, *A Godly Forme of Householde Government: For the Ordering of Private Families, According to the Direction of God's Word* (London: Thomas Man, 1612), p. 13.

99 Dod and Clever, *A Godly Forme of Household Government*, p. 19.

100 Dod and Clever, *A Godly Forme of Household Government*, p. 45.

101 Dod and Clever, *A Godly Forme of Household Government*, p. 104.

102 Dod and Clever, *A Godly Forme of Household Government*, p. 230.

103 Dod and Clever, *A Godly Forme of Household Government*, p. 88.

104 Dod and Clever, *A Godly Forme of Household Government*, p. 88.

105 Dod and Clever, *A Godly Forme of Household Government*, pp. 88–9.

106 Stone, *The Family, Sex and Marriage*, p. 170.

107 Friedman, *House and Household in Elizabethan England*, p. 65.

108 Dod and Clever, *A Godly Forme of Household Government*, p. 153.

109 Ian Archer, *The Pursuit of Stability: Social Relations in Elizabethan London* (Cambridge: Cambridge University Press, 1991), pp. 74–82.

110 Chris Wickham, 'Gossip and Resistance among the Medieval Peasantry', *Past & Present*, 160 (August 1998), pp. 3–24.

111 Jeremy Boulton, *Neighbourhood and Society: A London Suburb in the Seventeenth Century* (Cambridge: Cambridge University Press, 1987), p. 292; Keith Wrightson, *English Society 1580–1680* (London: Hutchinson, 1982), pp. 51–3; Cockayne, *Cheek by Jowl*, p. 21.
112 J. A. Sharpe, ' "Such Disagreements Betwyx Neighbours": Litigation and Human Relations in Early Modern England', in *Disputes and Settlements: Law and Human Relations in the West*, edited by John Bossy (Cambridge: Cambridge University Press, 1983), pp. 169–73; Tim Stretton, 'Written Obligations, Litigation and Neighbourliness, 1580–1680', in *Remaking English Society: Social Relations and Social Change in Early Modern England*, edited by Steve Hindle, Alexandra Shepard and John Walter (Woodbridge: Boydell Press, 2013), pp. 189–209.
113 Marjorie Keniston McIntosh, *Controlling Misbehaviour in England, 1370–1600* (Cambridge: Cambridge University Press, 1998), pp. 54–107.
114 Cited in David Herlihy, *Medieval Households* (Cambridge, MA: Harvard University Press, 1985), p. 117.
115 John L. Locke, *Eavesdropping: An Intimate History* (Oxford: Oxford University Press, 2010), p. 11.
116 Webb, *Privacy and Solitude*, pp. 195–6.
117 McIntosh, *Controlling Misbehaviour*, pp. 207–10.
118 Michel de Montaigne, 'An Apology for Raymond Sebond', in *The Complete Essays*, translated and edited by M. A. Screech (London: Penguin, 2013), II.12, p. 507.

Chapter 2 Privacy and Communication 1650–1800

1 Roger Chartier, 'The Practical Impact of Writing', in *A History of Private Life. III: Passions of the Renaissance*, edited by Roger Chartier (Cambridge, MA: Belknap Press, 1989), p. 111.
2 Chartier, 'The Practical Impact of Writing', p. 116. Also, Cecile M. Jagodzinski, *Privacy and Print: Reading and Writing in Seventeenth-Century England* (Charlottesville: University Press of Virginia, 1999), p. 2.
3 Clare Brant and Susan E. Whyman (eds.), *Walking the Streets of Eighteenth-Century London* (Oxford: Oxford University Press, 2007), pp. 36–7. On the growth of the metropolitan urban community, see Peter Earle, *A City Full of People: Men and Women of London 1650–1750* (London: Methuen, 1994), pp. 165–77; Jerry White, *London in the Eighteenth Century* (London: Vintage, 2013), p. 3.
4 Richard Sennett, *The Fall of Public Man* (New York: Alfred A. Knopf, 1977), p. 63.
5 James Sambrook, 'Ward, Edward [Ned] (1667–1731)', *Oxford Dictionary of National Biography*, Oxford University Press, 2004, http://www.oxforddnb.com/view/article/28682; Howard William

Troyer, *Ned Ward of Grubstreet: A Study of Sub-Literary London in the Eighteenth Century* (Cambridge, MA: Harvard University Press, 1946), pp. 29–60.

6   Ned Ward, *The London Spy*, edited by Paul Hyland (1698–1700; East Lansing: East Lansing Colleagues Press, 1993), p. 10.

7   Pierce Egan, *Life in London; Or, the Day and Night Scenes of Jerry Hawthorn, Esq. and his Elegant Friend Corinthian Tom, Accompanied by Bob Logic, the Oxonian, in their Rambles and Sprees through the Metropolis* (London: Sherwood, Neely, and Jones, 1821). See pp. 54–6.

8   Jane Rendell, *The Pursuit of Pleasure: Gender, Space and Architecture in Regency London* (London: Athlone Press, 2002), p. 31.

9   John Gay, *Trivia: Or, the Art of Walking the Streets of London* (London: Bernard Lintott, [1716]), p. 1.

10 John Bancks, 'A Description of London', in *Miscellaneous Works in Verse and Prose of Mr. John Bancks* (London: James Hodges, 1739), p. 337.

11 Gay, *Trivia*, p. 40.

12 Dennis Wheeler, 'Eighteenth Century History and the European Environment', in *A Companion to Eighteenth-Century Europe*, edited by Peter H. Wilson (Malden: Blackwell, 2008), pp. 14–15.

13 C. C. Knowles and P. H. Pitt, *The History of Building Regulation in London 1189–1972* (London: Architectural Press, 1972), p. 19; Peter Earle, *The Making of the English Middle Class: Business, Society and Family Life in London, 1660–1730* (London: Methuen, 1989), p. 207.

14 Jenny Gibbs, *Curtains & Drapes: History, Design, Inspiration* (London: Cassell, 1996), pp. 38–65.

15 Peter Guillery, *The Small House in Eighteenth-Century London: A Social and Architectural History* (New Haven: Yale University Press, 2004), p. 282.

16 Leonore Davidoff and Catherine Hall, *Family Fortunes: Men and Women of the English Middle Class 1780–1850* (rev. edn, London: Routledge, 2002), p. 377.

17 Tim Meldrum, 'Domestic Service, Privacy and the Eighteenth-Century Metropolitan Household', *Urban History*, 26, 1 (1999), p. 30; Alain Collomp, 'Families: Habitations and Cohabitations', in Chartier, *A History of Private Life. III: Passions of the Renaissance*, p. 507; Orest Ranum, 'The Refuges of Intimacy', in Chartier, *A History of Private Life. III: Passions of the Renaissance*, p. 225; Judith Flanders, *The Making of Home* (London: Atlantic Books, 2014), pp. 72–3.

18 For the even slower improvement in the housing of the poor in contemporary Paris, see Raffaella Sarti, *Europe at Home: Family and Material Culture 1500–1800* (New Haven: Yale University Press, 2002), p. 98.

19 N. W. Alcock, *People at Home: Living in a Warwickshire Village, 1500–1800* (Chichester: Phillimore, 1993), p. 203.

20 Guillery, *The Small House in Eighteenth-Century London*, p. 66.

21 Michael Paterson, *Private Life in Britain's Stately Homes* (London: Robinson, 2012), p. 60.

22 Bill Bryson, *At Home: A Short History of Private Life* (London: Doubleday, 2010), pp. 169–75.
23 Emily Cockayne, *Cheek by Jowl: A History of Neighbours* (London: Bodley Head, 2012), p. 33.
24 Emily Cockayne, *Hubbub: Filth, Noise and Stench in England 1600–1770* (New Haven: Yale University Press, 2007), pp. 107–12.
25 John Dunton, *The Night-Walker: Or, Evening Rambles in Search after Lewd Women* (London: James Orme, 1696), September, p. 4.
26 Gay, *Trivia*, p. 26.
27 Miles Ogborn, *Spaces of Modernity: London's Geographies, 1680–1780* (New York: Guilford Press, 1998), p. 76.
28 Ogborn, *Spaces of Modernity*, pp. 116–57.
29 Oliver Goldsmith, 'The Shabby Beau, The Man in Black, The Chinese Philosopher, &c., at Vauxhall', in *The Miscellaneous Works of Oliver Goldsmith, M. B.*, 6 vols. (London: John Murray, 1837), vol. II, pp. 286–7.
30 Gay, *Trivia*, p. 1.
31 Penelope J. Corfield, 'Walking the City Streets: The Urban Odyssey in Eighteenth-Century England', *Journal of Urban History*, 16, 2 (1990), p. 154.
32 *Spectator*, 131 (31 July 1711), reprinted in *The Spectator*, (12th edn, London: J. and R. Tonson, 1839), vol. II, pp. 184–5.
33 Ward, *The London Spy*, p. 16.
34 White, *London in the Eighteenth Century*, p. 118.
35 Cockayne, *Cheek by Jowl*, p. 33.
36 Amanda Vickery, *Behind Closed Doors: At Home in Georgian England* (New Haven: Yale University Press, 2009), p. 30. The 1604 ruling was in Sir Edward Coke's report of *Semayne's Case*. Walter F. Pratt, *Privacy in Britain* (Lewisburg: Bucknell University Press, 1979), p. 55.
37 Richard Burn, *The Justice of the Peace, and Parish Officer*, 2 vols. (London: A. Millar, 1755), vol. 2, pp. 104–6, 150–4.
38 Joseph Bramah, *A Dissertation on the Construction of Locks* (London: for the Author, 1787), p. 5.
39 William Blackstone, *Commentaries on the Laws of England*, 4 vols. (Oxford: Clarendon Press, 1765–9), vol. 2, p. 4.
40 Cited in Jeffrey Rosen, *The Unwanted Gaze: The Destruction of Privacy in America* (New York: Vintage, 2001), p. 28.
41 George Wilson, *Reports of Cases Argued and Adjudged in the King's Courts at Westminster* (2nd edn, London: P. Uriel and E. Brook, 1784), part 3, p. 62.
42 *Cherrington* v. *Abney*, 1709, cited in David J. Seipp, 'English Judicial Recognition of a Right to Privacy', *Oxford Journal of Legal Studies*, 3, 3 (Winter 1983), p. 336. Also, Cockayne, *Cheek by Jowl*, p. 34.
43 Earle, *The Making of the English Middle Class*, pp. 171–2.
44 David Garrioch, *Neighbourhood and Community in Paris, 1740–1790* (Cambridge: Cambridge University Press, 1986), p. 16.

45 Robert B. Shoemaker, 'The Decline of Public Insult in London 1660–1800', *Past & Present*, 169 (2000), pp. 99–103.

46 Arlette Farge, 'The Honor and Secrecy of Families', in Chartier, *A History of Private Life. III: Passions of the Renaissance*, p. 583.

47 Keith Thomas, *Religion and the Decline of Magic* (Harmondsworth: Penguin, 1973), pp. 631–2.

48 Susan Dwyer Amussen, *An Ordered Society: Gender and Class in Early Modern England* (Oxford: Blackwell, 1988), pp. 177–80; Martin Ingram, *Church Courts, Sex and Marriage in England, 1570–1640* (Cambridge: Cambridge University Press, 1987), pp. 369–74; Earle, *A City Full of People*, p. 177.

49 Marjorie Keniston McIntosh, *Controlling Misbehaviour in England, 1370–1600* (Cambridge: Cambridge University Press, 1998), p. 54.

50 Richard Gough, *The History of Myddle*, edited and introduced by David Hey (Harmondsworth: Penguin, 1981), p. 242.

51 Gough, *The History of Myddle*, p. 114.

52 Gough, *The History of Myddle*, p. 216.

53 Lawrence Stone, *The Family, Sex and Marriage in England 1500–1800* (Harmondsworth: Penguin, 1979), p. 22. For a proper stress on the social breadth of love as at least one element of marital relations, see Keith Wrightson, *English Society 1580–1680* (London: Hutchinson, 1982), pp. 74–92.

54 Linda A. Pollock, 'Living on the Stage of the World: The Concept of Privacy among the Elite of Early Modern England', in *Rethinking Social History: English Society 1570–1920 and its Interpretation*, edited by Adrian Wilson (Manchester: Manchester University Press, 1993), p. 88.

55 Gough, *The History of Myddle*, p. 140.

56 Gough, *The History of Myddle*, p. 104.

57 J. A. Sharpe, ' "Such Disagreements Betwyx Neighbours": Litigation and Human Relations in Early Modern England', in *Disputes and Settlements: Law and Human Relations in the West*, edited by John Bossy (Cambridge: Cambridge University Press, 1983), pp. 168–9.

58 Cited in Sharpe, ' "Such Disagreements Betwyx Neighbours" ', p. 169.

59 William Matthews (ed.), *The Diary of Dudley Ryder 1715–1716* (London: Methuen, 1939), p. 135.

60 Matthews, *The Diary of Dudley Ryder*, pp. 67, 72.

61 Ralph Houlbrooke (ed.), *English Family Life, 1576–1716: An Anthology from Diaries* (Oxford: Blackwell, 1988), p. 47.

62 William L. Sachse (ed.), *The Diary of Roger Lowe of Ashton-in-Makerfield, Lancashire 1663–74* (London: Longmans, Green, 1938), p. 20.

63 Linda A. Pollock, 'Parent–Child Relations', in *The History of the European Family. 1: Family Life in Early Modern Times 1500–1750*, edited by David I. Kertzer and Marzio Barbagli (New Haven: Yale University Press, 2001), p. 207. For a still higher estimate for the eighteenth century of two thirds, including apprentices, see Kristina Straub,

Domestic Affairs: Intimacy, Eroticism, and Violence between Servants and Masters in Eighteenth-Century Britain (Baltimore: Johns Hopkins University Press, 2009), p. 4.

64 Paterson, *Private Life in Britain's Stately Homes*, p. 172.

65 Earle, *The Making of the English Middle Class*, pp. 225–8.

66 Laura Gowing, *Domestic Dangers: Women, Words, and Sex in Early Modern London* (Oxford: Clarendon Press, 1996), p. 191.

67 D. A. Kent, 'Ubiquitous but Invisible: Female Domestic Servants in Mid-Eighteenth Century London', *History Workshop*, 28 (1989), pp. 120–1.

68 John MacDonald, *Memoirs of an Eighteenth-Century Footman* (London: George Routledge, 1927), p. 64.

69 MacDonald, *Memoirs*, p. 183. MacDonald's relations with a long sequence of employers are explored in Straub, *Domestic Affairs*, pp. 179–88.

70 David Cressy, 'Levels of Illiteracy in England 1530–1730', *Historical Journal*, 20, 1 (1977), pp. 1–23; Helen Jewell, *Education in Early Modern England* (Houndmills: Macmillan, 1998), pp. 146–54.

71 Roy McKeen Wiles, 'The Relish for Reading in Provincial England Two Centuries Ago', in *The Widening Circle: Essays on the Circulation of Literature in Eighteenth-Century Europe*, edited by Paul J. Korshin (Philadelphia: University of Pennsylvania Press, 1976), pp. 103–5.

72 Margaret Spufford, *Small Books and Pleasant Histories* (London: Methuen, 1981), pp. 91–101.

73 Naomi Tadmor, ' "In the Even My Wife Read to Me": Women, Reading and Household Life in the Eighteenth Century', in *The Practice and Representation of Reading in England*, edited by James Raven, Helen Small and Naomi Tadmor (Cambridge: Cambridge University Press, 1996), pp. 162–74.

74 David Vincent, *Literacy and Popular Culture: England 1750–1914* (Cambridge: Cambridge University Press, 1989), p. 79.

75 John Brewer, 'This, That and the Other: Public, Social and Private in the Seventeenth and Eighteenth Centuries', in *Shifting the Boundaries: Transformation of the Languages of Public and Private in the Eighteenth Century*, edited by Dario Castiglione and Lesley Sharpe (Exeter: University of Exeter Press, 1995), p. 15.

76 Thomas Brooks, *The Privie Key of Heaven; or Twenty Arguments for Closet-Prayer* (London: John Hancock, 1665), p. 2.

77 Chartier, 'The Practical Impact of Writing', p. 119.

78 Diarmaid MacCulloch, *Silence: A Christian History* (London: Allen Lane, 2013), p. 155.

79 François Lebrun, 'The Two Reformations: Communal Devotion and Personal Piety', in Chartier, *A History of Private Life. III: Passions of the Renaissance*, pp. 69–109.

80 Lancelot Andrews, *A Manual of the Private Devotions and Meditations of the Right Reverend Father in God, Lancelot Andrews, Late L. Bishop of Winchester* (London: A. Churchil, 1682).

81 Edward Wettenhall, *Enter into thy Closet: Or, a Method and Order for Private Devotion* (5th edn, London: John Martyn, 1676), p. 7.
82 Wettenhall, *Enter into thy Closet*, p. 36.
83 Richard Rambuss, *Closet Devotions* (Durham, NC: Duke University Press, 1998), p. 105.
84 Brooks, *The Privie Key of Heaven*, p. 3.
85 Peter Burke, 'Notes for a Social History of Silence in Early Modern Europe', in Peter Burke, *The Art of Conversation* (Cambridge: Polity, 1993), pp. 140–1.
86 Brooks, *The Privie Key of Heaven*, p. 109.
87 Michael Mascuch, *Origins of the Individualist Self: Autobiography and Self-Identity in England, 1591–1791* (Cambridge: Polity, 1997), pp. 120–1; MacCulloch, *Silence*, pp. 138–9.
88 1st edn, London: Henry Brome, 1672.
89 Leonore Davidoff, Megan Doolittle, Janet Fink and Katherine Holden, *The Family Story: Blood, Contract and Intimacy 1830–1960* (London: Longman, 1999), pp. 58–9.
90 Wettenhall, *Enter into thy Closet*, p. 2. See also William Coe, *The Diary of William Coe 1693–1729*, in *Two East Anglian Diaries 1641–1729*, edited by Matthew Storey (Woodbridge: Boydell Press, 1994), pp. 204–44.
91 Paul Delany, *British Autobiography in the Seventeenth Century* (London: Routledge and Kegan Paul, 1969), pp. 6–104.
92 David Vincent, *Bread, Knowledge and Freedom: A Study of Nineteenth-Century Working Class Autobiography* (London: Europa, 1981), pp. 14–19; Linda H. Peterson, *Victorian Autobiography: The Tradition of Self-Interpretation* (New Haven: Yale University Press, 1986), pp. 2–28, 15–19; Mascuch, *Origins of the Individualist Self*, pp. 55–96.
93 Thomas Tryon, *Some Memories of the Life of Mr. Tho: Tryon* (London: T. Sowle, 1705), p. 51.
94 Brant and Whyman, *Walking the Streets of Eighteenth-Century London*, pp. 37–8.
95 James Lackington, *Memoirs of the First Forty-Five Years of the Life of James Lackington ... Written by Himself: In a Series of Letters to a Friend* (London: for the Author, 1791).
96 Lackington, *Memoirs*, p. xiii.
97 Lackington, *Memoirs*, p. xvii.
98 Lackington, *Memoirs*, p. 4.
99 Lackington, *Memoirs*, pp. 1–2.
100 Cited in Duncan Campbell-Smith, *Masters of the Post: The Authorized History of the Royal Mail* (London: Allen Lane, 2011), p. 37.
101 James Daybell, *The Material Letter in Early Modern England: Manuscript Letters and the Culture and Practices of Letter-Writing, 1512–1625* (London: Palgrave Macmillan, 2012), p. 20; Pat Hudson, 'Correspondence and Commitment: British Traders' Letters in the Long Eighteenth Century', *Cultural and Social History*, 11, 4 (December 2014),

pp. 528–30; Brant and Whyman, *Walking the Streets of Eighteenth-Century London*, p. 44.

102 Lynn Hollen Lees, *The Solidarities of Strangers: The English Poor Laws and the People, 1700–1948* (Cambridge: Cambridge University Press, 1998), p. 167; Thomas Sokoll (ed.), *Essex Pauper Letters 1732–1837* (Oxford: Oxford University Press, 2001).

103 Susan Whyman, *The Pen and the People: English Letter-Writers 1660–1800* (Oxford: Oxford University Press, 2009).

104 Brant and Whyman, *Walking the Streets of Eighteenth-Century London*, p. 46.

105 Sachse, *The Diary of Roger Lowe*, p. 119.

106 Pollock, 'Living on the Stage of the World', p. 85; Gary Schneider, *The Culture of Epistolarity: Vernacular Letters and Letter Writing in Early Modern England, 1500–1700* (Newark: University of Delaware Press, 2005), p. 68.

107 Matthews, *The Diary of Dudley Ryder*, pp. 48–9.

108 Bruce Redford, *The Converse of the Pen: Acts of Intimacy in the Eighteenth-Century Familiar Letter* (Chicago: University of Chicago Press, 1986), p. 2.

109 Joan Wilkinson (ed.), *The Letters of Thomas Langton, Flax Merchant of Kirkham 1771–1788*. Chetham Society Publications, t.s. 38 (Manchester: Chetham Society, 1993), p. 131. Letter dated 15 October 1772.

110 Houlbrooke, *English Family Life, 1576–1716*, pp. 38–9.

111 Jürgen Habermas, *The Structural Transformation of the Public Sphere*, translated by Thomas Burger and Frederick Lawrence (Cambridge: Polity, 1992), pp. 57–66; Peter Lake and Steve Pincus, 'Rethinking the Public Sphere in Early Modern England', *Journal of British Studies*, 45, 2 (2006), p. 286.

112 Whyman, *The Pen and the People*, pp. 7, 217.

113 Vickery, *Behind Closed Doors*, p. 27.

114 Diane E. Boyd and Marta Kvande, 'Reading Women, Reading Public and Private', in *Everyday Revolutions: Eighteenth-Century Women Transforming Public and Private*, edited by Diane E. Boyd and Marta Kvande (Newark: University of Delaware Press, 2008), pp. 17–29.

115 Lawrence E. Klein, 'Gender and the Public/Private Distinction in the Eighteenth Century: Some Questions about Evidence and Analytic Procedure', *Eighteenth Century Studies*, 29, 1 (1996), pp. 100–4.

116 Brian Cowan, *The Social Life of Coffee: The Emergence of the British Coffeehouse* (New Haven: Yale University Press, 2005), p. 251.

117 Brewer, 'This, That and the Other', pp. 18–19.

118 PP 1844 (582) *Report from the Secret Committee on the Post Office*, p. 7.

119 On the 1710 Act see Seipp, 'English Judicial Recognition of a Right to Privacy', p. 338. Also, Frederick S. Lane, *American Privacy: The 400-Year History of Our Most Contested Right* (Boston: Beacon Press,

2009), pp. 18–20; David Flaherty, *Privacy in Colonial New England* (Charlottesville: University Press of Virginia, 1972), p. 120.

120 Alan Marshall, *Intelligence and Espionage in the Reign of Charles II, 1660–1685* (Cambridge: Cambridge University Press, 1994), pp. 78–95.

121 John Barrell, *The Spirit of Despotism: Invasions of Privacy in the 1790s* (Oxford: Oxford University Press, 2006), pp. 4–9 and *passim*.

Chapter 3 Privacy and Prosperity 1800–1900

1 George Orwell, *1984* (1949; Harmondsworth: Penguin, 1954), especially pp. 6, 168; Michel Foucault, *Discipline and Punish: The Birth of the Prison* (1975; London: Penguin, 1991), pp. 195–209.

2 Michael Froomkin, 'The Death of Privacy?', *Stanford Law Review*, 52, 5 (May 2000), p. 1463. Also, Daniel J. Solove, 'Privacy and Power: Computer Databases and Metaphors for Information Privacy', *Stanford Law Review*, 53, 6 (July 2001), p. 1397; John Naughton, *From Gutenberg to Zuckerberg: What You Really Need to Know about the Internet* (London: Quercus, 2012), p. 259; Manuel Castells, *The Internet Galaxy: Reflections of the Internet, Business and Society* (Oxford: Oxford University Press, 2001), p. 180.

3 Glenn Greenwald, *No Place to Hide: Edward Snowden, the NSA and the Surveillance State* (London: Hamish Hamilton, 2014), p. 175; Luke Harding, *The Snowden Files* (London: Guardian Books and Faber & Faber, 2014), p. 12.

4 Jeremy Bentham, *Panopticon; Or the Inspection-House* (1787), reprinted in *The Panopticon Writings*, edited by Miran Božovič (London: Verso, 1995), p. 34.

5 Miran Božovič, 'Introduction: "An Utterly Dark Spot" ', in Božovič, *The Panopticon Writings*, pp. 11–17; Robin Evans, *The Fabrication of Virtue: English Prison Architecture, 1750–1840* (Cambridge: Cambridge University Press, 1982), pp. 206–7.

6 Jeremy Bentham, 'Outline of the Plan of Construction of a Panopticon Penitentiary House: As Designed by Jeremy Bentham, of Lincoln's Inn, Esq.', in *The Works of Jeremy Bentham*, edited by John Bowring, vol. XI (Edinburgh: William Tait, 1843), Appendix, p. 96. The line is from the 139th Psalm.

7 Bentham, *Panopticon*, p. 45.

8 Michelle Perrot (ed.), *A History of Private Life. IV: From the Fires of Revolution to the Great War* (Cambridge, MA: Belknap Press, 1990), p. 2. Also, Edward Shils, 'Privacy in Modern Industrial Society', in *Censuses, Surveys and Privacy*, edited by Martin Bulmer (London: Macmillan, 1979), p. 29.

9 Leonore Davidoff, Megan Doolittle, Janet Fink and Katherine Holden, *The Family Story: Blood, Contract and Intimacy 1830–1960* (London: Longman, 1999), pp. 60–1.

10 John R. Gillis, *A World of Their Own Making: Myth, Ritual and the Quest for Family Values* (Cambridge, MA: Harvard University Press, 1996), pp. 30, 112.

11 James Baldwin Brown, *The Home Life: In the Light of its Divine Idea* (London: Smith, Elder, 1866), p. 8.

12 Janet Semple, *Bentham's Prison: A Study of the Panopticon Penitentiary* (Oxford: Clarendon Press, 1993), pp. 117–18.

13 PP 1810–11 (199) III, *Report from the Committee on the Laws Relating to Penitentiary Houses*, p. 15.

14 James Vernon, *Distant Strangers: How Britain Became Modern* (Berkeley: University of California Press, 2014).

15 First published in a single volume by Sherwood, Neely, and Jones, London, 1821.

16 Gregory Dart, ' "Flash Style": Pierce Egan and Literary London 1820–28', *History Workshop Journal*, 51 (Spring 2001), p. 185; David Vincent, *I Hope I Don't Intrude: Privacy and its Dilemmas in Nineteenth-Century Britain* (Oxford: Oxford University Press, 2015), pp. 90–1.

17 Charles Hindley, *The True History of Tom and Jerry* (London: Reeves and Turner, 1888), p. ii.

18 Jane Rendell, *The Pursuit of Pleasure: Gender, Space and Architecture in Regency London* (London: Athlone Press, 2002).

19 'Bernard Blackmantle' [Charles Westmacott], *The English Spy: An Original Work, Characteristic, Satirical, and Humorous. Comprising Scenes and Sketches in Every Rank of Society, being Portraits of the Illustrious, Eminent, Eccentric, and Notorious, Drawn from the Life…The Illustrations Designed by Robert Cruikshank*, 2 vols. (London: Sherwood, Jones, 1825, 1826), vol. 1, p. 3.

20 Ben Wilson, *Decency and Disorder: The Age of Cant 1789–1837* (London: Faber & Faber, 2007), p. 285.

21 Pierce Egan, *Life in London; Or, the Day and Night Scenes of Jerry Hawthorne, Esq. and his Elegant Friend Corinthian Tom, Accompanied by Bob Logic, the Oxonian, in their Rambles and Sprees through the Metropolis* (London: Sherwood, Neely, and Jones, 1821; Cambridge: Cambridge University Press, 2011), pp. 18–19. A 'Cyprian' was slang for a prostitute.

22 Richard Maxwell, 'Dickens's Omniscience', *ELH*, 46, 2 (Summer 1979), pp. 290–313.

23 Richard Altick, *The Shows of London* (Cambridge, MA: Belknap Press, 1978), pp. 141–50.

24 'Blackmantle', *The English Spy*, vol. 2, p. 260.

25 Max Schlesinger, *Saunterings in and about London* (London: Nathaniel Cooke, 1853), pp. 4–5.

26 Christopher Otter, 'Cleansing and Clarifying: Technology and Perception in Nineteenth-Century London', *Journal of British Studies*, 43, 1 (January 2004), pp. 40–64, 157–60.

27 M. J. Daunton, 'Public Place and Private Space: The Victorian City and the Working-Class Household', in *The Pursuit of Urban*

History, edited by Derek Fraser and Anthony Sutcliffe (London: Edward Arnold, 1983), p. 218.

28 M. J. D. Roberts, 'Public and Private in Early Nineteenth-Century London: The Vagrant Act of 1822 and its Enforcement', *Social History*, 13 (October 1988), pp. 273–94.

29 Patrick Joyce, *The Rule of Freedom* (London: Verso, 2003), p. 88.

30 Jo Guldi, *Roads to Power: Britain Invents the Infrastructure State* (Cambridge, MA: Harvard University Press, 2012), p. 20.

31 Vernon, *Distant Strangers*, pp. 30–6.

32 Anne D. Wallace, *Walking, Literature and English Culture: The Origins and Uses of Peripatetic in the Nineteenth Century* (Oxford: Clarendon Press, 1993), p. 166.

33 Morris Marples, *Shanks's Pony: A Study of Walking* (London: J. M. Dent, 1959), pp. 131–46; Rebecca Solnit, *Wanderlust: A History of Walking* (London: Verso, 2001), p. 120.

34 William Hazlitt, 'On Going a Journey', in *The Complete Works of William Hazlitt*, vol. 8, edited by P. P. Howe (London: J. M. Dent, 1931), p. 181.

35 Hazlitt, 'On Going a Journey', p. 185.

36 Marples, *Shanks's Pony*, pp. 144, 181–3.

37 John Lowerson, 'Brothers of the Angle: Coarse Fishing and English Working-Class Culture, 1850–1914', in *Pleasure, Profit, Proselytism: British Culture and Sport at Home and Abroad 1700–1914*, edited by J. A. Mangan (London: Frank Cass, 1988), pp. 105–27.

38 George Rowell, *The Victorian Theatre 1792–1914: A Survey* (2nd edn, Cambridge: Cambridge University Press, 1978), pp. 3–4; Michael R. Booth, *Theatre in the Victorian Age* (Cambridge: Cambridge University Press, 1992), p. 64.

39 'Blackmantle', *The English Spy*, vol. 1, p. 225.

40 Michael R. Booth, 'East End and West End: Class and Audience in Victorian London', *Theatre Research International*, n.s. 2 (1977), p. 103.

41 Vincent, *I Hope I Don't Intrude*, pp. 3–15.

42 Michael R. Booth, 'Early Victorian Farce: Dionysus Domesticated', in *Essays on Nineteenth Century British Theatre*, edited by Kenneth Richards and Peter Thomson (London: Methuen, 1971), p. 96.

43 Jacky Bratton, *New Readings in Theatre History* (Cambridge: Cambridge University Press, 2003), p. 169.

44 Altick, *The Shows of London*, pp. 319–22; Jerry White, *London in the Nineteenth Century: 'A Human Awful Wonder of God'* (London: Jonathan Cape, 2007), pp. 265–6.

45 Mark Girouard, *Life in the English Country House* (Harmondsworth: Penguin, 1980), p. 236.

46 Leonore Davidoff and Catherine Hall, *Family Fortunes: Men and Women of the English Middle Class 1780–1850* (rev. edn, London: Routledge, 2002), pp. 375, 383; Donald J. Olsen, 'Victorian

London: Specialization, Segregation, and Privacy', *Victorian Studies*, 17, 3 (March 1974), p. 272.

47 Bill Bryson, *At Home: A Short History of Private Life* (London: Doubleday, 2010), p. 148.

48 Girouard, *Life in the English Country House*, p. 219.

49 Victoria Posner, *Modernism and the Architecture of Private Life* (New York: Columbia University Press, 2005), p. 63.

50 Robert Kerr, *The Gentleman's House; Or How to Plan English Residences* (London: John Murray, 1864), p. 73.

51 Kerr, *The Gentleman's House*, pp. 74–5.

52 J. J. Stevenson, *House Architecture*, 2 vols. (London: Macmillan, 1880), vol. 2, p. 80.

53 John Burnett, *A Social History of Housing* (London: Methuen,1980), p. 102; Davidoff and Hall, *Family Fortunes*, pp. 360–1.

54 [Samuel Beeton], *The Book of Garden Management* (London: Ward Lock, 1871), pp. 83–4.

55 Stephen Constantine, 'Amateur Gardening and Popular Recreation in the 19th and 20th Centuries', *Journal of Social History*, 14, 3 (Spring 1981), pp. 388–90.

56 Deborah Cohen, *Household Gods: The British and their Possessions* (New Haven: Yale University Press, 2006), p. 34.

57 Edwin Heathcote, *The Meaning of Home* (London: Francis Lincoln, 2012), p. 151.

58 Posner, *Modernism*, pp. 95–6.

59 Michael Anderson, 'The Social Implications of Demographic Change', in *The Cambridge Social History of Britain 1750–1950. 2: People and their Environment*, edited by F. M. L. Thompson (Cambridge: Cambridge University Press, 1990), pp. 56–65.

60 [Thomas Wright], *Some Habits and Customs of the Working Classes: By a Journeyman Engineer* (London: Tinsley Brothers, 1867), p. 273.

61 Gervase Wheeler, *The Choice of a Dwelling: A Practical Handbook of Useful Information on all Points Connected with Hiring, Buying, or Building a House, with its Stables and Garden-Outbuildings* (London: John Murray, 1871), p. 127.

62 On the constant mobility of the London population see White, *London in the Nineteenth Century*, pp. 115–21.

63 Kerr, *The Gentleman's House*, p. 75.

64 Anderson, 'The Social Implications of Demographic Change', p. 58.

65 Martin Daunton, *House and Home in the Victorian City: Working-Class Housing 1850–1914* (London: Edward Arnold, 1983), pp. 280–1; Burnett, *Social History of Housing*, p. 168.

66 Flora Thompson, *Lark Rise to Candleford* (Harmondsworth: Penguin, 1973), p. 156.

67 Thompson, *Lark Rise to Candleford*, p. 21.

68 Frank Prochaska, *Women and Philanthropy in Nineteenth-Century England* (Oxford: Clarendon Press, 1980), pp. 97–137; Jane Lewis, *Women and Social Action in Victorian and Edwardian England*

(Aldershot: Elgar, 1991), pp. 32–46; Robert Whelan, *Helping the Poor: Friendly Visiting, Dole Charities and Dole Queues* (London: Institute for the Study of Civil Society, 2001), pp. 4–20; Margaret E. Brasnett, *Voluntary Social Action* (London: National Council of Social Service, 1969), pp. 4–15.

69　Vincent, *I Hope I Don't Intrude*, pp. 182–5.

70　John Tosh, 'From Keighley to St-Denis: Separation and Intimacy in Victorian Bourgeois Marriage', *History Workshop Journal*, 40 (Autumn 1995), pp. 193–206.

71　Susan Whyman, *The Pen and the People: English Letter-Writers 1660–1800* (Oxford: Oxford University Press, 2009), pp. 3–17 and *passim*.

72　Martin Daunton, *Royal Mail* (London: Athlone Press, 1985), p. 6.

73　Bernhard Siegert, *Relays: Literature as an Epoch of the Postal System* (Stanford: Stanford University Press, 1999), p. 100.

74　PP 1837–38 (658) II, I, *Second Report from the Select Committee on Postage*, Q. 10363.

75　Catherine J. Golden, *Posting It: The Victorian Revolution in Letter Writing* (Gainesville: University Press of Florida, 2009), p. 58.

76　David Vincent, *Literacy and Popular Culture: England 1750–1914* (Cambridge: Cambridge University Press, 1989), pp. 34–8.

77　On the early returns see Duncan Campbell-Smith, *Masters of the Post: The Authorized History of the Royal Mail* (London: Allen Lane, 2011), p. 140; Howard Robinson, *Britain's Post Office* (London: Oxford University Press, 1953), p. 155; Vincent, *Literacy and Popular Culture*, pp. 38–49. On nineteenth-century growth, see *Forty-Seventh Annual Report of the Postmaster General on the Post Office* (London: HMSO, 1901), Appendix A.

78　Frank Staff, *The Picture Postcard and its Origins* (London: Lutterworth Press, 1966), pp. 7–91; N. Alliston, 'Pictorial Post Cards', *Chambers' Journal* (October 1889), pp. 745–8.

79　W. H. Cremer, *St. Valentine's Day and Valentines* (London: W. H. Cremer, 1871), pp. 10–13; Frank Staff, *The Valentine and its Origins* (London: Lutterworth Press, 1969), pp. 25–38.

80　*Household Words*, 1, 1 (30 March 1850), p. 9.

81　Vincent, *I Hope I Don't Intrude*, pp. 196–8.

82　James W. Carey, 'Time, Space, and the Telegraph', in *Communication in History: Technology, Culture, Society*, edited by David Crowley and Paul Heyer (6th edn, Boston: Pearson, 2011), pp. 126–7; James Gleick, *The Information: A History, a Theory, a Flood* (London: Fourth Estate, 2011), p. 147.

83　George Sauer, *The Telegraph in Europe* (Paris: privately published, 1869), p. 145.

84　Jeffrey Kieve, *The Electric Telegraph: A Social and Economic History* (Newton Abbot: David & Charles, 1973), pp. 104–15.

85　*Pace* Tom Standage, *The Victorian Internet: The Remarkable Story of the Telegraph and the Nineteenth Century's Online Pioneers* (New York: Walker, 1998).

86 Richard R. John, *Network Nation* (Cambridge, MA: Harvard University Press, 2010), pp. 6–7.

87 R. Bond, *The Handbook of the Telegraph* (London: Virtue Brothers, 1862), p. 7.

88 David Kahn, *The Codebreakers: The Story of Secret Writing* (New York: Scribner, 1996), p. 189.

89 PP 1898 (383), *Report from the Select Committee on Telephones; Together with the Proceedings of the Committee, Minutes of Evidence, and Appendix*, p. iii.

90 On eavesdropping and party lines in the United States see S. H. Aronson, 'Bell's Electrical Toy: What's the Use? The Sociology of Early Telephone Usage', in *The Social Impact of the Telephone*, edited by Ithiel De Sola Pool (Cambridge, MA: MIT Press, 1977), p. 33; Claude S. Fischer, *America Calling: A Social History of the Telephone to 1940* (Berkeley: University of California Press, 1992), pp. 96, 241; John Brooks, *Telephone: The First Hundred Years* (New York: Harper & Row, 1976), pp. 116–17.

91 C. R. Perry, 'The British Experience 1876–1912: The Impact of the Telephone during the Years of Delay', in De Sola Pool, *The Social Impact of the Telephone*, p. 82.

92 Martyn Lyons, 'Love Letters and Writing Practices: On *Écritures Intimes* in the Nineteenth Century', *Journal of Family History*, 24, 2 (April 1999), p. 234.

93 *Etiquette for Ladies: A Complete Guide to Visiting, Entertaining, and Travelling; with Hints on Courtship, Marriage and Dress* (London: Ward, Lock, and Tyler, 1876), p. 80.

94 Lauren Berlant, 'Intimacy: A Special Issue', in *Intimacy*, edited by Lauren Berlant (Chicago: University of Chicago Press, 2000), p. 6.

95 Patrick Joyce, *The State of Freedom* (Cambridge: Cambridge University Press, 2013), pp. 100–43.

96 William Merrill Decker, *Epistolary Practices: Letter Writing in America before Telecommunications* (Chapel Hill: University of North Carolina Press, 1998), p. 49.

97 Vincent, *I Hope I Don't Intrude*, p. 39.

98 John Poole, *Paul Pry, A Comedy, in Three Acts* (New York: E. M. Murden, 1827), p. 68.

99 Barbara M. Benedict, *Curiosity: A Cultural History of Early Modern Inquiry* (Chicago: University of Chicago Press, 2001), p. 245.

100 Joyce, *The Rule of Freedom*, p. 4.

101 Richard Menke, *Telegraphic Realism: Victorian Fiction and Other Information Systems* (Stanford: Stanford University Press, 2008), pp. 13–20.

102 *Paul Pry: The Inquisitive, Satirical and Whimsical Epitome of Life as It Is*, 1, 3 (4 March 1826), p. 33.

103 Haia Shpayer-Makov, *The Ascent of the Detective: Police Sleuths in Victorian and Edwardian England* (Oxford: Oxford University Press, 2011), pp. 156–74, 187–200.

104   Melanie Tebbutt, 'Women's Talk? Gossip and "Women's Words" in Working-Class Communities, 1880–1939', in *Workers' Worlds: Cultures and Communities in Manchester and Salford 1880–1939*, edited by Andrew Davies and Steven Fielding (Manchester: Manchester University Press, 1992); Patricia Meyer Spacks, *Gossip* (Chicago: University of Chicago Press, 1985), p. 4.

105   Jörg R. Bergmann, *Discreet Indiscretions: The Social Organization of Gossip* (New York: Aldine de Gruyter, 1993), p. 146.

106   Ferdinand D. Schoeman, *Privacy and Social Freedom* (Cambridge: Cambridge University Press, 1992), p. 149.

107   Donald J. Gray, 'Early Victorian Scandalous Journalism: Renton Nicholson's *The Town* (1837–1842)', in *The Victorian Periodical Press: Samplings and Soundings*, edited by Joanne Shattock and Michael Wolff (Leicester: Leicester University Press, 1982), p. 328. For a parallel American market, see Lawrence M. Friedman, *Guarding Life's Dark Secrets: Legal and Social Controls over Reputation, Propriety, and Privacy* (Stanford: Stanford University Press, 2007), p. 93.

108   *Paul Pry: The Inquisitive, Satirical and Whimsical Epitome of Life as It Is*, 39 (11 October 1856), p. 4.

109   *Paul Pry: The Inquisitive, Satirical and Whimsical Epitome of Life as It Is*, 39 (11 October 1856), p. 6.

110   Cited in Angus McLaren, *Sexual Blackmail: A Modern History* (Cambridge, MA: Harvard University Press, 2002), p. 36. See also Peter Alldridge, '"Attempted Murder of the Soul": Blackmail, Privacy and Secrets', *Oxford Journal of Legal Studies*, 13, 3 (Autumn 1993), p. 372.

111   Deborah Cohen, *Family Secrets: Living with Shame from the Victorians to the Present Day* (London: Viking, 2013), p. xiv.

112   Cited in David J. Seipp, 'English Judicial Recognition of a Right to Privacy', *Oxford Journal of Legal Studies*, 3, 3 (Winter 1983), p. 344. Also, Raymond Wacks, *Privacy: A Very Short Introduction* (Oxford: Oxford University Press, 2010), p. 51.

113   Cohen, *Family Secrets*, pp. 38–73.

114   M. J. Cullen, *The Statistical Movement in Early Victorian Britain: The Foundations of Empirical Social Research* (Hassocks: Harvester Press, 1975), p. 137.

115   Oz Frankel, *States of Inquiry: Social Investigations and Print Culture in Nineteenth-Century Britain and the United States* (Baltimore: Johns Hopkins University Press, 2006), p. 1.

116   Theodore M. Porter, *The Rise of Statistical Thinking 1820–1900* (Princeton: Princeton University Press, 1986), pp. 5–11; Daniel R. Headrick, *When Information Came of Age: Technologies of Knowledge in the Age of Reason and Revolution 1700–1850* (Oxford: Oxford University Press, 2000), p. 86.

117   David Vincent, 'The Invention of Counting: The Statistical Measurement of Literacy in Nineteenth-Century England', *Comparative Education*, 50, 3 (August 2014), pp. 266–81.

118 Ian Hacking, *The Taming of Chance* (Cambridge: Cambridge University Press, 1990), p. 2.

119 Mary Poovey, 'Figures of Arithmetic, Figures of Speech: The Discourse of Statistics in the 1830s', *Critical Inquiry*, 19, 2 (Winter 1993), p. 268.

120 Mary Poovey, *A History of the Modern Fact: Problems of Knowledge in the Sciences of Wealth and Society* (Chicago: University of Chicago Press, 1998), pp. 308–18; Lynn Hollen Lees, *The Solidarities of Strangers: The English Poor Laws and the People, 1700–1948* (Cambridge: Cambridge University Press, 1998), pp. 121–3.

121 Cf. Anthony Giddens, *A Contemporary Critique of Historical Materialism. 2: The Nation-State and Violence* (Cambridge: Polity, 1985), p. 46.

122 Edward Higgs, 'The General Register Office and the Tabulation of Data, 1837–1939', in *The History of Mathematical Tables: From Sumer to Spreadsheets*, edited by M. Campbell-Kelly, M. Croarken, R. Flood and E. Robson (Oxford: Oxford University Press, 2003), pp. 209–32.

123 Edward Higgs, *The Information State in England: The Central Collection of Information since 1500* (Basingstoke: Palgrave Macmillan, 2004), pp. 72–4.

124 The Act built on the inspecting work of the National Society for the Prevention of Cruelty to Children (NSPCC), founded in 1884, whose nationwide body of inspectors focused their attention of the households of the poor. Louise Jackson, *Child Sexual Abuse in Victorian England* (London: Routledge, 2000), pp. 51–70.

125 Andrew Barry, Thomas Osborne and Nikolas Rose, 'Introduction', in *Foucault and Political Reason: Liberalism, Neo-Liberalism and Rationalities of Government*, edited by Andrew Barry, Thomas Osborne and Nikolas Rose (London: UCL Press, 1996), p. 8.

126 F. B. Smith, 'British Post Office Espionage, 1844', *Historical Studies*, 14, 54 (1970), pp. 189–203; Robinson, *Britain's Post Office*, pp. 47, 55, 91–2, 1–9; Walter F. Pratt, *Privacy in Britain* (Lewisburg: Bucknell University Press, 1979), pp. 64–6; David Vincent, *The Culture of Secrecy: Britain 1832–1998* (Oxford: Oxford University Press, 1998), pp. 1–9.

127 Torrens McCullagh Torrens, *The Life and Times of the Right Honourable Sir James R. G. Graham, Bart., G.C.B., M.P.*, 2 vols. (London: Saunders, Otley, 1863), vol. 2, p. 348.

128 Torrens, *The Life and Times of the Right Honourable Sir James R. G. Graham*, vol. 2, p. 288.

129 George W. M. Reynolds, *The Mysteries of London*, 2 vols. (London: Geo Vickers, 1845), vol. 1, p. 222.

130 Samuel D. Warren and Louis D. Brandeis, 'The Right to Privacy', *Harvard Law Review*, 4, 5 (1890), p. 196.

131 Warren and Brandeis, 'The Right to Privacy', p. 196.

132 Jeffrey Rosen, *The Unwanted Gaze: The Destruction of Privacy in America* (New York: Vintage, 2001), p. 7.

133 Daniel Solove, 'Conceptualizing Privacy', *California Law Review*, 90, 1 (2002), pp. 1099–102.

134 Warren and Brandeis, 'The Right to Privacy', p. 196.

Chapter 4 Privacy and Modernity 1900–1970

1 Alan Johnson, *This Boy* (2013, London: Corgi, 2014).

2 See, for instance, George Edwards, *From Crow-Scaring to Westminster* (London: Labour Party, 1922); Joseph Arch, *From Ploughtail to Parliament: An Autobiography* (1898; London: Cresset Library, 1986).

3 Johnson, *This Boy*, p. 141.

4 Johnson, *This Boy*, pp. 52–3.

5 Adam Kuper, *Incest & Influence: The Private Life of Bourgeois England* (Cambridge, MA: Harvard University Press, 2009), p. 82.

6 Anne Power, *Hovels to High Rise: State Housing in Europe since 1850* (London: Routledge, 1993), p. 376.

7 The Convention was issued for signatures in November 1950 and came into force in 1953. David J. Seipp, 'English Judicial Recognition of a Right to Privacy', *Oxford Journal of Legal Studies*, 3, 3 (Winter 1983), pp. 350–1.

8 Miles Glendinning and Stefan Muthesius, *Tower Block: Modern Public Housing in England, Scotland, Wales and Northern Ireland* (New Haven: Yale University Press, 1994), p. 1; A. H. Halsey, with Josephine Webb (eds.), *Twentieth-Century British Social Trends* (3rd edn, Basingstoke: Macmillan, 2000), p. 477.

9 Joanna Bourke, *Working-Class Cultures in Britain 1890–1960: Gender, Class and Ethnicity* (London: Routledge, 1994), p. 86.

10 John Burnet, *A Social History of Housing* (London: Methuen,1980), p. 278; Halsey, *Twentieth-Century British Social Trends*, p. 476.

11 Virginia Smith, *Clean: A History of Personal Hygiene and Purity* (Oxford: Oxford University Press, 2007), p. 311.

12 Claire Langhamer, 'The Meanings of Home in Postwar Britain', *Journal of Contemporary History*, 40, 2 (April 2005), p. 350.

13 Jerry White, *London in the Twentieth Century: A City and its People* (London: Viking, 2001), pp. 235–6.

14 Denise Lawrence-Zuñiga, 'Material Conditions of Family Life', in *The History of the European Family. 3: Family Life in the Twentieth Century*, edited by David I. Kertzer and Marzio Barbagli (New Haven: Yale University Press, 2003), p. 22.

15 Françoise Barret-Ducrocq, *Love in the Time of Queen Victoria* (Harmondsworth: Penguin, 1992), p. 24.

16 Witold Rybczynski, *Home: A Short History of an Idea* (New York: Viking, 1986), p. 24.

17 Maud Pember Reeves, *Round About a Pound a Week* (1913; London: Virago, 1979), p. 46. Also, Kathleen Dayus, *Her People*

(London: Virago, 1982), p. 3; Alison Light, *Common People: The History of an English Family* (London: Fig Tree, 2014), p. 240.

18 Margery Spring Rice, *Working-Class Wives: Their Health and Conditions* (1939; 2nd edn, London: Virago, 1981), p. 129.

19 Margaret Stacey, *Tradition and Change: A Study of Banbury* (London: Oxford University Press, 1960), p. 92.

20 Stacey, *Tradition and Change*, pp. 93–4.

21 Spring Rice, *Working-Class Wives*, p. 15.

22 Spring Rice, *Working-Class Wives*, p. 16.

23 Edwin Heathcote, *The Meaning of Home* (London: Francis Lincoln, 2012), p. 25.

24 Martha Loane, *From Their Point of View* (London: Edward Arnold, 1908), p. 34.

25 Dayus, *Her People*, p. 38.

26 Mass Observation, *People and Homes* (TS, 1943), p. 370.

27 Alan Johnson, *Please, Mister Postman: A Memoir* (London: Transworld, 2014), p. 59.

28 Mark Abrams, 'The Home-Centred Society', *Listener*, 1600 (26 November 1959), p. 915.

29 Michael Young and Peter Willmott, *Family and Kinship in East London* (Harmondsworth: Penguin, 1962), p. 35.

30 Young and Willmott, *Family and Kinship in East London*, p. 154.

31 Young and Willmott, *Family and Kinship in East London*, pp. 163–4.

32 On the very variable patterns of stability and mobility across 'traditional' working-class London, see White, *London in the Twentieth Century*, pp. 119–24.

33 Madeline Kerr, *The People of Ship Street* (London: Routledge and Kegan Paul, 1958), p. 23.

34 Andrew Seth and Geoffrey Randall, *The Grocers: The Rise and Rise of the Supermarket Chains* (2nd edn, London: Kogan Page, 2001), p. 18; Avram Taylor, *Working Class Credit and Community since 1918* (Basingstoke: Palgrave Macmillan, 2002), p. 73.

35 Charles Vereker and John Barron Mays, *Urban Redevelopment and Social Change* (Liverpool: Liverpool University Press, 1961), p. 74; Jerry White, *The Worst Street in North London: Campbell Bunk, Islington, Between the Wars* (London: Routledge and Kegan Paul, 1986), p. 78. On the long tradition of corner shops and credit, see, Michael J. Winstanley, *The Shopkeeper's World, 1830–1914* (Manchester: Manchester University Press, 1983), pp. 55–6; David Alexander, *Retailing in England during the Industrial Revolution* (London: Athlone Press, 1970), pp. 175–85.

36 Robert Roberts, *A Ragged Schooling* (1976; London: Fontana, 1978), p. 22.

37 Robert Roberts, *The Classic Slum* (Manchester: Manchester University Press, 1971), pp. 12, 60–1.

38 Selina Todd, *The People: The Rise and Fall of the Working Class 1910–2010* (London: John Murray, 2014), p. 203.

39 Kerr, *The People of Ship Street*, p. 95.

40   David Vincent, *Poor Citizens: The State and the Poor in Twentieth-Century Britain* (London: Longman, 1991), p. 186.

41   Margot C. Finn, *The Character of Credit: Personal Debt in English Culture 1740–1914* (Cambridge: Cambridge University Press, 2003), pp. 291–4; Josh Lauer, 'The Good Consumer: Credit Reporting and the Invention of Financial Identity in the United States, 1840–1940', *Enterprise & Society*, 11, 4 (December 2010), pp. 688–9. The Society for the Protection of Trade against Swindlers and Sharpers was founded in London as early as 1776, but a provincial network did not evolve until the 1820s.

42   *Manchester Guardian Society for the Protection of Trade, 1826–1926* (Manchester: Manchester Guardian Society, 1926), p. 4.

43   Finn, *The Character of Credit*, pp. 300–1.

44   C. McNeil Greig, *The Growth of Credit Information: A History of UAPT-Infolink plc* (Oxford: Blackwell, 1992), p. 109.

45   James B. Rule, *Private Lives and Public Surveillance* (London: Allen Lane, 1973), pp. 175–222.

46   Taylor, *Working Class Credit and Community*, pp. 108–42; Edward Higgs, *Identifying the English: A History of Personal Identification, 1500 to the Present* (London: Continuum, 2011), pp. 168–9.

47   Bourke, *Working-Class Cultures in Britain 1890–1960*, p. 86.

48   Judy Giles, *Women, Identity and Private Life in Britain, 1900–50* (Houndmills, Basingstoke: Macmillan, 1995), p. 68. On the enthusiasm of working-class tenants for houses with gardens, see, Mass Observation, *People and Homes*, p. 11.

49   Glendinning and Muthesius, *Tower Block*, p. 2.

50   Stephen Constantine, 'Amateur Gardening and Popular Recreation in the 19th and 20th Centuries', *Journal of Social History*, 14, 3 (Spring 1981), p. 387.

51   Mark Clapson, *Working-Class Suburb: Social Change on an English Council Estate, 1930–2010* (Manchester: Manchester University Press, 2012), pp. 184–7.

52   Geoffrey Gorer, *Exploring English Character* (London: Cresset Press, 1955), p. 43.

53   Margaret Willes, *The Gardens of the British Working Class* (New Haven: Yale University Press, 2014), p. 348.

54   Willes, *Gardens of the British Working Class*, p. 297.

55   Halsey, *Twentieth-Century British Social Trends*, p. 442.

56   Sean O'Connell, *The Car and British Society: Class, Gender and Motoring, 1896–1939* (Manchester: Manchester University Press, 1998), p. 87.

57   Mark Clapson, *Invincible Green Suburbs, Brave New Towns: Social Change and Urban Dispersal in Postwar England* (Manchester: Manchester University Press, 1998), p. 161.

58   Johnson, *Please, Mister Postman*, p. 124.

59   Abrams, 'The Home-Centred Society', p. 915.

60 Asa Briggs, *The BBC: The First Fifty Years* (Oxford: Oxford University Press, 1985), p. 278.

61 James Curran and Jean Seaton, *Power without Responsibility: The Press, Broadcasting and New Media in Britain* (6th edn, London: Routledge, 2003), p. 172; Clapson, *Working-Class Suburb*, p. 184.

62 Andrew Davies, 'Cinema and Broadcasting', in *20th Century Britain: Economic, Social and Cultural Change*, edited by Paul Johnson (London: Longman, 1994), pp. 263–80.

63 White, *The Worst Street in North London*, p. 83.

64 *Report of the Committee on Broadcasting, 1960* [Pilkington] Cmnd 1763 (London: HMSO, 1962), p. 21.

65 *Report of the Committee on Broadcasting, 1960*, p. 15.

66 Claire Langhamer, *The English in Love: The Intimate Story of an Emotional Revolution* (Oxford: Oxford University Press, 2013), p. 111.

67 B. R. Mitchell, *European Historical Statistics 1750–1975* (2nd edn, London: Macmillan, 1981), p. 697; Halsey, *Twentieth-Century British Social Trends*, pp. 444–5.

68 Johnson, *Please, Mister Postman*, p. 15.

69 Leonore Davidoff, Megan Doolittle, Janet Fink and Katherine Holden, *The Family Story: Blood, Contract and Intimacy 1830–1960* (London: Longman, 1999), p. 219.

70 Claude S. Fischer, *America Calling: A Social History of the Telephone to 1940* (Berkeley: University of California Press, 1992), pp. 47, 226.

71 Young and Willmott, *Family and Kinship in East London*, p. 159.

72 Carolyn Marvin, *When Old Technologies Were New: Thinking about Electric Communications in the Late Nineteenth Century* (Oxford: Oxford University Press, 1988), p. 64.

73 Ben B. Lindsey and Wainwright Evans, *The Companionate Marriage* (New York: Brentano, 1928).

74 O'Connell, *The Car and British Society*, p. 43

75 Martin Francis, 'The Domestication of the Male? Recent Research on Nineteenth- and Twentieth-Century British Masculinity', *Historical Journal*, 45, 3 (September 2002), pp. 645–6.

76 Johnson, *Please, Mister Postman*, p. 115. Andy Capp is a comic-strip character, created in 1957 and still carried by the *Daily Mirror* and *Sunday Mirror*. He neither has a job nor does anything around the house. In his later manifestations he and his long-suffering wife Flo are seeing a marriage guidance counsellor (see pp. 97, 113).

77 Davidoff et al., *The Family Story*, p. 216.

78 Langhamer, *The English in Love*, p. 4; David Kynaston, *Family Britain 1951–57* (London: Bloomsbury, 2009), pp. 55–9.

79 Adrian Bingham, *Family Newspapers? Sex, Private Life, and the British Popular Press 1918–1978* (Oxford: Oxford University Press, 2009).

80 Deborah Cohen, *Family Secrets: Living with Shame from the Victorians to the Present Day* (London: Viking, 2013), p. 192.

81 Maroula Joannou, 'Eyles, (Margaret) Leonora (1889–1960)', *Oxford Dictionary of National Biography*, Oxford University Press, 2004,

online edn, January 2012, http://www.oxforddnb.com/view/article/56952; Cohen, *Family Secrets*, pp. 194–6.

82 Mass Observation, 'Some Psychological Factors in Home-Building', *File Report 1919* (March 1943).

83 Cited in Kynaston, *Family Britain*, p. 530.

84 Johnson, *This Boy*, pp. 130–1.

85 Marie Stopes, *Married Love*, edited and introduced by Ross McKibbin (1918; Oxford: Oxford University Press, 2004), p. 22.

86 Aylmer Maude, *Marie Stopes: Her Work and Play* (London: Peter Davies, 1933), p. 137.

87 Marie Stopes (ed.), *Mother England: A Contemporary History Self-Written by Those Who Have Had No Historian* (London: J. Bale, 1929), p. 9. See also Ruth Hall's anthology of letters to Marie Stopes: *Dear Dr Stopes: Sex in the 1920s* (London: Deutsch, 1978).

88 David Vincent, *The Culture of Secrecy: Britain 1832–1998* (Oxford: Oxford University Press, 1998), pp. 158–66.

89 Kerr, *The People of Ship Street*, pp. 78–80; Diana Gittins, 'Married Life and Birth Control Between the Wars', *Oral History*, 3, 2 (1975), pp. 54–6; Elizabeth Roberts, *A Woman's Place: An Oral History of Working-Class Women 1890–1940* (Oxford: Blackwell, 1984), pp. 93–100; Davidoff et al., *The Family Story*, pp. 247–9; Bourke, *Working-Class Cultures in Britain 1890–1960*, pp. 32–41; Kynaston, *Family Britain*, pp. 551–2.

90 J. R. England, 'Little Kinsey: An Outline of Sex Attitudes in Britain', *Public Opinion Quarterly*, 13, 4 (1949–50), p. 598.

91 Simon Szreter and Kate Fisher, *Sex Before the Sexual Revolution: Intimate Life in England 1918–1963* (Cambridge: Cambridge University Press, 2010), p. 362.

92 Until the later 1920s, most cars were open to the elements.

93 Edward Higgs, *The Information State in England: The Central Collection of Information since 1500* (Basingstoke: Palgrave Macmillan, 2004), p. 112.

94 Martha Loane, *An Englishman's Castle* (London: Edward Arnold, 1909), p. 1.

95 Loane, *An Englishman's Castle*, pp. 1–2.

96 Lynn Hollen Lees, *The Solidarities of Strangers: The English Poor Laws and the People, 1700–1948* (Cambridge: Cambridge University Press, 1998), pp. 304–5.

97 Bourke, *Working-Class Cultures in Britain 1890–1960*, p. 14; Giles, *Women, Identity and Private Life in Britain*, pp. 66, 100.

98 For a positive estimation of the inspectors' role in an interwar Liverpool slum see Vereker and Mays, *Urban Redevelopment and Social Change*, p. 58.

99 Higgs, *Identifying the English*, pp. 153–6.

100 Sid Elias, *A Practical Guide to the Unemployment Acts* (London: National Unemployed Workers' Movement, [1931?]), pp. 1–14; Vincent, *Poor Citizens*, p. 75.

101 Victor George, *Social Security: Beveridge and After* (London: Routledge and Kegan Paul, 1968), p. 97.
102 Rule, *Private Lives and Public Surveillance*, pp. 122–74.
103 Elizabeth Bott, *Family and Social Network* (London: Tavistock, 1957), p. 100.
104 David Hooper, *Official Secrets: The Use and Abuse of the Act* (London: Secker & Warburg, 1987), pp. 29–31; Richard Thurlow, *The Secret State: British Internal Security in the Twentieth Century* (Oxford: Blackwell, 1995), pp. 37–42; Vincent, *The Culture of Secrecy*, pp. 116–28.
105 Bernard Porter, *The Origins of the Vigilant State* (London: Weidenfeld and Nicolson, 1987), pp. 67–78; Jane Morgan, *Conflict and Order: The Police and Labour Disputes in England and Wales, 1900–1939* (Oxford: Clarendon, 1987), pp. 93–4, 111.
106 *Report of the Committee of Privy Councillors Appointed to Inquire into the Interception of Communications* [Birkett], Cmnd 283 (1957), pp. 7, 29.
107 *Report of the Committee of Privy Councillors* (1957), p. 13.
108 *Report of the Committee of Privy Councillors* (1957), p. 14.
109 *Report of the Committee of Privy Councillors* (1957), p. 27.
110 Intelligence and Security Committee of Parliament, *Privacy and Security: A Modern and Transparent Legal Framework*, HC 1075 (12 March 2015), p. 11.
111 *Report of the Committee of Privy Councillors* (1957), p. 6.
112 Discussed in Deborah Nelson, *Pursuing Privacy in Cold War America* (New York: Columbia University Press, 2002), p. 9; Paul Ginsborg, *Family Politics: Domestic Life, Devastation and Survival 1900–1950* (New Haven and London: Yale University Press, 2014), p. 436.
113 George Orwell, *1984* (1949; Harmondsworth: Penguin, 1954), pp. 109–10.
114 Orwell, *1984*, p. 165.
115 Orwell, *1984*, p. 192.
116 Orlando Figes, *The Whisperers: Private Life in Stalin's Russia* (London: Allen Lane, 2007), pp. 2–10, 160; Oleg Kharkhordin, 'Reveal and Dissimulate: A Genealogy of Private Life in Soviet Russia', in *Public and Private in Thought and Practice: Perspectives on a Grand Dichotomy*, edited by Jeff Weintraub and Krishan Kumar (Chicago: University of Chicago Press, 1997), p. 353.
117 Paul Betts, *Within Walls: Private Life in the German Democratic Republic* (Oxford: Oxford University Press, 2010), p. 3.
118 Sheila Fitzpatrick, *Everyday Stalinism. Ordinary Life in Extraordinary Times: Soviet Russia in the 1930s* (Oxford: Oxford University Press, 1999), p. 165.
119 Roberts, *A Woman's Place*, p. 199; Rule, *Private Lives and Public Surveillance*, p. 156.

120 Robert Gellately, 'Denunciations in Twentieth-Century Germany: Aspects of Self-Policing in the Third Reich and the German Democratic Republic', *Journal of Modern History*, 68, 4 (December 1996), p. 931.
121 Mary Fulbrook, *The People's State: East German Society from Hitler to Honecker* (New Haven: Yale University Press, 2005), pp. 66–7.
122 Jonathan Steele, *Socialism with a German Face* (London: Jonathan Cape, 1977), p. 153.
123 Stephen Lovell, *Summerfolk: A History of the Dacha, 1710–2000* (Ithaca: Cornell University Press, 2003), pp. 122–52; Lawrence-Zuñiga, 'Material Conditions of Family Life', p. 46.
124 Betts, *Within Walls*, p. 14.
125 Gary Bruce, *The Firm: The Inside Story of the Stasi* (Oxford: Oxford University Press, 2010), p. 155.
126 Betts, *Within Walls*, p. 4.
127 Ginsborg, *Family Politics*, p. 443.
128 Orwell, *1984*, p. 53.

Chapter 5 Privacy and the Digital Age 1970–2015

1 Myron Brenton, *The Privacy Invaders* (New York: Coward-McCann, 1964).
2 Vance Packard, *The Naked Society* (London: Longmans, 1964), pp. 15, 43.
3 David J. Seipp, 'English Judicial Recognition of a Right to Privacy', *Oxford Journal of Legal Studies*, 3, 3 (Winter 1983), pp. 346–7.
4 Walter F. Pratt, *Privacy in Britain* (Lewisburg: Bucknell University Press, 1979), p. 5.
5 Jerry M. Rosenberg, *The Death of Privacy* (New York: Random House, 1969), p. 4.
6 Malcolm Warner and Michael Stone, *The Data Bank Society: Organizations, Computers and Social Freedom* (London: George Allen & Unwin, 1970), p. 225. See also P. Juvigny, 'Modern Scientific and Technological Developments and their Consequences on the Protection of the Right to Respect a Person's Private and Family Life, his Home and Communications', in *Privacy and Human Rights*, edited by A. H. Robertson (Manchester: Manchester University Press, 1973), p. 138.
7 Arthur R. Miller, *The Assault on Privacy: Computers, Data Banks, and Dossiers* (Ann Arbor: University of Michigan Press, 1971), p. 3.
8 Paul E. Ceruzzi, *A History of Modern Computing* (Cambridge, MA: MIT Press, 1998), pp. 14–15; Fritz Machlup, *The Production and Distribution of Knowledge in the United States* (Princeton: Princeton University Press, 1962), p. 319; Pratt, *Privacy in Britain*, pp. 154–6.
9 David Lyon, *The Electronic Eye: The Rise of the Surveillance Society* (Cambridge: Polity, 1994), p. 170.
10 John Naughton, *From Gutenberg to Zuckerberg: What You Really Need to Know about the Internet* (London: Quercus, 2012), pp. 45, 58.

11 For a critical survey of the revived death-of-privacy literature in the 1990s see Amitai Etzioni, *The Limits of Privacy* (New York: Basic Books, 1999), pp. 5–7.

12 On the intensity of the debate at the turn of the century, see Daniel J. Solove, *Understanding Privacy* (Cambridge, MA: Harvard University Press, 2008), p. 5; Patricia Meyer Spacks, *Privacy: Concealing the Eighteenth-Century Self* (Chicago: University of Chicago Press, 2003), p. 1.

13 Respectively by Reg Whittaker (New York: New Press, 1999); Simson Garfinkel (Sebastopol, CA: O'Reilly, 2000); Kieron O'Hara and Nigel Shadbolt (Oxford: Oneworld, 2008).

14 Michael Froomkin, 'The Death of Privacy?', *Stanford Law Review*, 52, 5 (May 2000), p. 1461.

15 David H. Holtzman, *Privacy Lost: How Technology Is Endangering Your Privacy* (San Francisco: Jossey-Bass, 2006), p. xix. Also, Charles J. Sykes, *The End of Privacy* (New York: St Martin's Press, 1999), pp. 4–5.

16 Jacob Morgan, 'Privacy is Completely and Utterly Dead, and We Killed It', Forbes.com (19 August 2014), p. 2. The most recent substantive study of the pervasive threat to privacy is Julia Angwin, *Dragnet Nation: A Quest for Privacy, Security, and Freedom in a World of Relentless Surveillance* (New York: St Martin's Press, 2015), pp. 1–20 and *passim*.

17 Malcolm Bradbury, *The History Man* (1975; London: Picador, 2012), p. 78.

18 Edmund Leach, *A Runaway World?* (London: British Broadcasting Corporation, 1968), p. 44.

19 Lily Pincus and Christopher Dare, *Secrets in the Family* (London: Faber & Faber, 1978), p. 9.

20 On Mark Zuckerberg's alleged utterance of this claim, see Connie Davis Powell, ' "You Already Have Zero Privacy. Get Over It!" Would Warren and Brandeis Argue for Privacy for Social Networking?', *Pace Law Review*, 31, 1 (Winter 2011), pp. 146–81. See also Scott McNealy's much-quoted remark of 1999, 'You have zero privacy anyway. Get over it.'

21 Dave Eggers, *The Circle* (London: Hamish Hamilton, 2013), p. 303.

22 Deborah Cohen, *Family Secrets: Living with Shame from the Victorians to the Present Day* (London: Viking, 2013), p. 235.

23 *Report of the Committee on Privacy* [Younger], Cmnd 5012 (London: HMSO, 1972), p. 10, para. 38. For a discussion of this focus in Younger see Pratt, *Privacy in Britain*, pp. 194–5; Seipp, 'English Judicial Recognition of a Right to Privacy', pp. 329–30.

24 *Report of the Committee on Privacy* (1972), p. 11, para. 22.

25 *Report of the Committee on Privacy* (1972), p. 118, para. 392.

26 *Report of the Committee on Privacy* (1972), p. 16, para. 54.

27 Christena Nippert-Eng, *Islands of Privacy* (Chicago: University of Chicago Press, 2010), p. 284.

28 *Report of the Committee on Privacy* (1972), p. 23, para. 74.
29 Alan F. Westin, 'Some Forecasts Based on US Experience', in *Privacy, Computers and You*, edited by B. C. Rowe (Manchester: National Computing Centre, 1972), p. 54.
30 See above, chapter 3, pp. 58, 77.
31 Amongst the many summaries, see Raymond Wacks, *Privacy: A Very Short Introduction* (Oxford: Oxford University Press, 2010), pp. 57–8.
32 On this emphasis see Judith W. DeCew, *In Pursuit of Privacy: Law, Ethics and the Rise of Technology* (Ithaca: Cornell University Press, 1997), p. 14.
33 Westin, 'Some Forecasts Based on US Experience', p. 54.
34 Martin Campbell-Kelly, 'Historical Reflections: Victorian Data Processing', *Communications of the ACM*, 53, 10 (2010), pp. 19–21.
35 Warner and Stone, *The Data Bank Society*, p. 21.
36 On the 1844 privacy panic, see David Vincent, *I Hope I Don't Intrude: Privacy and its Dilemmas in Nineteenth-Century Britain* (Oxford: Oxford University Press, 2015), pp. 222–3.
37 Claire Langhamer, *The English in Love: The Intimate Story of an Emotional Revolution* (Oxford: Oxford University Press, 2013), p. 4.
38 Göran Therborn, *Between Sex and Power: Family in the World, 1900–2000* (London: Routledge, 2004), p. 163.
39 Office for National Statistics, *Social Trends, No. 41, 2011 Edition* (Newport: National Statistics, February 2011), p. 4.
40 Office for National Statistics, *Social Trends, No. 41* (2011), p. 3.
41 Department for Communities and Local Government, *English Housing Survey: Headline Report* (London: Department for Communities and Local Government, February 2014), p. 70.
42 Department for Communities and Local Government, *English Housing Survey* (February 2014), pp. 28–9.
43 Department for Communities and Local Government, *English Housing Survey* (February 2014), p. 33.
44 Office for National Statistics, *Social Trends 30, 2000 Edition* (London: Stationery Office, 2000), pp. 173–4.
45 Paul Barker, *The Freedoms of Suburbia* (London: Francis Lincoln, 2009), pp. 26–7.
46 *Report of the Committee on Privacy* (1972), p. 26, para. 78.
47 Office for National Statistics, *Social Trends, No. 41* (2011), 'Lifestyles and Social Participation', pp. 3–4.
48 Office for National Statistics, *Social Trends, No. 40, 2010 Edition* (Newport: National Statistics, 2010), p. 170.
49 Office for National Statistics, *Social Trends, No. 41* (2011), 'Transport', p. 10.
50 Kate Fox, *Watching the English: The Hidden Rules of English Behaviour* (London: Hodder, 2004), p. 184.
51 Erving Goffman, *Behaviour in Public Places* (New York: Free Press of Glencoe, 1963), p. 84.

52 John R. Gillis, *A World of Their Own Making: Myth, Ritual and the Quest for Family Values* (Cambridge, MA: Harvard University Press, 1996), pp. 225–8.
53 Office for National Statistics, *Families and Households, 2013* (Newport: National Statistics, 2013), pp. 9–10, 12–13.
54 Langhamer, *The English in Love*, p. 7.
55 Angus McLaren, *Twentieth-Century Sexuality* (Oxford: Blackwell, 1999), p. 174.
56 Office for National Statistics, *Families and Households, 2013*, p. 3.
57 Office for National Statistics, *Families and Households, 2014* (Newport: National Statistics, 2015), p. 4. Data on the number of married same-sex families was not available at the time of writing.
58 Therborn, *Between Sex and Power*, pp. 196–8.
59 Jane Lewis, *The End of Marriage? Individualism and Intimate Relations* (Cheltenham: Edward Elgar, 2001), p. 89.
60 Gillis, *A World of Their Own Making*, p. 238.
61 Anthony Giddens, *The Transformation of Intimacy: Sexuality, Love and Eroticism in Modern Societies* (Cambridge: Polity, 1992), p. 40.
62 Giddens, *The Transformation of Intimacy*, p. 194.
63 Department for Communities and Local Government, *English Housing Survey* (February 2014), p. 33.
64 See the brilliant analysis of front-door etiquette in Nippert-Eng, *Islands of Privacy*, pp. 212–26.
65 Edwin Heathcote, *The Meaning of Home* (London: Frances Lincoln, 2012), p. 21.
66 YouGov, *YouGov/Co-operatives UK Survey Results* (2010), p. 1. http://cdn.yougov.com/today_uk_import/YG-Archives-Life-Coop-Neighbours-130510.pdf.
67 YouGov, *YouGov/Co-operatives UK Survey Results* (2010), pp. 1, 7.
68 YouGov, *Good Neighbours?* (2013), p. 7. http://cdn.yougov.com/cumulus_uploads/document/jwwdrlqsas/YG-Archive-neighbours-results-130513.pdf.
69 Nigel Parton, *Safeguarding Childhood: Early Intervention and Surveillance in a Late Modern Society* (London: Palgrave Macmillan, 2006), pp. 38–9.
70 Catharine A. MacKinnon, *Feminism Unmodified: Discourses on Life and Law* (Cambridge, MA: Harvard University Press, 1987), p. 100.
71 Patricia Boling, *Privacy and the Politics of Intimate Life* (Ithaca: Cornell University Press, 1996), pp. 4–14; Ruth Gavison, 'Feminism and the Public/Private Distinction', *Stanford Law Review*, 45, 1 (November 1992), pp. 1–45.
72 McLaren, *Twentieth-Century Sexuality*, p. 218.
73 *OECD Guidelines on the Protection of Privacy and Transborder Flows of Personal Data* (1980), p. 5. http://www.oecd.org/sti/ieconomy/oecdguidelinesontheprotectionofprivacyandtransborderflowsofpersonaldata.htm.

74 David Feldman, 'Privacy-Related Rights and Their Social Value', in *Privacy and Loyalty*, edited by Peter Birks (Oxford: Clarendon Press, 1997), p. 29.

75 Wacks, *Privacy*, pp. 63–4.

76 Mark Mazower, *Governing the World: The History of an Idea* (London: Allen Lane, 2012), pp. 101–2.

77 Respectively Articles 6 and 10.

78 Article 10.

79 James Michael, *Privacy and Human Rights: An International and Comparative Study, with Special Reference to Developments in Information Technology* (Aldershot: UNESCO, 1994), p. 122.

80 Daniel J. Solove, 'Privacy and Power: Computer Databases and Metaphors for Information Privacy', *Stanford Law Review*, 53, 6 (July 2001), p. 1441.

81 James B. Rule, 'Introduction', in *Global Privacy Protection: The First Generation*, edited by James B. Rule and Graham Greenleaf (Cheltenham: Edward Elgar, 2008), p. 4.

82 The project was eventually adopted by the United Nations. See 'Guidelines Concerning Computerized Personal Data Files' (adopted by the General Assembly 14 December 1990).

83 See, for instance, the 'Data Protection Principles' in the 1984 UK Data Protection Act, p. 35. *Data Protection Act 1984. Chapter 35.* http://www.legislation.gov.uk/ukpga/1984/35/pdfs/ukpga_10840035_en.pdf. On the general programme of reform, see David H. Flaherty, *Protecting Privacy in Two-Way Electronic Services* (London: Mansell, 1985), p. 9.

84 On the balance between convergence and variation, see Colin J. Bennett, *Regulating Privacy: Data Protection and Public Policy in Europe and the United States* (Ithaca: Cornell University Press, 1992), p. 222. On the UK's reluctance to legislate, see Michael, *Privacy and Human Rights*, pp. 100–8.

85 Raymond Wacks, 'Privacy in Cyberspace: Personal Information, Free Speech, and the Internet', in Birks, *Privacy and Loyalty*, p. 109.

86 Council of Europe, *Convention for the Protection of Individuals with Regard to Automatic Processing of Personal Data* (Strasbourg 1981), Preamble. http://conventions.coe.int/Treaty/en/Treaties/Html/108.htm.

87 Lee A. Bygrave, 'International Agreements to Protect Personal Data', in Rule and Greenleaf, *Global Privacy Protection*, pp. 21, 27.

88 *OECD Guidelines* (1980), Preface.

89 Froomkin, 'The Death of Privacy?', p. 1483.

90 Jon L. Mills, *Privacy: The Lost Right* (New York: Oxford University Press, 2008), pp. 226–7.

91 For an account of this event, see Christopher Moran, *Classified: Secrecy and the State in Modern Britain* (Cambridge: Cambridge University Press, 2013), pp. 136–76.

92 For surveys of the Snowden affair, see Luke Harding, *The Snowden Files* (London: Guardian Books and Faber & Faber, 2014); Glenn Greenwald, *No Place to Hide: Edward Snowden, the NSA and the Surveillance State* (London: Hamish Hamilton, 2014).

93 See above, p. 52.

94 Cited in Harding, *The Snowden Files*, p. 12.

95 Laura Poitras (dir.), *Citizenfour* (2014).

96 Intelligence and Security Committee of Parliament, *Privacy and Security: A Modern and Transparent Legal Framework*, HC 1075 (12 March 2015), p. 10.

97 David Anderson, *A Question of Trust: Report of the Investigatory Powers Review* (London: HMSO, June 2015), p. 8.

98 For a fuller exploration of this point see Vincent, *I Hope I Don't Intrude*, p. 245.

99 David H. Flaherty, 'Visions of Privacy: Past, Present, and Future', in *Visions of Privacy: Policy Choices for the Digital Age*, edited by Colin J. Bennett and Rebecca Grant (Toronto: University of Toronto Press, 1999), p. 23.

100 Clive Norris, 'There's No Success Like Failure and Failure's No Success At All: Some Critical Reflections on the Global Growth of CCTV Surveillance', in *Eyes Everywhere: The Global Growth of Camera Surveillance*, edited by Aaron Doyle, Randy Lippert and David Lyon (London: Routledge, 2012), p. 25.

101 Benjamin J. Goold, *CCTV and Policing: Public Area Surveillance and Police Practices in Britain* (Oxford: Oxford University Press, 2004), pp. 1–2, 108–9, 116–20.

102 Kelly A. Gates, *Our Biometric Future: Facial Recognition Technology and the Culture of Surveillance* (New York: New York University Press, 2011), p. 198.

103 Howard Rheingold, *The Virtual Community: Homesteading on the Electronic Frontier* (Cambridge, MA: MIT Press, 2000), pp. 315–16.

104 Adam Fox and Daniel Woolf, 'Introduction', in *The Spoken Word: Oral Culture in Britain 1500–1850*, edited by Adam Fox and Daniel Woolf (Manchester: Manchester University Press, 2002), pp. 8, 21.

105 Naughton, *From Gutenberg to Zuckerberg*, p. 138. See, for instance, Anderson and Tracey's study of how the early embrace of the internet added to rather than displaced existing patterns of communication: Ben Anderson and Karina Tracey, 'Digital Living: The Impact (or Otherwise) of the Internet on Everyday British Life', in *The Internet in Everyday Life*, edited by Barry Wellman and Caroline Haythornthwaite (Oxford: Blackwell, 2002), p. 149.

106 Office for National Statistics, *Social Trends, No. 41* (2011), 'Lifestyles and Social Participation', p. 3. The data was generated in response to the question put to adults of 18 and over, 'How often ... do you contact a close friend, relative or someone else close to you (apart from your spouse or partner) about how you're feeling or just to catch up?'

107 Robert S. Laufer and Maxine Wolfe, 'Privacy as a Concept and a Social Issue: A Multidimensional Development Theory', *Journal of Social Issues*, 33, 3 (1977), p. 37; Adam D. Moore, 'Privacy: Its Meaning and Value', *American Philosophical Quarterly*, 40, 3 (July 2003), pp. 222–3.

108 Mary Madden, Amanda Lenhart, Sandra Cortesi, Urs Gasser, Maeve Duggan, Aaron Smith and Meredith Beaton, *Teens, Social Media and Privacy* (Washington, DC: Pew Research Centre, 2013), p. 8.

109 See above, p. 49.

110 James B. Rule, *Private Lives and Public Surveillance* (London: Allen Lane, 1973), p. 336.

111 Dana Boyd, *It's Complicated: The Social Lives of Networked Teens* (New Haven: Yale University Press, 2014), p. 56.

112 Sonia Livingstone, 'Taking Risky Opportunities in Youthful Content Creation: Teenagers' Use of Social Networking Sites for Intimacy, Privacy and Self Expression', *New Media and Society*, 10, 3 (2008), p. 404.

113 Boyd, *It's Complicated*, p. 69.

114 Madden et al., *Teens, Social Media and Privacy*, p. 9.

115 Reported in Carmen Fishwick and Hannah Freeman, 'What Teenagers Think About Facebook's New Privacy Controls', *Guardian*, 25 October 2013.

116 Niklas Luhmann, *Introduction to Systems Theory* (Cambridge: Polity, 2013), pp. 212–32.

117 Daniel J. Solove, *The Future of Reputation: Gossip, Rumor, and Privacy on the Internet* (New Haven: Yale University Press, 2007), p. 165.

118 See, for instance, the argument in Barry Schwartz, 'The Social Psychology of Privacy', *American Journal of Sociology*, 75, 6 (May 1968), pp. 741–52.

119 Helen Nissenbaum, *Privacy in Context: Technology, Policy, and the Integrity of Social Life* (Stanford: Stanford University Press, 2010), p. 129 and *passim*.

120 Whether the term 'consent' has meaning any more in such transactions is addressed by James B. Rule, *Privacy in Peril* (Oxford: Oxford University Press, 2007), pp. 170–83. On the widespread sense that users lack sufficient control in the transactions, see 'Attitudes on Data Protection and Electronic Identity in the European Union', *Special Eurobarometer 359* (Brussels: European Commission, June 2011), p. 2; Mary Madden, *Public Perceptions of Privacy and Security in the Post-Snowden Era* (Washington, DC: Pew Research Centre, November 2014), Summary; ComRes/Big Brother Watch, *UK Public Research: Online Privacy* (London: Big Brother Watch, October 2013), p. 3.

121 Priscilla M. Regan, *Legislating Privacy* (Chapel Hill: University of North Carolina Press, 1995), p. 212.

122 Benjamin J. Goold, 'Surveillance and the Political Value of Privacy', *Amsterdam Law Forum*, 4 (2009), p. 4.

123 Solove, *Understanding Privacy*, p. 91.
124 Jeffrey Rosen, *The Unwanted Gaze: The Destruction of Privacy in America* (New York: Vintage, 2001), p. 8; Vincent, *I Hope I Don't Intrude*, p. 246,
125 Cited in Ronald Bergan, *Francis Coppola* (London: Orion, 1998), p. 44.
126 On the name, see Peter Cowie, *Coppola* (London: Faber & Faber, 1998), p. 86.
127 Dennis Turner, 'The Subject of "The Conversation"', *Cinema Journal*, 24, 4 (Summer 1985), p. 5; Lawrence Shaffer, 'The Conversation by Francis Ford Coppola', *Film Quarterly*, 28, 1 (Autumn 1974), p. 58.
128 Robert Phillip Kolker, *A Cinema of Loneliness: Penn, Kubrick, Coppola, Scorsese, Altman* (New York: Oxford University Press, 1980), p. 201.

Further Reading

❧

General

There are very few long-run histories of privacy. The only attempt to cover the entire chronological field remains the French-centred Philippe Ariès and Georges Duby (general editors), *A History of Private Life*, 5 vols. (Cambridge, MA: Belknap Press, 1987–94). Any scholar seeking to grasp the nature of privacy as a day-to-day practice should begin with Christena Nippert-Eng, *Islands of Privacy* (Chicago: University of Chicago Press, 2010). The most balanced recent contemporary surveys on privacy, with some history, are: James B. Rule, *Privacy in Peril* (Oxford: Oxford University Press, 2007); Daniel J. Solove, *Understanding Privacy* (Cambridge, MA: Harvard University Press, 2008); Raymond Wacks, *Privacy: A Very Short Introduction* (Oxford: Oxford University Press, 2010). Popular accounts of the evolution of the home are to be found in Judith Flanders, *The Making of Home* (London: Atlantic Books, 2014); Bill Bryson, *At Home: A Short History of Private Life* (London: Doubleday, 2010). Emily Cockayne, *Cheek by Jowl: A History of Neighbours* (London: Bodley Head, 2012) attempts a broad survey of an important aspect of the subject.

There is a large literature on the theory and concept of privacy, commencing in the modern era with Alan Westin's *Privacy and Freedom* (1967; London: Bodley Head, 1970). Thoughtful recent studies include: Anita L. Allen, *Unpopular Privacy: What Must We Hide* (New York: Oxford University Press, 2011); Judith W. DeCew, *In Pursuit of Privacy: Law, Ethics and the Rise of Technology* (Ithaca:

Cornell University Press, 1997); Julie C. Inness, *Privacy, Intimacy, and Isolation* (Oxford: Oxford University Press, 1992); Ferdinand D. Schoeman, *Privacy and Social Freedom* (Cambridge: Cambridge University Press, 1992); Helen Nissenbaum, *Privacy in Context: Technology, Policy, and the Integrity of Social Life* (Stanford: Stanford University Press, 2010); James Michael, *Privacy and Human Rights: An International and Comparative Study, with Special Reference to Developments in Information Technology* (Aldershot: UNESCO, 1994). The most accessible recent introduction to the concept, and to the range of contemporary attitudes to privacy, is to be found in David Anderson, *A Question of Trust: Report of the Investigatory Powers Review* (London: HMSO, June 2015), ch. 2.

Medieval/Early Modern

Diana Webb, *Privacy and Solitude in the Middle Ages* (London and New York: Hambledon Continuum, 2007), locates the existence of privacy at the beginning of the period. Lena Cowen Orlin, *Locating Privacy in Tudor London* (Oxford: Oxford University Press, 2007), is a model of how to treat the early history of the subject. Patricia Meyer Spacks, *Privacy: Concealing the Eighteenth-Century Self* (Chicago: University of Chicago Press, 2003), and Amanda Vickery, *Behind Closed Doors: At Home in Georgian England* (New Haven: Yale University Press, 2009), establish the framework of analysis in the eighteenth century. David Flaherty's early study of privacy in Britain's North American colony is essential reading: *Privacy in Colonial New England* (Charlottesville: University Press of Virginia, 1972). See also: Linda A. Pollock, 'Living on the Stage of the World: The Concept of Privacy among the Elite of Early Modern England', in *Rethinking Social History: English Society 1570–1920 and its Interpretation*, edited by Adrian Wilson (Manchester: Manchester University Press, 1993); Stephen Ozment, *Flesh and Spirit: Private Life in Early Modern Germany* (New York: Viking, 1999); John R. Gillis, *A World of Their Own Making: Myth, Ritual and the Quest for Family Values* (Cambridge, MA: Harvard University Press, 1996); Raffaella Sarti, *Europe at Home: Family and Material Culture 1500–1800* (New Haven: Yale University Press, 2002); Ralph Houlbrooke, *English Family Life, 1576–1716: An Anthology from Diaries* (Oxford: Blackwell, 1988); Annik Pardailhé-Galabrun, *The Birth of Intimacy: Privacy and Domestic Life in Early Modern Paris* (Cambridge: Polity, 1991. Two particularly useful surveys of society as a whole are Christopher Dyer, *Everyday Life in Medieval England* (London:

Hambledon, 1994), and Keith Wrightson, *English Society 1580–1680* (London: Hutchinson, 1982).

Religious observance provides suggestive parallels with modern privacy practices. Helpful studies are: Barbara H. Rosenwein, *Emotional Communities in the Early Middle Ages* (Ithaca: Cornell University Press, 2006); Andrew Cambers, *Godly Reading: Print, Manuscript and Puritanism in England, 1580–1720* (Cambridge: Cambridge University Press, 2011); Patricia Crawford, *Women and Religion in England 1500–1720* (London: Routledge, 1993); Jessica Brantley, *Reading in the Wilderness: Private Devotion and Public Performance in Late Medieval England* (Chicago: University of Chicago Press, 2007); Mary C. Erler, *Women, Reading, and Piety in Late Medieval England* (Cambridge: Cambridge University Press, 2002); Richard Rambuss, *Closet Devotions* (Durham, NC: Duke University Press, 1998). Diarmaid MacCulloch, *Silence: A Christian History* (London: Allen Lane, 2013), which runs through to the modern era, is especially interesting.

Spiritual practice is closely associated with the history of reading. On the early-modern period see: Gemma Allen, *The Cooke Sisters: Education, Piety and Politics in Early Modern England* (Manchester: Manchester University Press, 2013); Rebecca Krug, *Reading Families: Women's Literate Practice in Late Medieval England* (Ithaca: Cornell University Press, 2002); Naomi Tadmor, '"In the Even My Wife Read to Me": Women, Reading and Household Life in the Eighteenth Century', in *The Practice and Representation of Reading in England*, edited by James Raven, Helen Small and Naomi Tadmor (Cambridge: Cambridge University Press, 1996); Cecile M. Jagodzinski, *Privacy and Print: Reading and Writing in Seventeenth-Century England* (Charlottesville: University of Virginia Press, 1999). The tools of literacy are surveyed in R. A. Houston, *Literacy in Early Modern Europe: Culture and Education 1500–1800* (London: Longman, 1988).

Any understanding of the modern digital revolution needs to begin with the long history of correspondence. Particularly useful and thorough are James Daybell, *The Material Letter in Early Modern England: Manuscript Letters and the Culture and Practices of Letter-Writing, 1512–1625* (London: Palgrave Macmillan, 2012), and Susan Whyman, *The Pen and the People: English Letter-Writers 1660–1800* (Oxford: Oxford University Press, 2009). See also Bruce Redford, *The Converse of the Pen: Acts of Intimacy in the Eighteenth-Century Familiar Letter* (Chicago: University of Chicago Press, 1986), and William Merrill Decker, *Epistolary Practices: Letter Writing in America before Telecommunications* (Chapel Hill: University of

North Carolina Press, 1998). The most recent history of the machinery of postage is Duncan Campbell-Smith, *Masters of the Post: The Authorized History of the Royal Mail* (London: Allen Lane, 2011).

For the early history of the built environment, Jane Grenville, *Medieval Housing* (Leicester: Leicester University Press, 1999), provides a careful survey of recent research. Aspects of housing and how it was used are addressed in: Alice T. Friedman, *House and Household in Elizabethan England: Wollaton Hall and the Willoughby Family* (Chicago: University of Chicago Press, 1989); Michael Paterson, *Private Life in Britain's Stately Homes* (London: Robinson, 2012); Mark Girouard, *Life in the English Country House* (Harmondsworth: Penguin, 1980). London is a magnet for both people and historians. See: Peter Earle, *A City Full of People: Men and Women of London 1650–1750* (London: Methuen, 1994); Jeremy Boulton, *Neighbourhood and Society: A London Suburb in the Seventeenth Century* (Cambridge: Cambridge University Press, 1987); Clare Brant and Susan E. Whyman (eds.), *Walking the Streets of Eighteenth-Century London* (Oxford: Oxford University Press, 2007); Jerry White, *London in the Eighteenth Century* (London: Vintage, 2013); Miles Ogborn, *Spaces of Modernity: London's Geographies, 1680–1780* (New York: Guilford Press, 1998); Peter Guillery, *The Small House in Eighteenth-Century London: A Social and Architectural History* (New Haven: Yale University Press, 2004). Drains and related matters are examined in Virginia Smith, *Clean: A History of Personal Hygiene and Purity* (Oxford: Oxford University Press, 2007), and Emily Cockayne, *Hubbub: Filth, Noise and Stench in England 1600–1770* (New Haven: Yale University Press, 2007). Curtains are a neglected subject. For an introduction, see Jenny Gibbs, *Curtains & Drapes: History, Design, Inspiration* (London: Cassell, 1996). Locks await their historian, though there are references in many of the accounts mentioned here.

Legal aspects of the management of personal information in the early-modern period are studied in: Marjorie Keniston McIntosh, *Controlling Misbehaviour in England, 1370–1600* (Cambridge: Cambridge University Press, 1998); Robert B. Shoemaker, 'The Decline of Public Insult in London 1660–1800', *Past & Present,* 169 (2000); Martin Ingram, *Church Courts, Sex and Marriage in England, 1570–1640* (Cambridge: Cambridge University Press, 1987); J. A. Sharpe, '"Such Disagreements Betwyx Neighbours": Litigation and Human Relations in Early Modern England', in *Disputes and Settlements: Law and Human Relations in the West*, edited by John Bossy (Cambridge: Cambridge University Press, 1983).

The emergence of the public sphere was described in Jürgen Habermas, *The Structural Transformation of the Public Sphere*, translated by Thomas Burger and Frederick Lawrence (Cambridge: Polity, 1992). Amongst the large literature reviewing this thesis, John Brewer, 'This, That and the Other: Public, Social and Private in the Seventeenth and Eighteenth Centuries', in *Shifting the Boundaries: Transformation of the Languages of Public and Private in the Eighteenth Century*, edited by Dario Castiglione and Lesley Sharpe (Exeter: University of Exeter Press, 1995), is particularly useful. The physical locale of this new form of debate is examined in Brian Cowan, *The Social Life of Coffee: The Emergence of the British Coffeehouse* (New Haven: Yale University Press, 2005).

Modern

The conflicts and tensions embedded in the emerging landscape of privacy in the modern world are addressed in Deborah Cohen, *Family Secrets: Living with Shame from the Victorians to the Present Day* (London: Viking, 2013), and David Vincent, *I Hope I Don't Intrude: Privacy and its Dilemmas in Nineteenth-Century Britain* (Oxford: Oxford University Press, 2015). The best introduction to the middle-class family remains Leonore Davidoff and Catherine Hall, *Family Fortunes: Men and Women of the English Middle Class 1780–1850* (rev. edn, London: Routledge, 2002). See also Michael McKeon, *The Secret History of Domesticity: Public, Private, and the Division of Knowledge* (Baltimore: Johns Hopkins University Press, 2005). Useful introductions to the working-class experience are found in Elizabeth Roberts, *A Woman's Place: An Oral History of Working-Class Women 1890–1940* (Oxford: Blackwell, 1984), and Joanna Bourke, *Working-Class Cultures in Britain 1890–1960: Gender, Class and Ethnicity* (London: Routledge, 1994). The press of numbers and its consequences are examined in James Vernon, *Distant Strangers: How Britain Became Modern* (Berkeley: University of California Press, 2014). On Europe's largest city see, Jerry White, *London in the Nineteenth Century: 'A Human Awful Wonder of God'* (London: Jonathan Cape, 2007), and *London in the Twentieth Century: A City and Its People* (London: Viking, 2001). Amongst the large literature on the twentieth-century family, Göran Therborn, *Between Sex and Power: Family in the World, 1900–2000* (London: Routledge, 2004), is particularly useful. For surveys of the transformation of the built environment see John Burnett, *A Social History of Housing* (London: Methuen,1980), and Martin Daunton, *House and Home in the*

Victorian City: Working-Class Housing 1850–1914 (London: Edward Arnold, 1983). On the interiors, Deborah Cohen, *Household Gods: The British and their Possessions* (New Haven: Yale University Press, 2006), is a stimulating account.

The further history of literacy and written communication is examined in: David Vincent, *Literacy and Popular Culture: England 1750– 1914* (Cambridge: Cambridge University Press, 1989); Catherine J. Golden, *Posting It: The Victorian Revolution in Letter Writing* (Gainesville: University Press of Florida, 2009); Bernhard Siegert, *Relays: Literature as an Epoch of the Postal System* (Stanford: Stanford University Press, 1999). Attempts to place the new forms of electronic communication in perspective are made by: Tom Standage, *The Victorian Internet: The Remarkable Story of the Telegraph and the Nineteenth Century's Online Pioneers* (New York: Walker, 1998); James Gleick, *The Information: A History, a Theory, a Flood* (London: Fourth Estate, 2011); Jeffrey Kieve, *The Electric Telegraph: A Social and Economic History* (Newton Abbot: David & Charles, 1973); Richard R. John, *Network Nation* (Cambridge, MA: Harvard University Press, 2010); Carolyn Marvin, *When Old Technologies Were New: Thinking about Electric Communications in the Late Nineteenth Century* (Oxford: Oxford University Press, 1988). For oral forms of spreading information, particularly through gossip, see: Patricia Meyer Spacks, *Gossip* (Chicago: University of Chicago Press, 1985); Jörg R. Bergmann, *Discreet Indiscretions: The Social Organization of Gossip* (New York: Aldine de Gruyter, 1993); Melanie Tebbutt, 'Women's Talk? Gossip and "Women's Words" in Working-Class Communities, 1880–1939', in *Workers' Worlds: Cultures and Communities in Manchester and Salford 1880–1939*, edited by Andrew Davies and Steven Fielding (Manchester: Manchester University Press, 1992).

A balanced and informed guide to the digital revolution is provided by John Naughton, *From Gutenberg to Zuckerberg: What You Really Need to Know about the Internet* (London: Quercus, 2012). On computing more generally see Paul E. Ceruzzi, *A History of Modern Computing* (Cambridge, MA: MIT Press, 1998), and Arthur R. Miller, *The Assault on Privacy: Computers, Data Banks, and Dossiers* (Ann Arbor: University of Michigan Press, 1971). There has recently been extensive research on that most modern of figures, the teenage social media user. See Mary Madden, Amanda Lenhart, Sandra Cortesi, Urs Gasser, Maeve Duggan, Aaron Smith and Meredith Beaton, *Teens, Social Media and Privacy* (Washington, DC: Pew Research Centre, 2013), and Dana Boyd, *It's Complicated: The Social Lives of Networked Teens* (New Haven: Yale University Press, 2014).

The history of intimacy is critical to the evolution of privacy as a concept and a practice. For useful theoretical and methodological discussions, see: Lauren Berlant, 'Intimacy: A Special Issue', in *Intimacy*, edited by Lauren Berlant (Chicago: University of Chicago Press, 2000); William M. Reddy, *The Navigation of Feeling: A Framework for the History of Emotions* (Cambridge: Cambridge University Press, 2001); Anthony Giddens, *The Transformation of Intimacy: Sexuality, Love and Eroticism in Modern Societies* (Cambridge: Polity, 1992); Patricia Boling, *Privacy and the Politics of Intimate Life* (Ithaca: Cornell University Press, 1996). On the twentieth century, Claire Langhamer, *The English in Love: The Intimate Story of an Emotional Revolution* (Oxford: Oxford University Press, 2013), surveys a broad field. Much the most interesting recent oral history of intimate practices is to be found in Simon Szreter and Kate Fisher, *Sex Before the Sexual Revolution: Intimate Life in England 1918–1963* (Cambridge: Cambridge University Press, 2010).

The rise of the surveillance state has generated a large literature. An essential introductory text is Jeremy Bentham, *Panopticon; Or the Inspection-House* (1787), reprinted in *The Panopticon Writings*, edited by Miran Božovič (London: Verso, 1995). See also Janet Semple, *Bentham's Prison: A Study of the Panopticon Penitentiary* (Oxford: Clarendon Press, 1993), and Michel Foucault, *Discipline and Punish: The Birth of the Prison* (1975; London: Penguin, 1991). George Orwell's *1984* (1949; Harmondsworth: Penguin, 1954) should be read from end to end. Edward Higgs, *The Information State in England: The Central Collection of Information since 1500* (Basingstoke: Palgrave Macmillan, 2004), is a notably balanced and detailed introduction. James B. Rule's early study, *Private Lives and Public Surveillance* (London: Allen Lane, 1973), remains essential reading. See also David Lyon, *The Electronic Eye: The Rise of the Surveillance Society* (Cambridge: Polity, 1994). Studies of the secret state in all its forms begin with Alan Marshall, *Intelligence and Espionage in the Reign of Charles II, 1660–1685* (Cambridge: Cambridge University Press, 1994), and John Barrell, *The Spirit of Despotism: Invasions of Privacy in the 1790s* (Oxford: Oxford University Press, 2006). Works on the nineteenth and twentieth centuries include: Bernard Porter, *The Origins of the Vigilant State* (London: Weidenfeld and Nicolson, 1987); Richard Thurlow, *The Secret State: British Internal Security in the Twentieth Century* (Oxford: Blackwell, 1995); David Vincent, *The Culture of Secrecy: Britain 1832–1998* (Oxford: Oxford University Press, 1998); Christopher Moran, *Classified: Secrecy and the State in Modern Britain* (Cambridge: Cambridge University Press, 2013). The modern technology of surveillance is critically examined in: Clive Norris, 'There's No Success Like Failure and Failure's No Success At All: Some Critical Reflections on the Global Growth of CCTV Surveillance', in *Eyes Everywhere: The Global Growth of Camera Surveillance*, edited by Aaron Doyle, Randy Lippert and David Lyon (London: Routledge, 2012); Benjamin J. Goold, *CCTV and Policing: Public Area Surveillance and Police Practices in Britain* (Oxford: Oxford University Press, 2004); Kelly A. Gates, *Our Biometric Future: Facial Recognition Technology and the Culture of Surveillance* (New York: New York University Press, 2011). For accounts of the Snowden revelations, which have reset the current debate about the surveillance state, see: Glenn Greenwald, *No Place to Hide: Edward Snowden, the NSA and the Surveillance State* (London: Hamish Hamilton, 2014); Luke Harding, *The Snowden Files* (London: Guardian Books and Faber & Faber, 2014); and the film by Laura Poitras, *Citizenfour* (2014).

For those whose principal concern is the erosion of civil liberties in the West, the history of privacy in the twentieth-century European dictatorships provides a critical point of reference. The growing literature on this subject includes: Paul Ginsborg, *Family Politics: Domestic Life, Devastation and Survival 1900–1950* (New Haven and London: Yale University Press, 2014); Orlando Figes, *The Whisperers: Private Life in Stalin's Russia* (London: Allen Lane, 2007); Paul Betts, *Within Walls: Private Life in the German Democratic Republic* (Oxford: Oxford University Press, 2010); Sheila Fitzpatrick, *Everyday Stalinism. Ordinary Life in Extraordinary Times: Soviet Russia in the 1930s* (Oxford: Oxford University Press, 1999); Robert Gellately, 'Denunciations in Twentieth-Century Germany: Aspects of Self-Policing in the Third Reich and the German Democratic Republic', *Journal of Modern History*, 68, 4 (December 1996); Mary Fulbrook, *The People's State: East German Society from Hitler to Honecker* (New Haven: Yale University Press, 2005); Stephen Lovell, *Summerfolk: A History of the Dacha, 1710–2000* (Ithaca: Cornell University Press, 2003).

Privacy out of Doors

This study has emphasized the importance to the history of privacy of gentle outdoor pursuits. Pedestrians are still largely studied through the lens of literary accounts: see Rebecca Solnit, *Wanderlust: A History of Walking* (London: Verso, 2001), and Anne D. Wallace, *Walking, Literature and English Culture: The Origins and Uses of*

Peripatetic in the Nineteenth Century (Oxford: Clarendon Press, 1993). Morris Marples, *Shanks's Pony: A Study of Walking* (London: J. M. Dent, 1959), is an early attempt to open up the subject. The history of gardening is a burgeoning field, ranging from John Harvey, *Mediaeval Gardens* (London: B. T. Batsford, 1981), to Margaret Willes, *The Making of the English Gardener* (New Haven: Yale University Press, 2011). The study of privacy could be transformed by a thorough, long-run social history of recreational fishing. For the time being, see Charles Chenevix Trench, *A History of Angling* (London: Hart-Davis, MacGibbon, 1974), and John Lowerson, 'Brothers of the Angle: Coarse Fishing and English Working-Class Culture, 1850–1914', in *Pleasure, Profit, Proselytism: British Culture and Sport at Home and Abroad 1700–1914*, edited by J. A. Mangan (London: Frank Cass, 1988).

Index